PRAVDA HA HA

PRAVDA HA HA

True Travels to the End of Europe

RORY MACLEAN

BLOOMSBURY PUBLISHING

LONDON · OXFORD · NEW YORK · NEW DELHI · SYDNEY

BLOOMSBURY PUBLISHING
Bloomsbury Publishing Plc
50 Bedford Square, London, WC1B 3DP, UK

BLOOMSBURY, BLOOMSBURY PUBLISHING and the Diana logo are trademarks of
Bloomsbury Publishing Plc

First published in Great Britain 2019

To find out more about our authors and books visit www.bloomsbury.com
and sign up for our newsletters

Pravda (Правда) *n.* **1**. Truth. **2**. Disposition to speak or act truly or without deceit; truthfulness, veracity, sincerity [- Russ. э́то пра́вда? Is it true?] **3**. Russian broadsheet newspaper, formerly the official newspaper of the Communist Party of the Soviet Union [f. Proto-Slavic *pravьda*, from *pravъ* = right, correct]

'But I tell you, Winston, that reality is not external.
Reality exists in the human mind, and nowhere else...
Whatever the Party holds to be the truth, is truth.'

George Orwell, *Nineteen Eighty-Four*

Contents

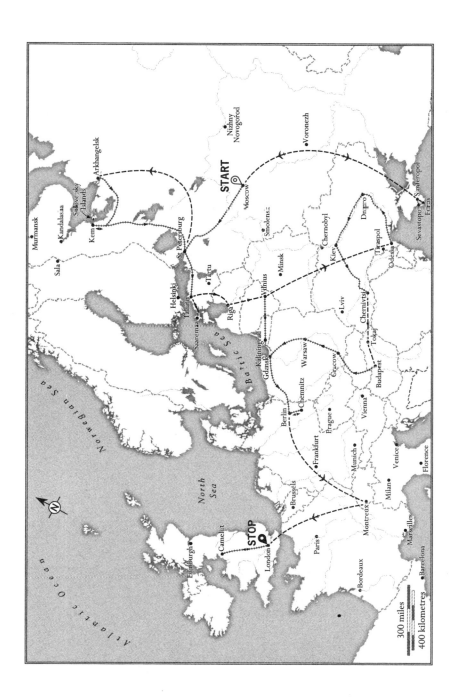

Russia

I

Under Moscow

Underground there was no horizon. Underground the people moved in halting steps, moved as one, moved four abreast to ride down, deep down beneath the city. The earth swallowed them, corralled them, unnamed them as the metallic shriek rose up to strike them dumb. No one talked above the whine of the motors. No one stood out. Once or twice the odd traveller dared to shout, leaning towards his fellows, his warm breath brushing their ears. Otherwise the mass – ten million souls every day – moved through the deafening noise, unable or unwilling to be heard.

I stepped among them, shuffled with them down the banks of escalators to the platform. In the pale milky light waited office clerks and stallholders, weary shop cleaners and crisp police recruits, pedlars with sacks of tourist tat and widows in frumpy Soviet dresses who'd seen their sons shot dead in the chaos after capitalism's triumph. Two hundred feet below ground the surging crowd elbowed aside a frightened, almond-eyed Yakut woman. Three white policemen approached her, backed her against the wall, demanded identity papers with a gesture that needed no words. Another traveller, a sharp-nosed Uzbek with his furious moustache, shepherded his young son around them without a look. The boy carried a plastic Russian flag. The scream of brakes echoed off the cold Crimean marble.

At peak times the trains arrived every minute at every one of Moscow's 224 underground stations, grating to a stop, flinging open their gaping doors, sucking in the *bydlo*. That's what Moscow's elite call the common people, the countless commuting offspring of provincial peasants, the rabble from the city's margins who'll never stand tall, never escape the shadows. *Bydlo*. Proles. Cattle. Scum.

At Taganskaya the throng heaved itself off the platform, carrying me with it into the metal carriage, crushing me against three identikit blondes. The women – slender and curvy with violet nails and long straightened hair – batted me away with their lashes. A buffed twentysomething in T-shirt and jeans carried his crumpled security guard uniform in a plastic bag. Beside him a grey-haired, grey-skinned academic noted his earnings in a diary, a leaky biro stain on his threadbare pinstripe. On a seat behind them a bricklayer at the end of his shift squinted at two ancient Nokias nestled like matchboxes in his big hands, his sausage fingers punching out the wrong number on one of them again and again.

Then I saw the bird.

It came out of nowhere, flying in through a closing door, inches above our heads. It was starling-sized and short-tailed with buff-grey plumage. As the train accelerated out of the station, I guessed that it had flown down into the underground – above the escalators' deep rolling rumble – and become trapped. Two men tried to grab it. The identikit blondes shrieked and ducked their heads. A stocky youth in bow tie began to swat at it with a folded newspaper. Other passengers held his arm, started to laugh, to yell, gazing in awe at the beautiful, frightened creature as it swept back and forth through the snaking carriages, shitting on the head of the failed academic in its terror.

Next the strangest thing happened.

After half a dozen fast flights, somewhere between Taganskaya and Kurskaya, the bird realised that there was no escape. Quite suddenly it stopped flying, and perched on a young man's shoulder by the door. He seemed to be a random choice, not distinctive at first glance, neither handsome nor bad-looking either: slight build, tracksuit top and high, chiselled cheekbones under deep brown eyes. Not exceptional at all, apart from his stack of hair, his unruffled calm, and being black in Moscow.

The man's stillness, and the frailty of the bird's trembling chestnut breast, brought a sudden serenity to the carriage. Commuters stared at the astonishing sight, met each other's glances, took hardly a breath so as not to break the spell, oblivious to the rising squeal of the brakes as the train slowed to pull into the next station. When the doors opened no one moved, until the man jerked backwards out of the carriage and onto the platform. Then the bird took off, its long flight feathers flashing with red and yellow tips.

I stared as well, before shaking myself out of my reverie. I wanted to follow him, to get off the train. I searched for my voice. 'Are you getting off now?' I said, pushing against the blondes. *Vy seichas vykhodite?* Let me off. But no one heard me, no one looked up as the crush of incoming passengers blocked my exit, entombing me again. Too soon the doors slammed shut and both man and bird were gone. With a scream the train plunged back into a darkness beyond which there was no horizon, no distant hill, no grand shadow cast in sudden valleys, only longsome tunnels that led from sleep to work and back again, day after day, night upon night.

2

Over Russia

'She told you about mushroom?' said Dmitri Denisovich with a swift intake of breath.

'I want to *taste* the mushroom,' I told him again.

Russia's chicken tsar fixed his hooded blue eyes on me. He leaned forward in his graphite Aeron office chair. I held his gaze. He obviously hadn't expected my request. Beyond his panoramic window a jet-black helicopter climbed into the cloudless summer sky. The Kremlin's teeth like crenellations took a bite out of the firmament.

'No problem,' he said with forced nonchalance, not breaking the stare. His vowels were dark, his voice as thick as tar. 'One million dollars...' he added, twisting the diamond ring on his finger. I could hear the cogs whirring and crunching in his brain. '...Or one book.'

Dmitri Denisovich meant business. A week earlier our mutual friend had called him from the balcony of her London penthouse, gazing out over Regent's Park, and asked him to look after me. Russian hospitality may be legendary but Dmitri had refused her, until she'd mentioned that I was a writer.

'One book?' I asked him, not having a million dollars to hand. 'What do you mean?'

'We make deal and you enjoy mushroom,' he said again in fractured English, waving away my question, leaving too much unsaid. 'No problem, my friend. I like you.'

There was something magnetic about Dmitri, something mercurial and seriously shady too. He seemed unable to keep still, cracking his neck, rolling his shoulders, rising to his feet to prowl around his plush burgundy office, like a caged beast in Givenchy. He was bigger than I'd expected, and better dressed. His trim blazer and flashy floral shirt hinted at both flair and vulgarity. His black hair was crew-cut short. I guessed that he was on the cusp of fifty.

But I didn't wonder if he packed a pistol, for his clothes were too tailored to hide a holster, unlike those of his unsmiling, kasha-fed bodyguard. That man balanced on shiny pointy-toed shoes by the door in front of a lacquered, hyper-real, faux-Rousseau painting of a wolf's head, saying nothing.

It was a lucky start to my journey. On my first day back in Russia, I'd landed myself an affable (and dodgy) oligarch who now stepped towards me, laid his hand on my shoulder and said, 'You trust me with your life.'

Then he smiled. I had never seen such ugly teeth. They were like broken rocks.

Thirty years had passed since my last visit to Moscow, at the dawn of a new age. In 1989 Eastern Europe had risen up against its Red Army occupiers and sent them packing. The fall of the Wall was followed by the collapse of the Soviet Union. Seventy years of totalitarianism ended almost overnight. McKinsey management consultants flew in to Sheremetyevo to guide spunky go-getters towards pluralist capitalism. Russia became a member of the Council of Europe. NATO expanded towards its borders, hinting that in time it could join the club. Europeans embraced the idea of a borderless continent, believing that they had changed the world.

In those euphoric days I'd travelled from Berlin to Moscow, exploring lands that were – for most Westerners – the forgotten half of Europe. In East Germany, Poland, Hungary, Romania and Russia, I'd met people who hadn't spoken to a foreigner in decades, who opened their hearts and told me stories of lost years, ruined lives and secret policemen. In Czechoslovakia, I'd heard Václav Havel – the imprisoned playwright who'd become president – herald the birth of 'a Europe in which no one more powerful will be able to suppress anyone less powerful, in which it will no longer be possible to settle disputes by force'. I'd placed my faith in the healing power of openness, compassion and reconciliation.

How could it have been otherwise? My generation had grown up in the shadow of the Second World War, haunted by the ghosts of its sixty million dead. We'd come of age during the Cold War, with half a continent imprisoned behind a wall. Our response was to value individual liberty above tribalism. We couldn't have borne the loss of more fathers and uncles, to see our brothers die in the name of the old demons. So we celebrated when former adversaries drew back the Iron Curtain. We applauded as East and West Germans danced together in no-man's-land. Some of us even dared to imagine the end of the nation state.

Now I'd returned to Moscow to try to understand what had gone wrong. Why – after liberating themselves from Soviet tyranny – had Russians surrendered their freedom for Dictatorship 2.0? Why – after that promising dawn – had the Kremlin redoubled its efforts to undermine European unity? And how could so many in the West have fallen for the lies and spin, dragging democracy to this precarious present moment?

My plan was to retrace my original journey, backwards. I would travel from Moscow to Berlin and London, through countries confronting old fears and fresh challenges, divided again by chauvinism and xenophobia. I wanted to learn how refugees, the dispossessed and cyberhackers had been used by nationalists. I needed to understand why Europe's unspeakable past couldn't be kept at bay.

There was also a personal reason for my journey. Thirty years ago I'd travelled with the certainty of a young man, living by certain principles, prizing certain values. Over the decades those certainties – those ethics – had sustained me, and I'd continued to live by them as much as possible. But now tolerance, empathy and even the promise of the future were under attack. I had to find a way to keep faith in them, despite the echo of marching boots, and the shadow of Brexit, and the collapse of a European dream.

'You come to my dacha Saturday,' said Dmitri Denisovich, more used to issuing orders than invitations. 'It will be trip you never forget.'

3

Putin's Pecker

In the wild woods west of Moscow, slender birch saplings leaned together, leaned apart, like elegant dancers swaying to the music of the wind. Beneath them in the dark Russian soil lay buried treasure. More valuable than gold, as seductive as pleasure, it was a prize said to evoke sensations of profound euphoria. Officials denied its existence. Its mention had been purged from the internet. Yet word of every new discovery was whispered between the country's elite. In nouveau-riche palaces and bulletproof Bentleys, oligarchs tenderly fed it to their lovers, washed down by vintage Dom Pérignon. Oil magnates infused it in vodka to gift deputies of the State Duma. And men died in bloody turf wars fought over its secret copses.

So potent and coveted was this rare subterranean *Ascomycete fungus* – an irresistible blond truffle that brought on delusions of invincibility – that Russia's born-again nationalists had named it *pipiska putina*. Putin's Pecker.

I'd learned about it from my Russian friend in London. She had exiled herself there, a moneyed non-dom who filled her time with lunches at the Connaught and with Chelsea Centre evening classes: French literature, Italian cookery and Forex Trading for Beginners. She'd joined one of my creative writing workshops, and then another and another, scribbling with breathless urgency about her Soviet childhood, about the vast land haunted by absences and – in an unguarded moment – about the phallus-shaped fungus.

On the drive to his dacha, Dmitri confirmed what she had told me about it, adding with his rocky smile, 'If I tell you more, I must kill you.'

He'd collected me that luminous morning in a pair of black Range Rovers. In the West a businessman might show off his bespoke Savile Row suits but in Russia it's the number of top-of-the-range Range Rover Sentinels that impresses, as well as bodyguards. Vasya was with us at the wheel of the lead, luxury, armour-plated, all-terrain fortress, said to be able to withstand grenade attacks without mussing a passenger's hair.

'But money no longer falls from sky,' Dmitri admitted with unexpected modesty. *Ty chto dumayesh, den'gi s neba padayut?* 'I can afford only basic model.'

Dmitri's 'basic' Range Rovers accelerated into the sweltering traffic, hitting 60 mph in six seconds, pushing me back in my hand-tooled Windsor leather seat. At that speed Moscow unfolded like a flipbook, in a flash of sharp images that simulated an impression of change: newly gilded onion domes, low-slung Maseratis and Little Potato fast-food stalls. In late summer, Europe's largest city felt like a pressure cooker, shimmering with heat and with its residents ready to explode. Sirens echoed off its Stalinist skyscrapers. Queues of dusty labour coaches idled outside its new building sites. Fuming policemen swaggered across the broad boulevards, their truncheons knocking against their jackboots.

Beyond the tinted windows I caught sight of wrecking balls, crumpled beggars and the bare bronze head of Peter the Great, the eighth tallest statue in the world. A few years ago its sculptor had tried to sell the fifteen-storey behemoth to the United States as Christopher Columbus. When he failed, he repurposed the work as a tsar and flogged it to his friend the mayor. In Russia, as in the rest of the world, it matters who you know.

'Bush legs,' said Dmitri in response to my question. 'I made my money on George Bush's legs.'

Now I understood why a portrait of the late US president sat on his desk.

'Sorry for my English bleeding your ears but you are writer.' He picked a hair off his baby-blue Jaeger cashmere jumper. He could have done without the camouflage khaki cravat. 'I tell you my story and you write it. Understand?'

I also now had an inkling of what Dmitri meant by 'one book'.

When the Soviet Union collapsed in the early 1990s, Russians started to starve. In response the European Community donated much of its butter mountain and milk lakes to the rump empire. The Salvation Army, banned during the communist years, opened hundreds of soup kitchens. And George H. W. Bush flooded the place with chicken.

'Never before had anyone seen such beautiful fat legs, not even on their own babushka,' recalled Dmitri, making a crude gesture with his manicured hands.

To hungry Russians, the plump pink thighs and drumsticks were manna from Heaven (or at least from Arkansas). With their gift for wit and repartee, they dubbed the phosphate-filled imports 'Bush legs'.

'I tell you, my childhood was grey: grey clothes, grey school, grey pot of cabbage soup on cooker,' recalled Dmitri. His words seemed to be formed at the back of his mouth, stumble across his tongue and then tip syllable by syllable over his lips. 'When glorious Soviet Union went to dog, people suddenly can buy everything they ever dreamed of, like bananas. To get them they started to hustle, selling salami, vodka, women.'

'Me, I was nineteen year old. I wanted to be rich. I wanted to escape grey. So I sold chicken. I made office in my uncle apartment. I slept on floor. And no matter how much I sold, no matter how much I charged, people wanted more. More and more Bush legs, which I kept in courtyard in freezer truck. In one month I bought myself cordless telephone. I was so proud. In three months I bought apartment. In one year I had first factory. Now I send my nephew to school at Eton.'

American philanthropy had an ulterior motive, Dmitri explained. Its charity crushed the Russian poultry industry, cornering the market for US farmers, until chancers like Dmitri seized back control. At breathtaking speed – and on borrowed cash – he built his own hatcheries, farms, feed mill and portioning plant. Across Russia hundreds of similar stories could be told of brazen opportunism, criminal acumen and amenable relatives in the KGB. As Dimitri put it, in the 1990s anyone with balls and the right connections could 'bag couple of oil wells'.

There is a story from those days of two mafia gangs vying to blackmail the same bank. The banker made it known that he'd pay protection money only to the stronger of the two. To prove themselves worthy, the first gang immediately set about kneecapping its opponents. The second gang opted to use brains rather than brawn. It scooped a homeless drunk off the streets, cleaned him up, dressed him in designer clothes and put it about that he was the head of an especially ruthless *third* gang. He was seen in the best restaurants, spotted buying serious weapons from a KGB fence and overheard boasting about annihilating the competition. Then, with the scene set, and in full sight of the banker, the second gang executed the drunk in cold blood. Some say that he was roasted to death in a burning Mercedes. Others that he was buried up to the neck and decapitated with a scythe. But no matter how the poor man met his end, the ruthlessness of the second gang so impressed the banker that he chose them.

'Balls *and* brains,' Dmitri said, tapping his temple.

Dmitri wasn't one of the hard boys (and odd girl) who'd moved in such circles. But like them, his life had been propelled from pathetic Soviet grey to inconceivable wealth in a few dramatic months.

'I wanted all and I took all,' he boasted. 'My life was no more grey. My life became history. You write down these words,' he ordered, gesturing at my notebook. 'Capitalism is free wolves living among free sheep, for sure.'

Our convoy swept west through Moscow's so-called sleeping districts. In between the great white apartment blocks and ranked maisonettes, mothers pushed prams around abandoned statues of Lenin. Pensioners sat in the shade of acacia trees. A stray dog lay in a tepid pool of water, struck dumb by the heat. Soon the yawning suburbs gave way to truck lots and karaoke bars, the ugly sprawl leavened by an odd copse of birches and filthy wooden village clinging to life between the carriageways.

Communism's collapse had led to the redistribution of wealth, but not in a way that anyone could have foreseen. In the early 1990s privatisation vouchers – and then a fraudulent 'loans-for-shares' scheme – had divvied up the riches of the Soviet Union. The vouchers gave ordinary Russians a share of state enterprises but few had a clue how to use them. Many changed hands on the street, often for no more than a few dollars or a bottle of vodka. Con artists, entrepreneurs and organised crime syndicates capitalised on public ignorance, amassing millions of vouchers. Boris Yeltsin then sold them control of the country's largest companies, in return for their support during an election campaign.

'Some people got bagel, others got bagel hole,' Dmitri said to explain the rise of the first oligarchs, two dozen of whom came to own 40 per cent of the country.

Then the 2008 financial crisis – the global caesura that would reshape the world – concentrated wealth in even fewer hands, sidelining mid-size operators like Dmitri Denisovich. He had taken out 'balloon loans' from both Russian and Western banks, using shares in his own company as collateral to fund its expansion. With the meltdown of the Moscow stock market, and the collapse of his company's share price, he had to sell his holdings at a crippling loss.

'I became poor like church rat,' he insisted with more mock modesty. When I pointed out that the poor tend not to wear Givenchy he snapped in irritation, 'Real oligarchs own fifty million dollars plus. In book you call me minigarch.'

Along the Rublyovo–Uspenskoye Highway, odd-job men waited by parked cars with Ukrainian licence plates and, further on, underdressed women in high boots and short summer skirts also offered their services. Beyond them traffic policemen idled in the shade, stopping older Ladas, checking papers, asking the driver to breathe on them and pocketing a bribe if they smelt alcohol.

Thirty minutes later the forest began to close in around us, looming so close to the road that it seemed to cut off the light. Family cars pulled onto the gravel shoulder, parents and children with wicker baskets vanishing between the massed conifers. Soon we too turned off the highway and onto a dirt track. I peered ahead in the hope of catching sight of a weathered wooden villa with high balconies and intricate fretwork. I imagined – thanks to Chekhov – long walks in its apple orchard with the scent of hay and the sound of a piano in the air. Instead I saw only deadening pinewoods.

'Is this the road to your dacha?' I asked.

'My dacha?' replied Dmitri, calm again, playing with the word and me. 'For sure, you see no dacha at all.'

I recalled my London friend warning me that Dmitri had wildness in him, flooding his veins, beating under his skin, and that I had to be careful. Already ours was a volatile relationship, changing as he asserted himself and I submitted so as to glean his story. On the seat beside him I sensed more than his capriciousness, and pongy aftershave.

'First we make fun,' he went on, enjoying his control of the situation, nodding at his bodyguard. 'Is why we need Vasya.'

Our convoy stopped in the middle of nowhere and five strangers emerged from the other Range Rover. I couldn't tell who belonged to whom but I guessed the young woman might have been his wife or partner, if he was married. Dmitri made no introductions. No one met my eye.

Vasya – who I'd imagined carried a pistol – opened the lead Range Rover's tailgate and took out four empty yellow tubs. As he handed them to the group, Dmitri issued instructions in Russian. All responded with a respectful '*Sudar*'. The Tsarist 'Sire'. Vasya then unloaded a coil of rope, black bin bags, a hose … and half a dozen Kalashnikovs.

Dmitri revelled in my alarm.

'Like I say, if I tell too much, I must kill you,' he repeated with his broken-rock laugh.

Around us the trees lay at wild angles like giant spillikins, the oldest pines having fallen, rotted and fed the saplings that sprouted on their remains. Vasya vanished between them with the guns as the group split into pairs. In the open glades the air was wild with heat, cut through by darting horseflies. Dimitri and I walked together between the shimmering streaks of brightness and patches of shade, buckets in hand, with heads down.

Every Russian child knows the names of a dozen forest mushrooms. Boys and girls are said to be able to follow the rich musty fragrance into the darkest glades, and to recognise the tastiest, rarest and most poisonous fungi.

I, on the other hand, couldn't stop thinking about the guns.

'*Lisichki!*' Dmitri cried almost at once, spotting a cluster of yellow 'little vixen' chanterelle. 'My favourite.'

As we wandered further away from the vehicles, the frowning trees closed in again to shut out the sky. No sound disturbed the vast silence, apart from distant voices calling out their discoveries. On rising ground amid young pines we found small, oily *maslyata*. At the foot of birch trees grew brown-capped *podberyozovik* and – in a nearby stand of aspen – its orange-capped cousin *podosinovik*. In a stretch of open grassland the woman tripped over a plate-size, sweet-tasting *champignon de Paris* – Russians use its French name – which is said to erupt from the earth with such force that it can break through asphalt.

In a damp copse of firs, I kicked over a rotted branch and found a batch of *belly*. I called out but Dmitri told me that *belly* – a kind of massive white porcini – becomes poisonous at the end of a humid summer.

'No *pipiska putina*?' I asked him.

'Not here, for sure,' he answered.

It was hot and sweaty work, raking through the mouldering leaves, stumbling over fallen trunks, my eyes peeled for either honey-coloured *opyonok* or an imagined assassin. As we picked through the undergrowth, I recalled a theory that fungi exist in subtle symbiosis with a forest, weaving themselves into the tips of roots, sharing sugar, nitrogen and – remarkably – transmitting warnings of approaching diseases or aphid attack. If the web of roots and filaments beneath my feet were a kind of sylvan defence system, I wished it would give me a sign. If I vanished in the forest, no one would ever know.

Dmitri sensed my vulnerability and said, 'I like you. You are ambitious. So I make you offer.'

'What offer?'

'I want you to write book.'

'I am writing a book.'

'*Important* book,' he emphasised, lifting his voice. 'Like *Nineteen Eighty-Four*. You write new *Nineteen Eighty-Four*.'

Dmitri claimed to have a thing about literature, although I doubted he read much other than the Frankfurt edition of the *Financial Times*. He waxed lyrical about Tolstoy and Dostoevsky and the importance of words but I suspected his real interest was posterity. *His* posterity. Even though I had no intention of reworking Orwell for him, I couldn't resist asking, 'What's your book about then?'

'*Your* book is about Europe, and me. It is, how you say, allegory. You write it. You put your name on cover. You win big Pulitzer Prize.'

'And you?' I asked, hardly believing my ears. 'Are you the star of this book?'

'I talk, for sure,' he said. 'I talk so you can tell my story. You hear much blah blah blah but you make it best possible.'

I groped for words. I thought of Orwell's fear of 'the very concept of objective truth … fading out in the world'. At last I managed to say, 'Dmitri Denisovich, with all due respect I don't think…'

'Do not refuse me,' he interrupted, stabbing a finger at me in a flash of anger. 'You are my guest. You will honour me.'

Over the next hour we walked in silence, describing a broad circle through the woods, arriving together in a sun-chequered clearing as if on cue. Dmitri inspected the others' spoils with approval. In the buckets were five or six kilos of chunky ceps, yellow chanterelles and brightly capped birch boletes with grey-flecked stalks. A good haul for the time of year.

Then Vasya handed out the guns. He gave the last AK-47 to Dmitri. Of all the men I alone did not have one. Beads of sweat rolled down my back. I looked around for cover, judging which way to run. The forest was silent apart from the babble of a nearby stream. Pointlessly I checked that my passport was in my pocket.

'Now for fun,' said Dmitri.

He lifted the Kalashnikov, and passed it to me. Only now did I see the rope, strung between the treetops and suspending a dozen swollen bin bags high above our heads. The woman started to laugh with sudden, girlish excitement. The men snuffed out their cigarettes and jostled for position beneath the bags. On a signal from Dmitri, they started to shoot. The woods crackled with rapid gunfire and in an instant the bags exploded, showering the party with cool fresh water, which had been syphoned from the stream by Vasya. Terrified birds took flight from the surrounding trees. Wood splinters and broken branches tumbled onto the forest floor. The air stank of cordite and pine sap.

'To God's great Russia,' shouted Dmitri above the laughter, in a kind of blessing, soaked to the skin like the rest of us, 'May it never die.'

4

Russia, My Russia

Rublyovka is Moscow's Henley or Hamptons, an exclusive colony of multi-million-dollar dachas, fifty-room French chateaux and red-brick manor houses overlooking landscaped English parks. Vladimir Putin and Roman Abramovich own turreted villas on the river. Olympic ice skater Tatiana Navka shares her mini-palace with Kremlin press spokesman Dmitry Peskov.* Property magnate Vladislav Doronin built a spaceship-shaped home for supermodel Naomi Campbell there. Guests set down on private helipads, leave their fur coats in climate-controlled closets, swim in Carrara marble infinity pools, then step into surround-sound pulsar showers with a toy boy or two. At the local Barvikha shopping mall they can also pick up a Ferrari.

After blasting the bin bags, we backtracked to Rublyovka, swinging into the high-end enclave through its double-barrier security gate.

'Your dacha is here?' I asked Dmitri again, picking another splinter out of my hair.

* Peskov, one of Vladimir Putin's right-hand men, is alleged to have controlled the dossier of *kompromat* – compromising material – on Donald Trump and Hillary Clinton that was used to influence the 2016 US presidential election, according to former British intelligence officer Christopher Steele. In 2019 his daughter Elizaveta Peskova worked as an intern to Aymeric Chauprade, a French MEP who used to be a member of Marine Le Pen's Front National.

'*Was* here,' he replied.

Moscow has more billionaires than any other capital in the world. Most own estates in Rublyovka but all that I glimpsed of them was the odd mock-Elizabethan chimney pot. In the gated citadel every building, every road, every glass-and-barbed-wire security tower was boxed in by seven-metre-high steel barriers. Our convoy cruised along its narrow, treeless alleys as if between parallel Berlin Walls. We slowed at a blind corner so as not to collide with a speeding Bentley Mulsanne. No one was on the streets, apart from a squad of groundskeepers sweeping the road with birch twig brooms.

'Better than old Khrushchyovka box, for sure,' said Dmitri, thinking of the Khrushchev-era prefabs in which he – and most Russians – had been raised.

As I could see no buildings, I didn't disagree. Instead I wondered if Dmitri's country home – given his propensity for bling and bluster – would be an ersatz-Thai palace with gopping Gothic tower? Or perhaps a Beverley Hills knock-off topped with Disneyland water slide? I didn't know, but I didn't have to wait long to find out. Vasya pulled up to a concealed entrance, the steel gate swung open and we drove onto an empty lot.

'I tore down dacha,' he said, as we bounced over the rutted earth. 'I never looked back.'

The size of the property was modest for a chicken tsar – about a hundred *sotka* (or two acres) – but more shocking was the state of it. The soil had been churned like butter, chewed over by JCB diggers and spat out into huge ugly mounds. Long, jagged cuts had been slashed around its trees. In some places rough ladders dropped down into the wounds as if into First World War trenches. The building itself had been reduced to rubble.

We stepped down from the Range Rover and into the open. The sun burned through the motionless air and ricocheted off the broken earth. The remaining oaks – unsettled by the digging – had lost their leaves, so offered little shade. Man is endowed with reason and the power to create, wrote Chekhov in *Uncle Vanya*, yet so often all he seems to do is destroy.

'Why?' I asked Dmitri as we walked alongside a shallow trench.

·

'Because of mushroom,' he replied.

'*Pipiska putina?*' I asked. 'Here?'

'Here,' he answered, gesturing at the ground. 'One metre deep.'

After the recession, Dmitri had faced eviction. His debtors were after his blood, on the point of seizing his property, threatening his life.

'In Russia one life is worth nothing,' he explained, snapping his fingers. 'But if you owe money, Shylock Jews keep you alive to get it back.'

Dmitri's debt seemed to have been compounded by offence (of what nature he would not be drawn but it seemed to involve at least one Kremlin official). As a result he was awoken every midnight by menacing phone calls. Chickens were impaled on the railings of his townhouse. His Learjet's tyres were slashed. He began to suspect that he'd be murdered as soon as he settled the debt. So, with that ancient Russian sense of mission – and a defiant two-finger flick at his foes – he set about devaluing his greatest remaining asset. He demolished the Rublyovka dacha.

And that was his windfall, an inexplicable miracle of the sort that so often arises in – and possesses – this land. As he began to obliterate its foundations, one of his demolition men – a local woodsman – spotted in the newly exposed earth a blond, phallus-shaped 'pecker'. And then another. And another.

'My second fortune was under my nose.'

In parts of temperate Europe – central France, Croatia, Spain and even rural Wiltshire – truffles grow close to the surface, usually in alkaline soil around the bases of beech, hazel and oak trees. None can survive the harsh northern winter, or so most people believe. Yet Russia's elite have long known that truffles like no other grow in the wild woods west of Moscow. Their remarkable *Ascomycete fungus* is said by them to be more potent than SS-X-29 Satan missiles, as irresistible as Tverskaya prostitutes, as unique as the nation itself. Of course the Russian variety is no common fungus, nestling among superficial surface roots. Instead it survives below the frost line, by wrapping itself around a tree's primary taproot. At that depth it also protects itself from both wild boar and domesticated pigs, the latter having been used by generations of truffle hunters elsewhere in Europe.

In Rublyovka a series of clandestine test holes had revealed the hidden wealth of Dmitri's land, and its enormous value. He ordered the digging-up of his whole property, sold the treasure in secret and paid off his debts – plus a bounty of bribes for safety's sake.

'I know I know, trees died,' he admitted with a shrug. 'But Putin's Pecker made me rich again.'

I looked across the stark, walled wasteland. Dmitri's crazy tale echoed Russians' belief in themselves as a chosen people, as well as their willingness to ravage the land for a quick buck.

'It is not this hot in Hell,' he then said, leading me towards a lobster-red marquee that was as out of place as a merry-go-round on a battlefield. At its entrance waited our fellow mushroom hunters, changed into domestic uniform. Inside the air-conditioned tent, another member of his staff – in white chef's apron and hat – sorted through the fungi, brushing away debris and cutting off the base of the stalks.

'Now we talk, we drink, we eat,' said Dmitri, gesturing to a nest of armchairs beside the field kitchen. Vasya stationed himself by the door as a raven-haired hostess approached us carrying a silver salver. Her boss snapped open the bottle and poured. 'First and last glass you swallow in one,' he instructed. 'All others are up to you.'

As we talked, the cool air filled with the smell of fragrant *lisichki* and oily *maslyata*. Canned music played from somewhere at the back of the tent. When the first delicate plates were laid before us – delicious mouthfuls of fruity chanterelle with an aftertaste of apricots and pepper – I mentioned the difficulty in distinguishing poisonous from non-poisonous mushrooms.

'You must have courage,' advised Dmitri.

'Like Putin?' I asked to draw him out. The man was so wildly popular that no Russian seemed capable of having a conversation without mentioning his name.

'I don't like big word like patriotism but President Putin has vision. Your leaders have Twitter. They think in days, not years.

Write this down,' he instructed me. 'Our president has fifteen-year plan. He chases it, no matter.'

I was taking notes, trying to catch his turn of phrase, yet I detected a slight guardedness in his response. I asked him, 'What is his plan?'

'To make Russia great again.'

'I've heard that one before.'

'In Russia is good plan.' He knocked back another vodka and went on, 'America and Europe always want to make Russia small, everyone knows. Remember "gift" of Bush legs? It was trick to destroy our chicken farmers.'

As well as strategic vision, Putin – who has ruled Russia longer than any leader since Stalin – was said to be loved for his modesty, a quality that might have been questioned had the Russian media been allowed to report on his billions or his estimated twenty residences including a couple of Black Sea palaces.

'Plus he respects church,' Dmitri added, as if quoting some official tract. 'You know last Christmas he went as Mr Anybody to church in Nizhny Novgorod?'

I did know, and I pointed out that he had made sure that the networks knew as well. His private act of worship had been broadcast live on national television.

'Listen, my friend. Russians never experience democracy in one thousand years. So he is best leader in one thousand years. Write this also please.'

'Do you really believe that, Dmitri?' I asked, the mechanical tone in his voice bringing to mind the old Soviet habit of praising communism in public while condemning it in private.

'What I believe is my business. What you write is also my business.'

I didn't trust Dmitri. It was all but impossible to back up his assertions. I simply had to take him at his word, and I did that for I was intrigued, not by his wealth or audacity, but rather by a part of him that he could not – or would not – expose. I sensed that through him I'd start to understand chippy, lying, modern Russia.

I also sensed something else in the air. It wasn't the sudden buzz of the alcohol in my head or the aroma of honeyed *opyonok* bubbling in sour cream. I felt a rising pressure, a shift in the atmosphere outside the tent. Dmitri was too intent to notice it, carrying on blah blah blahing as he refilled our glasses.

'I love my homeland but no one can know Russia with their brain. You can understand it only with heart. *Lyubite Rodinu, mat' vashu!*' he cried out, striking his chest like a well-dressed Tarzan. 'Those words mean "Love your Homeland as your mother!" But to Russian ear it also sounds like "Love your Homeland, you motherfuckers!"'

Dmitri raised his glass to homelands, taking in both his united Russia and my fractured Europe. The toast brought tears to his eyes as more mushrooms arrived at our table, including a salver of black trumpets sautéed in garlic and topped with chopped parsley.

'All people who eat mushrooms are stupid,' he declared, propelling himself further into good spirits. 'But people who do not eat mushrooms – who do not have courage – are more stupid. They become grey people, grey dust.'

I closed my notebook. I laid down my pen. I took in my host, warts and all. I met his eyes and said, 'That is why I want to taste the pecker.'

Dmitri's face darkened in a heartbeat. He fell as quiet as he had done in his Moscow office. A whiff of menace – and alcoholic breath – hung between us. He repeated, syllable by syllable: 'One million dollars.'

'I don't have anything like that sort of money,' I admitted.

'Then you write for me one book,' he replied with a victorious laugh.

Oligarchs were meant to be 'uncultured ignoramuses'. They 'don't read books. They don't have time. They don't go to art exhibitions. They think the only way to impress anyone is to buy a yacht,' according to Alexander Lebedev, owner of the *London Evening Standard* and the *Independent*. Yet Dmitri wanted me to think him different. Yes, his character could transform itself in the blink of an eye. Yes, his volatility heightened my sense of unease.

But as he started to recite a piece of prose from memory, my view of him began to change. His Russian was suddenly rich and pliable, flowing straight from the heart. His voice rose in joy and fell in sorrow, whether recalling an extract from a Gogol novel, a portrait of a sad, romantic Turgenev hero, or indeed an article on Gazprom from the *Weekend FT*.

'I grew up with books. We all grew up hungry for books. Every new book was way to escape Soviet grey,' he confessed in English, talking of how literature had opened a door out of the closed country.

In his voice was real passion and I was impressed. At the same time I recalled the Russian saying that free cheese is only found in mousetraps.

'Now don't be frightened,' he said to me. 'We work together.' Then he called over his shoulder, 'Anna?'

The raven-haired hostess glided to his side. He spoke softly to her and she – a serious twenty-year-old with child-like eyes set in a pale face – stepped away then returned with a small silver box. Dmitri opened it to reveal a solitary truffle. It was the colour of ripe wheat. It had no smell. It was *pipiska putina*.

'It doesn't look special,' I said.

'Wait,' said Dmitri.

He brushed off a speck of soil. He reached for a small walnut-handled knife. He did not peel the truffle. He cut off a wafer-thin slice and laid it on the middle finger of Anna's outstretched hand.

'Try,' he said, as she lifted her hand towards me.

I thought it was a joke.

Dmitri rolled his eyes and spoke again in Russian. In response Anna turned back to him, lifted her finger to his lips and he sucked the truffle off it.

'Like so,' he said, then cut a second sliver and laid it on her index finger. He added, 'Her hands are very clean.'

Again Anna raised her fingers to me. We bent towards each other. I opened my mouth. I took the fungus. On my tongue it tasted of musk and earth, darkness and even sex, if sex has an aftertaste of vanilla.

'Now give time,' said Dmitri, leaning back in his armchair and casually mentioning that the effect could last for weeks, even months. I relaxed into my seat as well.

'Today I tell you all, and you write all, because all is finished,' he admitted, gesturing towards the silver box. 'No more secrets. No more guard at gate. No more *putina* on my land.'

I hazarded a guess that his Rublyovka neighbours might also be sitting on a fortune of fungi.

'Maybe they become even richer but you know, I don't give fuck for them.' He laughed again – a deep, animal cackle – then he turned to Anna and said, 'Dance'.

The words were spoken with a trace of tenderness but in a way that could not be mistaken for anything other than a command. The woman obeyed without question. She stood before us and moved with taut grace, not so much dancing as unwinding herself, twisting and turning to some inner tension as Vasya cranked up the volume on the sound system.

Dmitri knew the song – the corny Slavic hit 'Combine Harvester' – and started to sing along to the lyrics, paraphrasing them while rocking his head back and forth in happy intoxication.

'I feed pig, I plough field, I beat barley…' he crooned. 'I am not fool who dreams of glitzy life…'

I was struck by the ditty's simplistic sentimentality and the naff notion of unappreciated 'real guys' who spit on modern culture and defend the Motherland.

'We are real guys who man the army,' he sang on. 'Driver of harvester! Driver of tractor! Packer of watermelon truck!'

Another song followed with even more idiotic lyrics and Dmitri sprang to his feet, casting off his reserve as the truffle began to take hold of him.

'Russia, my Russia, from Volga to Yenisei…' he piped, taking into his heart *Rossiya, moya Rossiya*. The lead singer of Putin's favourite rock band – whose other hits include 'Soldier' and 'Kombat' – often wore a Second World War uniform at his jingoistic performances. Dmitri's emotions swelled with the music as he sang of accordions playing and girls smiling at their sweethearts under the moonlight.

Then we heard the thunder. It silenced Dmitri, shook Anna out of her submissive routine. In an instant they made for the entrance like animals on a scent, bursting out into the naked heat.

I followed.

Enormous black clouds massed on the horizon, spilling towards us, bloated with rain. A fresh breeze stirred the air. Moscow – with its humid continental climate – can be subject to sudden summer downpours, and we were in for a drenching.

As the storm rolled forward, a madness overcame us. The vodka and dance had been hypnotic. The loony lyrics had moved us even though they were quite meaningless. On top of which I could not judge – I was not capable of judging – the effect of the truffle on my now-sizzling brain.

Dmitri did not hold himself back. Thrill shot through him like an electric shock. As the first raindrops hissed onto the baked earth, he began to dance again, while tearing off his clothes. Off came his Church's brogues and Harvie & Hudson shirt. Away went his Hackett chinos and the camouflage cravat. As the skies opened he was all but naked, gesticulating to the beat of the rain and Russian rock. A whopping tattoo of another wolf leapt across his torso, its breath raging red up his arm, its ruff and throat slashed with Russian pine trees.

Anna – whether hostess, companion or concubine – followed him, to an extent. She slipped off her uniform jacket and rolled her bare shoulders against the cooling drops, giving nothing of herself away.

Then the rain grew much heavier, thundering against the marquee, drumming off the black Range Rovers. Rivulets began to form underfoot, snaking across the churned ground, turning the site into a mud bath. Vasya stepped across the pools with an open umbrella but Dmitri batted it away. Lightning flashed in the gloom, freezing his dance in crazy gestures: a disco jerk, an air guitar riff, a lunge at both Anna and Vasya. He splattered their uniforms with mud, pushed them onto their knees, and ran his filthy hands through their sodden hair. At least that's what I thought happened. I couldn't be sure. By then I could hardly see a thing.

In any case it was my turn not to care. The truffle was also having its effect on me. I slipped back inside the lobster-red tent. Light and shadow played across its polyester walls. I settled into an armchair. I closed my eyes and, as the rain beat out its rhythm, I fell into a trance.

5

Terrible Beauty

Beat of drums, crack of guns; the killing machines were on the move. On the outskirts of Moscow a dozen hulking T-90 battle tanks shook the earth, rent the air and caused a child to drop her banana ice-cream cone. A rank of spanking new T-14 Armatas, the world's most deadly tracked combat vehicle, pushed into the column. Their 125 mm smoothbore cannon can fire a dozen Vacuum-1 rounds per minute, every one capable of penetrating one-metre-thick steel at a distance of two miles. Atop each turret stood a Russian tankman: proud, defiant and gazing ahead to victory, as well as at the unmarked pedestrian crossing. Spectators darted between the raucous machines, videoing them through the billows of diesel exhaust. Ground Forces soldiers in full battle kit jogged alongside them, and around a young mother jerking a pram through the track ruts.

I was spellbound, bewitched, deafened and blasted, especially when Anna, the raven-haired hostess, leaned forward in her seat and said, 'Beautiful, yes?'

Msta-S howitzers and mobile rocket launchers followed the tanks onto the open plain, among them a vicious Buk-M2 surface-to-air missile system that could – according to my programme – 'perform multiple missions with greater mobility and simultaneously engage a maximum of 24 targets'. In 2014 a similar Buk, with

five-metre-long SA-11 guided missile, had brought down Malaysia
Airlines flight MH17, killing all 298 passengers and crew.

'Beautiful in their duty,' she repeated as armour and infantry
assembled in front of the grandstands.

I'd awoken with the morning half gone. The sun had shone
into Dmitri's gazebo and my eyes, as well as onto the flies that
had hatched overnight in the dampened earth. I'd shifted in the
armchair and they had risen in an iridescent cloud, turquoise heads
and thoraxes tracing mad patterns around my head.

I couldn't yet explain *pipiska putina*'s power. I knew that Siberian
shamans had long used the fly agaric *Amanita muscaria* to reach
a trance state. In Chin Dynasty China, herbalists recorded that
the psilocybin mushroom 'makes one laugh unceasingly'. Plato
was said to have drunk its tea at the ancient Greek rites of Eleusis
and similar fungi had roused Viking warriors to battle. But to
my knowledge nothing had been written about truffles inducing
delusions of invincibility, except in Russia.

In dreamy half-sleep, I wondered if *Ascomycete fungus* had inspired
Lenin to pep up the hallucinatory power of the communist project?
Perhaps it had fed Stalin's mighty and murderous delusions? Could
it even have led Tsar Alexander II to declare that scientific fact had
never limited Russian certainties or faith? 'All countries abide by
the law but Russia abides by sayings and proverbs,' he'd once said.

All I knew for sure was that a writer promises to tell a reader
what he or she believes to be true. But what to do when one's
senses are all aflutter? How to square actual events with skewed
memories of them? And isn't every account of the past – whether or
not animated by *pipiska putina* – eventually revealed to be a story,
written as all histories, of and for their time? The truffle's effect on
me was at once invigorating and strangely subtle: clammy palms,
racing heart, dilated pupils. I felt energised and level-headed at the
same time. Certainly I was no cool and objective reporter, although
I wouldn't go so far as to say that it had made me unreliable. In any
case, I reasoned, truth has always been much stranger than fiction
in Russia.

At some point in the night I'd woken to see Dmitri sprawled across the sofa like some Gogol caricature, deep in 'that marvellous slumber which is known only to those fortunate beings who are bothered neither by haemorrhoids, nor fleas, nor overdeveloped mental faculties'. He had departed early, hell-bent on some secretive mission, leaving behind a Range Rover, a driver and Anna. She'd brought me a cup of black tea, explaining that she had been instructed to take me to the Patriot Park Army Show.

'He said that we may do as you wish,' she added in a soft monotone voice.

Patriot Park was Russia's military Disneyland, a grandiose estate of glitzy exhibition halls and plush conference venues surrounding a mass of nasty military hardware. Hundreds of ultramodern tanks, futuristic mine-clearing robots and innovative Arctic hovercraft loomed over a vast courtyard the size of two football pitches. Around it salesmen from Arsenal Arms, Kalashnikov Industries and UVZ Uralvagonzavod demonstrated armed drones and Balkan grenade launchers. Children clambered over artillery pieces and Terminator fire-support combat vehicles. Grandparents struck poses at the controls of huge S-400 Triumph anti-aircraft missile launchers. On a Ural Typhoon's dusty windscreen, a patriotic visitor had written 'Russia', irony not being a local virtue.

As well as a place for 'family fun', Patriot Park was Russia's foreign arms sales bazaar. When Vladimir Putin opened the 13,500-acre park, he'd called it 'an important element in our system of military-patriotic work with young people'. He'd also used the occasion to announce the addition of forty advanced ballistic missiles to the nuclear arsenal.

Anna and I had pushed through the crowds at the Berlin Reichstag replica, built for Yunarmia cadets to practise their assault techniques, and skirted the Innovative Weapons Technology tent to reach the vast Alabino range. The previous day's rain had taken the sting out of the heat and both grandstands were packed with excited merry-makers: decorated veterans in waterproof shells, toddlers holding red and blue balloons, teenage girls wearing short summer dresses and souvenir army caps set at jaunty angles. Anna wore a silk shirt, black skirt and no make-up, except on her toenails which were painted pink. As we searched for our seats, she'd talked about herself, about life in Moscow and about the country itself.

'Russia must educate its children,' she said, nodding towards an animated school group sharing buckets of Robopop popcorn. 'Or America will do it for us, as they tried in Ukraine. We must defend ourselves against US aggression and other terrorists.'

'Terrorists?' I asked.

'Like those who killed my father.'

Martial music and black exhaust then cut across our conversation, spewing 'The March of Soviet Tankmen' into the air, filling it with boasts of courageous men and invincible armour. A column of fighting vehicles thundered past the grandstands at full speed, a T-80 turned on a rouble and a BTR-80 armoured personnel carrier released a squad of infantrymen. Next a T-90 forded the adjoining lake, with only its snorkel and cannon breaking the surface. Two TOS-1 heavy flamethrowers followed, blazing an arc of fire across our field of vision. When a Smerch multiple rocket launcher took aim at a distant target, and it erupted with an ear-splitting roar, I realised it wasn't only my senses that were explosive. Live ammunition was fired at the annual show.

'Thundering with fire, glinting with steel...' enthused another patriotic song as a phalanx of Mi-35 Hind helicopter gunships appeared above our heads and paratroopers sailed down to the ground, forming up to advance swiftly on an imagined enemy.

On the field, television cameramen darted between the machines, moved in for close-ups, then set up for the 'tank ballet' where Bolshoi dancers pirouetted around a ring of T-80s. Their video feed was projected onto both huge screens around the park and the network.

Overhead the Swifts and Falcons aerobatic teams – flying MiG-29s and Sukhoi Su-30 fighter bombers – laid red, white and blue smoke trails across the sky, their loops, barrel rolls and fly-pasts accompanied by heavy rock music.

'Welcome our pilots!' commanded the announcer, calling out the names of the high-flying airmen. 'Welcome Team Commander

Viktor Selutin! Wingman Ivan Osyaikin! Master Pilot Sergey Vasiliev! Applaud louder, people, so they can hear you!'

The aircraft climbed and stalled, released dazzling magnesium flares, tumbled towards the ground and then relit their engines to dive at the ecstatic, awestruck crowd. People stood on their chairs, applauding the spectacle. In the grand finale the audience touched their hearts for the national anthem and Anna repeated, 'Beautiful'.

At the end of the show we walked away through a haze of jet fumes, along a corridor of sparkly red plastic stars, pausing at an historical display of 'captured' Second World War German armour.* At Patriot Park, as elsewhere in Russia, the victory over Nazism was sacred. Why? Because after the gulags, after the economic failure, after the humiliation of millions under the Soviet system, it was the one achievement of which all Russians could be proud.

'We can do it again!' read a young man's baseball cap, the jingoistic catchphrase printed beneath the hammer and sickle that perpetrated – as it did on every military vehicle in the park – the glorious memory of the Great Patriotic War.

At the park canteen, a security goon patted me down for a concealed weapon as heavy artillery rounds flashed on the horizon. Lunch consisted of borsch, army rations and *ptichye moloko* marshmallow cake. Anna only wanted a coffee, saying that she had to watch her figure, and chatted at length about making one's own way in life. The truffle hadn't made me want to invade Germany but it had emboldened me, so – prompted by her willingness to talk – I asked about her father's death.

'It's tied to my birth,' she said, tossing her plaited hair over her shoulder with a sigh.

---

* In fact all the German vehicles at Patriot Park were replicas, newly made in Russian factories as there were no longer enough originals to go round. In 2018 the Kremlin had even repatriated from Laos thirty of its own vintage T-34s to star in military parades and film shoots.

In 1999 Anna's parents had lived in south-east Moscow, she told me. Her mother had worked at a local supermarket until the last week of her pregnancy. She'd had no choice as her husband hadn't been paid for months.

In the first years after the collapse of communism, Russia's gross domestic product had fallen by half, more than America's during the Great Depression. Bank savings had been wiped out by inflation. Free health care ceased to exist. Male life expectancy crashed to fifty-seven years, the lowest level in the industrial world. People struggled to survive, asking if there was such a thing as right and wrong, while criminals lorded it over both their streets and the Kremlin. Anna's parents knew that they would need every kopek to buy a good life for their first-born.

When her mother had gone into labour, her father found a taxi to run them to the hospital. But in the rush her overnight bag was left behind in the kitchen. Once she was admitted to the ward, he'd popped back to retrieve it from their apartment. He never returned.

Around midnight, the dead and dying of Guryanova Street began to arrive at the hospital, their bloody stretchers lining the white-tiled corridors. Medics and nurses swirled around the injured, stemming haemorrhages, commandeering beds. As her contractions increased, Anna's mother had been wheeled through the gory melee towards the delivery room. She was screaming by now, both in pain and for her husband. An hour or two later Anna was hauled out of her weeping, widowed mother into an age desperate for certainty.

On that pivotal birth night, their Guryanova Street apartment building had been destroyed. Some 400 kilograms of explosives had been detonated on its ground floor and the nine-storey structure had collapsed, killing and injuring hundreds in a horror of flying glass and crumbled concrete. A charmless and little-known bureaucrat – a former FSB (Federal Security Service) head, successor of the KGB – then stepped forward to announce to the traumatised nation that the perpetrators were terrorists who had been trained in Chechnya. 'We will pursue the terrorists everywhere,' he declared at a news conference. 'If they are in an airport, then in an airport and, forgive me, if we catch them in the toilet, then we'll *mochit* them – rub them out – in the toilet.'

No matter that the Chechens insisted that they had nothing to do with the bombings. Overnight the Russian people had an enemy on which to focus their anger, and the popularity of the charmless bureaucrat – whose name was Vladimir Putin – soared in the wake of his televised revenge attack on Chechnya. Three months later he stood in the country's presidential election, and won.

Anna grew up in his world, a pale and serious girl haunted by the shock of her terrible first night. Its tension – her mother's pain – had been absorbed into her body, gripping her muscles, subjecting her to severe migraines throughout childhood. Every birthday reminded her of what she had lost. Yet she never questioned that her father had been taken by anyone other than 'terrorists'. Russia's new leader had said it was so, and he was too exemplary, too powerful, to be doubted.

On my travels I try to be invisible. I aim to be a kind of conduit, asking the reader not to look at me but to look with me. I want to portray the people who I meet as they are, not to try to change them, which means I tend to keep my opinions to myself. But with Anna I couldn't stay quiet. I couldn't let her continue to live a lie. Instead I blundered in.

In 1999 a terrible beauty had been born in Russia, I told her. In that fatal September the die had been cast for her country's future. The Guryanova Street bombing had been one of a series of coordinated attacks on civilian targets in Moscow as well as in Buynaksk and Volgodonsk. None of them had been perpetrated by 'terrorists'.

At the time, politicians and oligarchs alike were hated for their pillage of the country. For them to survive, faith had to be restored in the regime. The FSB was instructed to make people afraid. One of its vehicles and two employees – both of whom later died in mysterious circumstances – were even caught transporting sacks of explosives to the cellar of a sixth target, in the city of Ryazan south-east of Moscow. In addition, RDX hexogen, the key ingredient in all the bombs including at Guryanova Street, was held in facilities under the exclusive control of the FSB.

'What? Blow up our own apartment buildings? You know, that is really … utter nonsense! It's totally insane,' said Putin when the facts came out, and in response to accusations of complicity. 'No one in the Russian Special Services would be capable of such a crime against his own people.'

Then he shut down the public enquiry.

In the Patriotic Park cafe, I told Anna that the Russian apartment bombings had been the greatest political provocation on the continent since the burning of the Reichstag. It was an event – a conscious and decisive act – that obsessed me, both because of its iniquity and because of how much it had changed Europe.

When I had finished talking, she stared at me. She blinked her child-like eyes. She seemed unable to grasp my meaning as if I'd been speaking in tongues. Then she must have decided that the truffle had distorted my reason. She tossed her plait over her shoulder again and said, 'This is not true.'

To kick off the afternoon's entertainment, balaclava-wearing dancers in Spetsnaz SAS uniforms performed a robot ballet on the main stage. Families checked out riot-control vehicles and inflatable, full-size MiG decoys, useful to confuse enemies at times when deceit alone won't do. In the souvenir shop knick-knack hunters bought Putin fridge magnets and bomber jackets adorned with the word 'Victory'. A baby's cot in the form of a Buk missile launcher was among the weekend's specials. Nearby a child ate a hot dog beside an intercontinental ballistic missile (ICBM) capable of destroying an entire country.

To ease the enmity that had come between us, I asked Anna how she had come to work for Dmitri. Again with candidness she volunteered that she had never joined the *tiolki* – the 'cattle' – at the Gaudi Club or the Lookin Rooms, flirting with wealthy strangers, hoping to be spotted by a 'sponsor'. She wouldn't trade on her body, she assured me, not even in exchange for the best love-nest apartment on Rublevka – Moscow's billionaires row.

'For me this is just a job,' she said, adding that she planned to study psychology at night school. 'Dmitri Denisovich has promised to pay the fees.'

At the Kalashnikov stand, thrill-seekers queued to test the new AK-74M assault gun. A demonstration of the firing performance of the company's RSHG-2 rocket grenade launcher was delayed until after tea. Beyond them, at the far end of the exhibition hall, a father berated a child. I hadn't noticed the misdemeanour but it couldn't have been serious: a thoughtless joke or dropped piece of cake. Yet the man seemed to want to make a point. He towered over the silent boy, who lowered his head in shame. He yelled at his son, swelling in his boots as he diminished him. I remembered a story of the daughters of an Irish farmer. Their father had owned a pig and, one day, without provocation, in a game, the young girls had hit it with a stick. Its squeals amused them so they struck it again, and again. They beat the pig until it was dead.

At the end of the day I didn't have the stomach to visit the nearby Kubinka Tank Museum, said to be the world's largest collection of armoured war machines. Instead I decided to head back to Moscow, alone. Anna's absence of doubt disturbed me, and a sudden wave of anger washed over me. I asked myself if she might argue that a strong leader had a duty to wield power, even to commit crimes, for the good of the nation. I wondered if she'd accept that the murder of 293 people, including her own father, had been the price to pay for Russia's resurrection.

We parted at the centre of the park beneath a statue of Georgy Zhukov, the Red Army commander who had captured Berlin in 1945. A simple inscription appeared on the plinth, but not Zhukov's name. The deliberate omission of his name transformed the statue's meaning. It was a code that every Russian understood. 'To the Marshal of the Victory' did not refer to Zhukov, but rather to Stalin … and by extension to the once little-known bureaucrat who'd unveiled the statue a few years earlier.

6

Tell Me Another One

We all like a good story. We all need a narrative for our lives. The most potent stories give us an idea or individual to believe in, as well as someone to blame when things go wrong: Stalin loved little children, Jews caused Germany's ills, Middle East migrants bring cholera into Europe, Brussels strips the UK of its independence. Today many Russians have come to fancy that there was a golden age that can be reclaimed, that the whole Soviet people marched in step on Red Square on May Day, calling out in a single voice 'Glory! Glory to the victorious people!'

The Second World War wasted Europe. Over six hellish years the Soviet Union lost 1,700 towns, 70,000 villages and 26 million men, women and children. Leningrad was besieged for 872 days. More than half of Russian POWs died of starvation or neglect in German camps. Eleven million more lives were snuffed out in the Holocaust. Warsaw was dynamited street by street, neighbourhood by neighbourhood. One in five Poles died, as did one in six Lithuanians. In the war's final fortnight, 40,000 tons of Soviet shells fell on Berlin. In Hitler's pulverised capital, the vengeful conquerors raped at least 100,000 women (about two million in Germany as a whole). Then the Red Army marched over three million German prisoners to Siberian gulags, some of whom would not return for a decade.

With the defeat of Nazism, the devastated continent was split like a rotten melon. Its western half was flooded with American dollars and defended by Allied armies. Its Soviet east was sustained by fear. At Yalta, Stalin had agreed to free elections for all Europeans but, as most communist parties were too unpopular to gain power through the ballot box, he used coercion to tighten their grip. First the Red Army refused to withdraw, then communists allied themselves with interim governments. Every day, from within, they demanded more and more power, cutting away elected authority like salami, thin slice after thin slice. Next they secured control of the police, aided by the threat of Russian bayonets. Opponents were arrested and their leaderless parties absorbed. Finally the elections, fettered by fraud and police terror, were rigged. Within two or three years, communists took over every government east of the Brandenburg Gate. It was an effective system.

Stalin's objective was to create a buffer zone, as had Catherine the Great when she'd seized Crimea and parts of Poland, as had Tsar Alexander I after Napoleon's defeat. To protect Moscow, Uncle Joe annexed Bessarabia and northern Bukovina from Romania. He peeled away a slice of Hungary. Estonia, Latvia and Lithuania lost their independence so he could have access to the Baltic. He severed uranium-rich Ruthenia, the eastern tail of Slovakia. He lopped off yet more Polish territory and incorporated it into Soviet Ukraine.

He also tried to draw Berlin – and then the whole of Germany – into the communist orbit. In 1948 he blockaded the city in an effort to drive the Americans out of Europe. But the Allies retaliated by launching an airlift to sustain the city's freedom. Stalin was forced to back down, and the Cold War turned hot.

Over the next forty years the end of the world was nigh. MAD, or mutual assured destruction, was a pyrrhic military strategy that ensured any attack doomed both the aggressor and the defender. At the touch of a button life on Earth could be extinguished. The suicidal nuclear deterrent sustained an edgy status quo through the Hungarian Revolution and Cuban missile crisis, Prague Spring and Vietnam War, until 1989 and the fall of the Wall.

In that optimistic year, Eastern Europeans embraced the democracy that Stalin had denied them. As the Red Army withdrew, they chose 'a historically new kind of order through the process of unification' (Václav Havel again), aligning themselves with the borderless, cooperative European Union. Two years later the USSR itself – the world's largest nation – imploded, liberating further millions from Soviet tyranny, ending generations of repression, bringing unfamiliar freedoms and responsibilities.

Mikhail Gorbachev had come to power in 1985 to revitalise the USSR. He'd championed restructuring and openness. He'd relaxed censorship and encouraged truth-telling. His reforms – and unwillingness to use force – freed Eastern Europe. But at home his changes floundered and slipped out of control: first because administrators had neither the experience nor the enterprise to carry them forward – decades of terror had wiped free thinking out of the civil service; and second because of shame.

With the collapse of communism, and the release of secret files, Russians could no longer deny that they were complicit in Soviet crimes: loading innocents into cattle trucks, lifting rifles in a firing squad, spying on neighbours, turning a blind eye. The truth was too much to bear and, in response, unrepentant hard-liners imprisoned Gorbachev and tried to seize control of parliament. Their coup was thwarted by mass protests and hijacked by the shrewd and impulsive Boris Yeltsin.

'Behind our backs there was treachery. Behind my back,' recalled Gorbachev, who later told the BBC that he'd recognised the real danger of civil war. 'A split in society and a struggle in a country like ours, overflowing with weapons, including nuclear ones, could have left so many people dead and caused such destruction. I could not let that happen just to cling to power.'

At the Kremlin the Soviet flag was lowered for the last time, taking with it the illusion of a people's Utopia. The seductive dream that had shaped the country was exposed as a deception and Russians found themselves with no ideology to cling to, and no vision for the future.

Individuals, often young and cynical, always with connections, stepped into the moral vacuum. Power and public property fell into their hands, weakening the state. They positioned themselves as the new 'authorities', forming the only bodies to hold society together. Bribery and violence consolidated their position. Critics and competitors were ruined, killed or co-opted into the profiteering new elite.

As food costs tripled and inflation wiped out nominal savings, Moscow became the global capital of inequality (the richest 10 per cent came to own 87 per cent of all the country's wealth). Ordinary people began to long for their Soviet past. Their nostalgia was manipulated – by the compliant media – into a public acceptance of the restoration of Soviet political practices. The apartment building bombings perpetrated the myth that enemies surrounded Russia. Once again NATO was cast as an aggressor thrusting into Russia's historical buffer zone.

Of course the propaganda worked because people needed something to believe. Russians were in trauma, their collective memory racked by historical suffering and guilt. There was no appetite for the Freudian idea – which had so transformed Germany after the Second World War – that the repressed (or at least unspoken) will fester like a canker until it is brought to light.

Hence in Russia there were no Nuremberg trials. No one accepted responsibility for the gulags, for carrying out Stalin's orders, for KGB snatch squads, for snitching on a neighbour to save one's own skin. Any idea of collective repentance vanished.

Instead, in their need for a new identity, Russians embraced a mythologised version of history: deifying Stalin, welcoming the restoration of the Soviet national anthem, printing school textbooks that glorified the Red Army and condemned its withdrawal from Germany as a 'fatal mistake'. They accepted – or at least considered possible – untruths such as the idea that it was Gorbachev who destroyed the Soviet Union, that Ukrainian nationalists crucified ethnic Russian children and Malaysia Airlines flight MH17 had been pre-loaded with 'rotting corpses' in Amsterdam. Their sense of belonging was restored by old blood-and-soil nationalism.

'DON'T LIE! DON'T PARTICIPATE IN LIES, DON'T SUPPORT A LIE!' the novelist and Nobel laureate Aleksandr Solzhenitsyn had written in an open letter after the publication of *Gulag Archipelago*. 'In our country, the daily lie is not the whim of corrupt nature, but a mode of existence, a condition of the daily welfare of every man. In our country, the lie has been incorporated into the state system as the vital link holding everything together, with billions of tiny fasteners, several dozen to each man.'

No one listened.

At the start of the twenty-first century, many Russians – and then many Westerners – lost their appetite for the truth. They chose not to ask questions, preferring the easy choice of falsehood, of being fed simplistic solutions to complicated problems, of championing leaders who had – who have – the power to reshape reality in line with their stories.

Lies became the glue that held people together.

7

Stranger in Moscow

Kremlin means fortress. For almost a thousand years the Moskovskiy Kreml has been a bastion. Slavic tribes, grand dukes and tsars made it their citadel. Stalin envisioned it as the sacred heart of his supreme world capital. As the self-proclaimed 'father and the sun of the nation' he occupied its Corpus No. 1, until his wife Nadezhda shot herself on the building's third floor. Once a boggy, thirty-metre-wide moat separated it from the *bydlo* – the rabble – of Moscow town. Today only the moat is gone.

I circled the fortress, stepped onto the trim grass verge and strode forward to touch the looming walls, until driven back to the pavement by a policeman's whistle. In 1839 the French traveller Marquis de Custine described the sixty-eight-acre stronghold as a 'satanic monument … that would suit some of the personages of the Apocalypse'. Its bricks, mortar and iconic spires still radiated a demonic air, and not only in my buzzing brain. The dead permeated the place. Myriad mortal remains festered in its earth and walls; in the bones of beheaded boyars and disgraced patriarchs, in the ashes of murdered servants and charred cosmonauts, in the dust of Bolshevik revolutionaries dumped by the hundred into mass graves. Lenin lay in his dark mausoleum, a fallen Soviet god in glass sarcophagus with right hand clenched into a fist. Stalin was here too, his cursed – yet revered – skeleton entombed beneath a stone bust with eyes downcast in false humility.

Beyond its walls, within which Uncle Joe had signed sheaves of death warrants, the body count defied reason: a million 'enemies' imprisoned or exiled during his first years in power, ten to twelve million peasants forced off their land in his murderous collectivisation programme, six or seven million starved to death during his artificial famine, yet more executed or dispatched to forced labour camps during the Great Terror, ten to twelve million innocents then relocated in the Second World War, and a final million arrested for 'political crimes' in the months before Stalin's own death. All of them, all of Russia's victims and victors, its duped and deified, haunted this place, magnifying its air of menace, casting a shadow over the city and the country.

'Glory! Glory to the victorious people!'

In Red Square I stopped and stared, stopped and stared and shivered for – beneath those looming walls – Russian day trippers ate double-scoop chocolate ice-cream cones and laughed. In the summer sunshine I was shocked by their casual smiles, by their careless pleasure, by their forgetfulness.

It was then that my journey turned, in one serendipitous moment, in a rush of emotion and good fortune. I looked across Red Square and recognised the man I'd seen with the bird on the metro. He was scurrying around the edge of the crowd with his head down and shoulders hunched, hobbling like a wounded animal, wearing headphones.

I dropped my haunted thoughts as he vanished behind the newly revised State Historical Museum. I darted between school groups, organised tours and a pair of Lenins in characteristic flat cloth-worker's cap. Next to them other unemployed actors were dressed as Stalin, smoking cherry-root pipes as they worked the happy-go-lucky crowd, posing for photographs and pocketing dollar-bill tips. I jogged on, elbowing aside Genghis Khan, the genocidal ruler preferred by Chinese visitors, but lost sight of the hobbling stranger in the crush at Resurrection Gate. On a whim

I turned right towards Revolution Square. That was the nearest metro station and, I guessed, his destination.

Across the square, beyond Moscow's last remaining monument to Karl Marx, stood the Hotel Metropol. Over the years Lenin and Trotsky had given speeches in its Great Hall. Bertolt Brecht, Mao Zedong and Marlene Dietrich had stayed in its luxury suites (although not at the same time). It was here that the Russian lyric poet Sergei Yesenin had declared his love for Isadora Duncan, and John Steinbeck worked with Robert Capa on *A Russian Journal*. I don't know why I noticed the hotel now but as my eyes slid across its art nouveau facade, I spotted the man again, descending a flight of steps in front of it. With Putin's Pecker still swelling my courage, I shot after him, back under ground and, at the head of the escalators, I reached out to tap his shoulder.

'*Ot'yebites!*' he said, spinning around to face me, at once defiant and fearful. Fuck off. Strangers never touch Muscovites, unless the stranger is intoxicated, which I was of course.

'The bird,' I said, catching my breath. '*L'oiseau*,' I tried, grasping for a common language. '*J'étais là dans le métro*.' I didn't know the word in Russian, let alone in Arabic, Hausa or Yoruba. 'I saw you on the metro.'

The man was thirtyish, loose-limbed, lean and lithe with dark brown eyes and full lips set in a slender face. His sunglasses were pushed back into his thick black hair. A 'Patriotic Russia' tracksuit top was slung around his neck, its arms dangling at his sides.

'What do you want?' he asked with the distinctive musical lilt of West African English.

I told him and he laughed, his eyes widening above the deep shadows. 'My friend, I am sorry. I am too busy,' he replied, cutting me dead. As annoyed commuters shoved by us, he stepped back and turned away with an unexpected spin. His movement was nimble and strangely familiar, apart from a peculiar hesitancy in his right foot.

'Michael Jackson!' I blurted excitedly, trying my own (lame) spin, and the man stopped in his tracks. His backwards glide had reminded me of the singer's iconic moonwalk. I'd also recognised

Jacko's 'Billie Jean' ringing in his headphones. 'Michael Jackson stayed at the hotel on this square,' I went on, clutching at straws, gesturing above our heads, my fascination with cross-cultural pop trivia finding some use at last. I guessed that the man was a fan. 'He played the piano in its foyer,' I added.

The African stared at me for an age. He searched my face. He took half a step forward and for a moment I thought he was going to hit me. Then he turned up his collar with a studied flick and said, 'Show me.'

Africans are as rare as hen's teeth in Moscow, apart from students who'd been drawn by bargain basement tuition fees. Once thousands had studied in the USSR but the man was too young to be a fraternal nations relic, and too poorly dressed to be a modern businessman. I wanted to know why he was in the city.

The Metropol's maître d' pointed us to a corner table hidden behind a pillar. Sami didn't hang back from the lavish buffet, working his way along it. As he loaded his plate with salmon pancakes, crêpes and pastries, his nest of hair – gathered, coiled and woven into a dense stack as if by a precise subtropical bird – tilted on his head like a living black turban. In his plastic carrier bag was a single pot of instant noodles.

As he'd ploughed through his second helping, I told him that Jackson's piano stood by the entrance to the Grand Hall beneath the ornate stained-glass roof, pointing to a harpist playing Chopin Preludes beside it. I said that in 1993 Jacko had been the first American pop star to perform in post-Soviet Russia. After the show he'd written 'Stranger in Moscow' in his room.

'Upstairs, here?' he replied, raising an index finger. His hands were so fine as to appear sculpted. 'Man, that's inspirational.'

I half expected him to bolt at any moment but instead he told me that years earlier (and before the accusations of sexual abuse) he'd seen a video of that same concert, 4,000 miles away in northern Nigeria. At a corner drinks stall he and his teenage friends had tried to mimic Jackson's dance moves, perfecting circle slides and MJ spins along Sokoto's alleyways.

'At home I was like a street dancer, like the kid who got up first to get some moves off his chest,' he said, leaning forward, relaxing back into English. 'Jackson sang, "Beat It". He taught that no one should be defeated.'

I refilled our cups and heard then, and over our many later meetings, that Sami's father had been a plantation manager, supervising irrigation projects, advising on the rotation of maize and millet. His mother had been a housemaid at one of the larger farms. As his parents worked away from home, Sami was raised by his mother's sisters on the outskirts of the city. He did well at school, I learned, graduating top of his year in mathematics and deciding to study bookkeeping because he'd kept his father's accounts for years.

'I didn't think of it as work. I saw it as my duty.'

Sami had wanted to see something of the world but that wasn't an option, especially after his mother suffered kidney failure during his second year at college. The cost of her treatment, drugs, syringes and a full-time carer to turn her over in the hospital bed ruined his father. When she died the aunties, who'd mortgaged their land to fund Sami's education, also wanted to be paid.

'This happened in my life and it cut me deep,' he said, not taking his eyes off mine.

I saw no anger lines etched across his face, heard no defeat in his voice. In time I would come to know him as one of the most hopeful people I've ever met, yet suffering must have marked him, for overnight, Sami and his father had been cast into debt. They'd been forced to sell the truck, could afford neither an agricultural licence nor tuition fees. Their best chance to make a new start was at the nearby Bukkuyum mines, one of the hottest places on Earth.

Day after day father and son had laboured beside each other, dropping into the deep shafts by gripping grooves dug in the wall. There were no safety ropes to break a fall, no support struts to protect them in the narrow, stifling galleries. Eleven hours a day and seven days a week, they hacked away at the rock face looking for a seam of gold. At any moment the mine could collapse, burying them alive.

Yet somehow throughout the seven terrible months, Sami – with a certain glorious energy – kept dancing.

'People thought I was crazy, but that's the thing that kept me sane. I'd tell myself: how good can our days be, if we waste them on dead feelings?'

Every evening, he'd moonwalked and side-slid across the clay-hard riverbeds and around the desperate work camp, entertaining the heavy-eyed itinerants as well as the tagalong sex workers. He'd thrilled to 'Thriller', trusted 'You Are Not Alone', played 'Bad' over and over until the pirated cassette tape stretched and wowed in the baking heat. Only when he began to lose the spring in his step did he realise that he had to make a choice. Join the exodus, or stay and die.

'My father told me, look at the man in the mirror,' said Sami, paraphrasing Jackson's lyrics. 'He told me to look at myself, then to make a change.'

Sami's escape became possible when his father unearthed a single, thumb-sized nugget. They traded it with the boss man (a Hausa with plump, ringed fingers and black pointed shoes), paid shares to their fellow miners and, with the balance, hired a 'travel agent'. Sami wanted to try for England, the ideal of generations of Nigerians (and Ghanaians, Gambians and Ugandans). He wanted to better himself, to make money and then to come home. He had an uncle in London, or some city to the north. The English were tolerant and welcoming, he'd heard. He also knew that Jackson had once planned to live there.

The agent advised Sami against land and sea routes. Turkey and the Aegean had ceased to be reliable, or rather more impossible. Russia had emerged as an obliging transit country, if one was able to pay.

Sami took a leap of faith, into the unknown, towards a world that offered to sustain his hope. He flew to Mexico then backtracked to transit through Madrid's lax airport controls. He had never before been on an aircraft, didn't sleep during the three-day journey and hoarded all the in-flight meals to see him through the coming week.

At Moscow's Sheremetyevo airport, his (fake) return ticket secured him a twenty-day tourist visa. But the promised ride to Belarus and the Polish border wasn't waiting for him. In his exhaustion he stepped out onto the terminal's approach road, looked the wrong way and was struck by a minibus.

'My father sacrificed everything for me but the accident was a rightful curse,' he said at the Metropol. 'A rightful curse.'

The minibus had belonged to the Martha and Mary Convent of Mercy. A century earlier the order had been founded to assist sick and wounded soldiers, as well as to provide for the needs of local poor. I learned later that the October Revolution had put paid to its good works, the Bolsheviks looting and desecrating its churches, turning one of them into a cinema. After the collapse of communism, the sisterhood was restored and a moneyed laywoman (in irreverent short skirt, Hermès silk scarf and with the right connections) had been appointed its prioress. But her mission had little to do with saving souls, and the one-and-a-half-hectare central Moscow site was sold for millions of roubles ... on the very day that Sami was wheeled into its infirmary.

'The nuns set my leg in plaster, then went on strike,' he explained.

A sister convent – which Sami would not name – took him in. It was a much poorer outfit, its handful of malnourished novices squatting in an abandoned Young Pioneers dormitory in the suburbs with broken windows and rising damp. Its chapel was a converted garage. There was little food to eat. But it gave Sami the time and space to recuperate, as his tourist visa expired and he became an illegal. In exchange for doing odd jobs, the prioress promised to look after him, and to keep him hidden.

'I worked hard for them, but they did not treat me with respect. That was a realisation for me.'

As the weeks passed and he regained his strength, the nuns – and their regular handyman – demanded more and more of Sami: ordering him to dig over the kitchen garden, to clear rubbish from the cellar, to repair the chapel (garage) roof. Once again he set about plotting his escape. He managed to contact the agent who was to have met him at the airport and arranged a new meeting point near to Red Square. But his conversation was overheard.

On his last evening at the convent he fell down the cellar steps. He didn't see who pushed him and his new injuries were not severe, no more than a badly twisted ankle, but the nuns – and the handyman – insisted on his lying down, and then sedated him. Overnight he was strapped to the bed, a cloth stuffed in his mouth and one of his toes cut off. Sami's labour had become valuable for them and, when he awoke, they threatened to call the police if he tried again to escape.

'Bitches,' he said.

Sami's story sent a chill through me. I'd read somewhere that at any one time an estimated fifteen million migrants are passing through (or trying to settle in) Russia. Migrants often embellish – even invent – narratives in the belief that their chances for asylum increase with added drama. But Sami had no reason to spin me a yarn, unless he imagined that I could help him. He also had a limp.

In the rotten convent he'd played the nuns' game for three more weeks – cowed, subservient and grateful – until one day when they were at vespers. He locked them into the former body shop and hobbled away. A few hours later I saw him on the metro.

'That bird was a rightful sign for me,' he said. 'A sign.'

As he'd told his story, his voice had grown louder, prouder, until it drew the maître d' to our table, with the bill. He explained that our table was reserved, even though there was hardly another soul in the restaurant. His arrogant air brought an immediate change in Sami. He seemed to shrink before my eyes, wrenching back his openness and rising to his feet obediently. He was anxious to avoid the attention of authority, and the bully had intimidated him.

As I paid, he hurried away with shoulders hunched once again, past Michael Jackson's piano, around the marble fountain and beneath the hotel's elaborate Princess of Dreams ceramic facade. The mosaic panels depicted the legend of a beautiful princess who fell in love with a traveller. When he died the princess renounced her worldly life and became a nun.

At the door Sami wouldn't give me his mobile number. He told me that he'd said too much. He regretted letting down his guard. I scribbled my address on a page torn from my notebook and asked him to contact me in a few days.

'Forget it, man,' he said, then looked back at the panels and repeated, 'Bitches.'

8

Beat It

I did want to help Sami and so went in search of Dmitri. He would have the means to get him back on his feet, so to speak. He might order his Learjet to fly him straight to London. At least that's what I fancied. By good fortune Dmitri was also looking for me.

'I have new offer you cannot say no,' he said on the phone.

We met at VDNKh, pronounced 've-de-en-kha', Stalin's tragi-comic Exhibition of Achievements of National Economy. VDNKh was a vestige of the worker's paradise gone awry, created by the great dictator himself with triumphalist pavilions, earnest agricultural exhibitions and endless heroic statues of miners and farm labourers clutching pickaxes or sheaves of wheat to their swelling chests. Nothing was understated in its – or Dmitri's – world.

'Some people born great. Others make great, like me,' he enthused, garbling Shakespeare. His self-importance remained as inflated as his hallucinogens. 'Today great is coming to you.'

I knew where he was going so, as we strode together along the Alley of the Cosmonauts (shadowed by Vasya and a Range Rover), I sidestepped his ghost-writing proposal to tell him about Sami. He humoured me until I said that the nuns had cut off Sami's toe.

'Did they test for AIDS?' he asked.

'AIDS? Why on earth would they have tested him for AIDS?'

'All Africans must test to keep Russia pure.'

I tried to explain that Sami wasn't ill, that he had taken the chance – found the courage – to try to improve his life. 'Just like you,' I ventured.

Dmitri spat at the ground, shocking me. 'But he is black, you say.'

'Yes.'

'Listen, I am not racist. I am realist. Business needs foreign workers. In my chicken factory were many Ukrainians and Moldovans. They were not so different. They worked for peanut. But black? Muslim? No, thank you,' he said, working himself into a lather.

'In Europe you let in too many foreigners,' he went on before I could respond. 'You know what will one day happen? Jesus and Madonna will go from church. Sharia law will become European law. But never in Russia. Never. We want purity so if you are not pure, get out.'

Millions of Russians have chosen to do just that, I pointed out. Over the last thirty years, emigration – which had been all but impossible during the communist era – has drained the country of its brightest and best. Since the fall of the Wall, more than three-quarters of Russia's Jews have moved abroad. In the last couple of years alone a quarter of a million other Russians have applied for US green cards. Today there are as many holders of Soviet-era doctor of science degrees working in the United States as in Russia itself. And as the country nudges towards a nationalistic future, the Kremlin does not complain. Moscow seems happy to see the backs of freethinkers and potential protesters, who leave behind them a more compliant and passive population.

'Sami also needs help to leave,' I said, appealing to Dmitri's humanity. 'Can you at least suggest how he can get to the border?'

'*Chelovek bez rodiny, kak solovei bez pesni,*' he replied roughly. A man without a homeland is like a nightingale without a song.

Dmitri had been shaped by communism's failure, and by the cut-throat cynicism that had succeeded it. He had fought to survive in a society where craftiness and ruthlessness were more vital than integrity. He wouldn't help Sami but something I'd said had struck a chord.

We walked on, circling the Friendship of Peoples' Fountain, a frothy confection of sixteen gilded female figures dressed in ethnic costumes and representing the old Soviet republics. Ahead rose the freshly painted 'Russia – My History' museum with three-storey-high portraits of Catherine the Great and Putin. Next to it stood the abandoned Ukrainian pavilion, its padlocked doors flanked by crumbling statues and cracked concrete hammers and sickles.

'Now I talk,' said Dmitri. 'I said before you are ambitious.'

'Yes, and so is Sami,' I replied, refusing to give up.

'I talk about you now. You have smart thinking face. You can double your cleverness if you listen to me. What are *The Thirteen*, *The Great Snake* and *White Sun of the Desert*?'

'They're movies.'

'Yes. Russian movies. Russian *Western* movies.'

White Sun of the Desert was a retelling of *The Magnificent Seven*. In *The Thirteen* nasty capitalist bandits set upon cowboy-like Red Army soldiers. In *At Home Among Strangers* the Apaches are portrayed as Civil War anti-communists.

'I love Russian Westerns and your book – my story – can be movie, for sure.'

In years past American cowboy films had been hugely popular in the USSR. Even Stalin was a fan, ordering Soviet cineastes to remake John Ford's *The Lost Patrol*. But after the old villain's death, the genre was deemed to be counter-revolutionary, in its praise of white colonialists and portrayal of Native Americans as bloodthirsty savages. Hence the birth of *Red* Westerns, produced in the Soviet Union and East Germany, substituting the Urals for Nevada and subverting Western clichés in order to criticise foreign culture.

'Tell me, what are two biggest victories in European history? Not Great Patriotic War. Not 1917 Revolution. No. Bigger and more great are victories over Mongol and Muslim.'

'That was in the fifteenth century,' I pointed out.

'Yes. After 700 *years'* occupation,' he replied, not overly burdened with historical accuracy. 'People must know danger is coming again.'

'And you're making a movie about it?'

'Red Western movie.'

'And this is also a reworking of *Nineteen Eighty-Four*?'

'Both is allegory, like I say.'

This then was Dmitri's agenda, and it stopped me in my tracks, along with Vasya and the shadowing Range Rover. Somehow he'd learned about my time in the film business.

'You'll direct it?' I asked.

'Acting too.'

'Can you ride a horse?'

'I get stunt double.'

Tinny music echoed through the park's ubiquitous loudspeaker system. A team of North Korean guest workers in wide-brimmed hats weeded between the pebbles in Young Naturalists Square. Children swept by them on bicycles and roller blades. A bridal couple posed for wedding photographs in front of the Stone Flower Fountain.

I'd played Dmitri along for too long. I'd drawn him out so as to hear what lunacy might next spill from his lips, to try to fathom that unspoken part of his personality. But my game had gone far enough. 'Dmitri Denisovich,' I told him, 'there won't be a book or film script for you, at least not written by me.'

'Give and take, if you know what I mean,' he replied in warning. 'I pay what you want. I buy you nice apartment in London or Berlin. No problem. Every man has price.'

'I can't do it,' I said.

The chicken tsar looked at me with disdain, staring as one might at a urinating dog. Then with a dark laugh the arch-opportunist said, 'I help your black man too.' He stretched his lips around his broken teeth in a semblance of a smile and added, 'I warn you, do not spit on my soul.'

The two buildings formed a rectangle around a small sloping Moscow square. Along the upper edge rose a monumental Stalinist block, its pantheon of Soviet gods gazing down across the courtyard at their broken Sixties sister. I rented a room in the lower block, without statues, beyond a copse of birch trees, behind a dirty, panelled balcony and double security door. My building's geometric steel frame rusted at its edges. Its raw concrete walls blocked out the sun.

Often at dawn I was awoken by the sound of fallen tiles, cracking underfoot beneath my jammed window. Early risers stepped around them on their way to the metro, ahead of the heat of the day. Schoolchildren dodged them, mounting the square's steps with heavy satchels and tread, chased by street-sweepers and the rising sun. Next came the squeak of prams, the yap of lapdogs and – just before ten – sure-footed bureaucrats striding towards a ministry building on the far-off riverbank. Later, a breath of air stirred the smell of boiled cabbage and meat-stuffed *golubtsy*, wafting it around the square as an aged veteran shuffled into town. He wore a black tie and medals (including the Afghan Order of the Star) when destined for another funeral, his silvery spectacles enfolded in his dark-veined hands.

After lunch the drunks lifted themselves from the corral of benches and staggered away in search of their next drink. An hour later they returned, bickering around the birches, cadging lights from passers-by, squatting on untended concrete planters that sprouted with wind-blown grasses. Come late afternoon the sun found a gap between the buildings, and residents gathered to catch its light. Old men played dominoes, grandmothers cracked open sunflower seeds and Uzbek labourers shared news from home. The feuding couple from House 2, Apartment 49 found a kind of privacy out in the open, away from the confines of their small family flat. Beyond them in the playground young mothers shepherded toddlers around a Kremlin tower climbing frame – known to residents as 'the ogre's castle' – until their husbands tramped home carrying shopping bags of onions and pickles.

With dusk the blue light of hundreds of televisions flickered on sheer nylon curtains. Water pipes gurgled between floors. The Korean nail salon closed its door and the old soaks fell into a half-hearted fistfight on the abandoned basketball court.

Two evenings I waited in the square. I waited not for the housewife, who ambled out after supper to sit cross-legged on a wall and smoke a cigarette, nor for the drunks snoring towards oblivion on the benches. Again and again I turned to look through the Stalinist archway, and between the trees, as if someone had called my name, or been there only a moment before, then melted into shadow.

On the third evening the shadow came to life and I recognised the familiar limp. Sami looked more tired than he had at our last meeting. The bags under his eyes seemed heavier. In his fist he clutched my address. We shook hands and I told him that Dmitri would be no help. He wasn't surprised, yet – as he sat down beside me – he seemed to crumple, his shoulders and head drooping in disappointment.

'It can't be rightfully so,' he said quietly. 'Can't be so.' I hadn't realised how much store he'd put in my mention of the chicken tsar. He took a deep breath and went on, 'You know, my father had a heavy hand but he kept me out of trouble. He wouldn't let me hang out with knuckleheads and problem-makers. He gave me my compass so I always found the right path.' Again he held my eye.

I remembered another story from thirty years ago. On that earlier trip I'd met a woman who, as a child, had caught three ants and put them into a jar. When they'd started to climb out, she'd shaken them back down to the bottom. Every time they'd tried to escape she'd made them fall. Finally, after many hours, the ants had given up, like the bird on the metro.

'It happened quite suddenly,' the woman had told me. 'I watched them for a long time, but they made no more attempts to get away. I left the jar outside for days in the rain and sun, but the ants just stayed in a circle and twitched their whiskers.'

In the shadowed courtyard, sitting in silence beside Sami, a deep sadness overcame me. All my life I've been free to travel as I've pleased. I've made plans, boarded aircraft and trains, reached back and forth across oceans and continents. I've been drawn towards the horizon, to the place just out of sight, driven forward by curiosity, by questions, by the need to understand the lives of others. I've inhabited a world of open doors, never imagining that those doors would close. And now new borders were rising again between people, keeping apart the haves and the have-nots, protecting the rich and damning the poor, mocking my naive notions of a family of man.

I looked at Sami and wondered what would make him give up his journey. How many times would he be shaken and pushed down? He told me that he was sleeping rough, that without a visa he'd soon be arrested. His only option was to carry on, he said. 'I keep on my path.'

I reached for my wallet and gave him $250. I didn't know what else to do, other than to wish him well.

'Good luck on your trip too, my friend,' he said to me.

9

Tentacles

At dusk the Black Sea swells into dark bays and hidden coves. Its currents twist around Stygian submarines, butt against rocking frigates, wash my ferry towards the wide stone landing-steps of Russia's great naval port.

I stepped ashore through Sevastopol's colonnaded gateway, stirring a wave of night birds to swirl above the shadowy villas. Ahead, sailors on shore leave and murmuring couples sauntered along the sea's inky edge, beneath rustling pines, towards Primorsky Boulevard. I followed in their wake, drawn forward by ripples of music.

In a waterside park, two dozen dancers whirled around the wheeled amplifier of a street entertainer. He crooned into a handheld microphone, chiding young and old onto their feet. In a medley of 1980s Russian pop songs – 'A Million Scarlet Roses', 'Lavanda', 'Broken Heart Tango' – he sang of love, loss and happiness ever after. Passers-by twirled for a happy moment or two, gripping partners or shopping bags. Holidaymakers clutched at the lyrics and each other. Swaying housewives waved their mobiles to the beat, calling home to explain that dinner would be late. A crew-cut mariner grasped the hand of a white-haired woman in a bright red dress. Two drunks staggered into the throng, steeped in delight, joining in the high-volume dance.

I stood at its periphery, reaching for my own mobile to record the event, until my hand too was seized and I was sucked into the whirlpool.

'You are a terrible dancer,' the twenty-something shouted into my ear after a moment. '*Kakoi zhe ty slon neuklyuzhiy.*' You move like an elephant.

She was small and well muscled with wide blue eyes and cropped copper-red hair. She spoke a mixture of Russian, Ukrainian and English. In her heeled motorcycle boots she stood no higher than my chin, but – as I discovered when she tried to spin herself around me – her spark made up for her short stature.

'Elephant,' she teased again, pushing me away. Yet come the next day I was sitting behind her on a Kawasaki.

Crimea lends itself to stories. Its history is a story based on fact, but not all the facts, woven together with creativity of one sort or another. In ancient times pirates and giant seafaring cannibals dropped anchor here, according to Homer. Greeks from a city named after (mythical) Hercules then settled on the (real) peninsula. In its murky inlets, Vladimir the Great is said to have chosen to be baptised, founding in AD 988 the Russian Orthodox Church (according to the legend he rejected Islam only because of its taboo against alcohol). Along the coast Lord Cardigan's Light Brigade charged into (poetic) infamy and the tsar's last loyalists escaped from prosaic reality aboard lines of steamships.

Tales true and half-true continued to be told up to the present day of course. Outside the capital's 'parliament' stands a new bronze statue of a bulked-up soldier receiving a flower from a young girl. It is dedicated to the 'polite people' who had liberated Crimea.

At a press conference after the 2014 invasion, Putin denied that the men who'd seized Crimea had been Russian soldiers. When a journalist pointed out that they had been heavily armed, carrying new Russian Army 7.62 mm PKP machine guns and driving military GAZ-2975 Humvee-type all-terrain vehicles, the president had speculated – with characteristic sardonic humour – that these 'polite people' were 'merely spontaneous self-defence groups who may have acquired their weapons and uniforms from local Voentorg military surplus shops'.

Across the millennia Crimea has never failed to fire imaginations, and now its stirring sea air – and the ongoing waxing and waning effect of the truffle – also sped me on a merry dance.

'Gorbachev was a war criminal who destroyed the Soviet Union and reunited our enemy Germany,' Katja shouted over her shoulder as we accelerated out of the city. 'He should have been locked up.'

I'd come to Crimea to visit the spot where Gorbachev had been imprisoned for three days in 1991. For me, it was the moment when Russia's tentative steps towards democracy had suffered their first body blow. I didn't yet know that I would come to within spitting distance of the man who'd then delivered the final knock-out punch.

We motored south across a bone-dry prairie. The arrow-straight road cut between bleached salt pans and scorched limestone escarpments, bending only when it met the mountains. Katja shifted into low gear and leaned into the turns, canyon-carving uphill with terrifying speed.

She was a local guide and interpreter whose ad for motorbike tours had been tacked on the tourist office noticeboard. She was also a rebel, of sorts. Born in Sevastopol after the collapse of the Soviet Union, she described herself as 'Ukrainian by blood, Russian in my heart'. After Crimea's annexation, or 'the coming back' as she called it, she'd carved out a living by taking visitors on 'a sightseeing tour of the century': Civil War battlefields, coastal batteries and Facility 825 – a once-secret Cold War nuclear submarine base. Behind its nine-metre-thick blast doors, along a curved half-mile tunnel within a rocky isthmus, up to seven subs could be hidden nose-to-tail, repaired and prepared for Armageddon.

Katja's tour price? A hundred dollars a day. Cash.

The scream of the Kawasaki killed all further conversation, as did the spectacular view that unfolded when we breached the mountain pass. The Black Sea sparkled like mica in the heat haze, its gleam mottled by the shadows of clouds swept inland by the breeze. To left and right, magnificent cliffs rose steeply from the deep. Overhead, alpine swifts turned in the wind while linnets and yellowhammers fussed in the gorse around us.

'Stunning,' I said when she killed the engine.

'Russian,' replied Katja.

At our feet a thin strip of asphalt snaked down from the Baydar Gate, through bushy pinewoods, around narrow defiles and a tiny gold-domed church perched on a crag, to a narrow ledge of lush shoreline.

For generations Russian royals had built their summer palaces in this place of stark beauty, as had first secretaries of the Communist Party and their henchmen. Stalin had spent his summer days flitting between its finest villas, carving up Europe with Roosevelt and Churchill while at the Livadia Palace. Khrushchev had favoured Dacha No. 1, also known as Wisteria, where Brezhnev later entertained US President Richard Nixon. When he became first secretary, Gorbachev had taken over Dacha No. 2 on the hillside below the last tsar's summer bolthole. But his wife, Raisa, hadn't fancied it and so Dacha No. 3 was built for them among the acacias and magnolias in Foros.

We glided downhill without helmets, the balmy air soft on the skin, the wind running its fingers through Katja's hair. On the handlebars fluttered ribbons: the red, white and blue of Russia and the orange and black of St George. Orange and black – the colours of fire and smoke – were the only military decoration to have been preserved throughout both tsarist and Soviet times.

At first Foros was a disappointment, revealing itself as a ramshackle settlement of crumbling pavements, walls and yawning watermelon vendors. At the water's edge dozens of 'temporary boathouses' – so called to sidestep planning regulations – had been converted into five-storey villas, their wire fences blocking access to the sea. A decade earlier hired hands had toted machine guns along the public beach, but now the late-season holidaymakers knew the rules, and clumped together on a far stretch of stony shore.

There were no signs to direct us to Dacha No. 3, of course. A local man advised us to look out for its terracotta roofs. Another said that the main villa's roof was green. We were told that the complex had been built in a year, its construction workers and staff housed in a specially built apartment block. The cliff-top dacha was said to have a grand living room with sweeping views of the coast, indoor and outdoor swimming pools and an elevator to the sea.

'Police and sharpshooters still patrol it,' volunteered a fruit seller, his wares spread out on cardboard by the local park. Katja translated that its grounds were encircled by a mesh security fence 'that a mouse couldn't get through'.

Mikhail Gorbachev had changed the world, then the world turned its back on him. In 1985, the year in which the dacha was built, the US military had ramped up its budget to bankrupt the USSR. Moscow had raced to match American weaponry, squandering an unsustainable third of GDP on its military. At the Foros dacha, after the Red Army's devastating defeat in Afghanistan, Gorbachev had told Raisa, 'We cannot go on living like this.'

Gorbachev had wanted to slash the military budget so as to concentrate on economic and social reform. At their 1986 Reykjavik summit, he told US President Ronald Reagan, 'I am convinced that if you and I have different ideological ideas, that is not a reason for us to shoot at one another. On the contrary, I am convinced that, in addition to political relations, purely human relations between us are also possible.'

Gorbachev's courage – and his realism – led to him and Reagan signing the most important nuclear arms agreement of the Cold War. His domestic policies freed political prisoners and permitted private ownership for the first time since Lenin's New Economic Policy. But his reforms were rejected by reactionaries and exploited by opportunists.

On a sweltering Sunday in August 1991, five black Volgas drove over the pass and down to the gates of the dacha. Gorbachev was not expecting visitors, let alone high-ranking Communist Party hardliners. His visitors told him that they opposed his reforms. They invited him to join them to save the Soviet Union. When he refused they arrested him.

At dawn the next day a column of tanks rumbled down Moscow's broad Kutuzovsky Prospekt to surround the Russian White House.

But rather than surrender, Boris Yeltsin walked out of the building and climbed on top of one of the tanks. He denounced the hardliners' attempted takeover, then hijacked it to propel himself to power. His bold gesture was calculated to look good on TV. Three days later the coup collapsed with hardly a shot fired. Come the end of the year Mikhail Gorbachev was history, the hardliners were under arrest and Yeltsin was president.

Katja and I biked up broken lanes, skirted the ruins of a sanatorium and came to grinding stops at looming rocky barriers. I knew that the dacha complex had been built with its own power and water supply, both of which were backed up with duplicate systems. I guessed that it would also have had a top-notch communication network. On the outskirts of town, at the foot of Mount Mshat-Kaya, we spotted a high tower bristling with antennae. We left the bike beneath it and crossed the coast road towards the sea. We found traces of an old path. Katja walked ahead, telling me to keep quiet. We skirted a rocky hummock, stepped out of a shallow ravine and came face to face with a soldier.

'This path is closed,' he said in Russian. He was armed.

'We're going for a swim,' Katja said, taking my hand as if we were naughty teenagers off on a jolly jape. I kept my mouth shut.

'This path is closed,' he said again, not amused.

Beyond him I saw the tops of cypress and redwood trees. I caught sight of terracotta roofs and covered walkways. I spotted a naval frigate at anchor in the glittering bay. I also saw that it was time to go back.

'*Konechno, ne volnuites*', *ukhodim*,' said Katja. We're leaving, don't worry. We turned on our heels. Jasmine and lavender scented the air. Two policemen waited by the Kawasaki. Again Katja talked us out of trouble. Along the coast we spotted the dacha's access road, blocked by three police cars.

'I thought the dacha was empty these days,' I shouted to her as we sped away.

In town we stopped at a bar to ask questions. Nobody told us who was staying at the dacha but everyone knew.

'Helicopters come and go,' said the barman, refilling our glasses, admitting nothing, revealing everything. 'We can only guess who rides inside them.'

'Do you think *he* is there?' I asked Katja.

'If so, we welcome him with open arms,' she replied with a sudden, giddy laugh. 'He is a hero of the people. He has given us back our Motherland.'

'So he did get the dacha,' I realised, aloud.

After the break-up of the Soviet Union, Dacha No. 3 – along with Crimea – had become part of independent Ukraine. But Vladimir Putin had eyed the complex for years. Somehow it came into the ownership of the Kremlin-friendly state bank VTB* and Putin began to summer at Gorbachev's former holiday home, until its dubious acquisition was revealed in the aftermath of Ukraine's Orange Revolution. Putin's visits came to an abrupt end. Then, a couple of years later, he managed to take back the dacha, along with all of Crimea – by force.

'If you really are interested in history, I'll take you to meet my father,' said Katja as we climbed back on her bike. 'He *is* history.'

Our headlight picked out the gleam of blackbirds rising through the twilight to roost in high trees. An ancient Lada, its open trunk stacked with freshly picked sweetcorn, rattled by roadside grape vendors. In a dusky field a solitary cow tugged at its tether beneath a vast billboard. On it Putin beamed alongside the new Kerch Strait road–rail bridge. The billboard's patriotic text made no mention of Arkady and Boris Rotenberg, the president's childhood friends (and former judo teachers) who'd been awarded the $4.36 billion construction contract to link the peninsula and Russia.

---

* Vneshtorgbank or VTB was no ordinary bank, according to the *Guardian*'s Luke Harding. Two successive FSB/KGB spy chiefs sent their sons to work for it, and its deputy chief executive chaired the FSB's public council. The bank also agreed to make many expedient loans, including for the proposed (and then aborted) Trump Tower Moscow, claimed Harding in his book *Collusion*.

Beyond the billboard was the Night Wolves festival ground. Here every summer the notorious motorcycle gang re-enacted the Second World War. In pyrotechnic fantasies and high-octane motorcycle stunts, 'heroic' Red Army bikers battled 'heartless' Wehrmacht BMW riders before taking on goose-stepping 'pro-Western' demonstrators. In last year's performance the Statue of Liberty even made an appearance, spewing a fiery retch of dollars 'to poison, separate and kill the Slavic peoples'.

The Night Wolves had special ties with Putin, who'd ridden a Harley-Davidson trike onto the stage at the inaugural show. They'd supported his annexation of Crimea, patrolling its streets alongside the unmarked Russian soldiers. They'd fought in the Donbas War. They parroted his nationalistic narrative, running down liberals, homosexuals and other ne'er-do-wells. 'Wherever the Night Wolves are, that should be considered Russia,' declared its leader Alexander 'The Surgeon' Zaldostanov, who ran the club as if it were an auxiliary of the state.

Katja and I rode into the dark and onto a rough track. When she cut the engine, the night was quiet and still. We crossed an orchard knee-deep in summer-scorched grass. In its light the rising moon caught fruit trees flecked with lichen, abandoned ploughs and a hand-built hut backed by a rank of willows. Its upper windows were surrounded by jigsaw-cut fretwork. Peculiar metal tools hung from nails hammered at haphazard spots in the tongue-and-groove wall. A split oil-drum barbecue glowed on the porch. Katja stepped around it and pushed open the back door.

'In our dacha there are only two rules,' said Katja's father in welcome as we entered the chaotic kitchen, holding out his hand, handing me a brimming wine glass. 'Live every night as if to wake the dead, and wake no one but the dead in the morning.'

'And never discuss politics,' added Katja with a knowing laugh, the uneven floorboards juddering as she dropped into a chair. 'Unless you want to sleep in the shed.'

Katja's father, Andrei – a tall and unusually thin sexagenarian with tousled grey hair – had been waiting for us. Katja had called ahead, telling me that he hungered for conversation since his retirement from Moscow. Dinner with him appeared to be an optional part of her tour package, for an inevitable extra payment.

Dachas – *real* dachas – tend to be either inherited village houses or log-walled cottages built on 10 x 10 plots gifted to the party faithful by Khrushchev. At least half of Russia's city dwellers own or have the use of one, growing potatoes, pickling cucumbers, collecting berries and apples. Katja's father had acquired his in 1991, in exchange for a second-hand video recorder.

'How was that possible?' I asked.

'Nothing in this country can be understood without context,' he replied.

No educated Russian can answer an historical question without mentioning slavery, serfs or the Great Patriotic War. Within five minutes Andrei had mentioned all three, explaining that his grandparents – Katja's great-grandparents – had been 'well-off' peasants who'd owned a nearby plot of land and a cow. Both were taken from them during Stalin's murderous collectivisation. To survive they'd lived off berries scavenged in the forest.

'They lost a cow but their son became an officer in the Red Army,' shrugged Katja, cutting across the conversation, stirring it up even before finishing her first glass. 'That strikes me as progress.'

'As you will have gathered, Stalin – who was feared during his lifetime – is now revered by *some* people as "an effective manager",' smiled Andrei from the grill. *Some* people obviously included Katja. 'Please excuse my daughter,' he added. 'Every family has its cockroach.'

She stuck out her tongue at him, adding with another laugh: 'When the forest is cut down, wood chips fly.'*

'Charming, no?' said Andrei with an amused air of defeat, like a man sharing a joke on his walk to the gallows. 'Let me refill your glass.'

---

* In some quarters the victims of Stalin's many purges are known as 'Stalin's chips'. *Stalinskiye shepki*. A 2019 opinion poll indicated around 25 per cent of Russians believe his campaign of political terror was 'historically justified'. No mention of Stalinist terror is made in the official school curriculum.

The wine was red, heavy and Georgian. On the kitchen counter, platters of home-made, salted *suluguni* cheese rounds, scattered with handfuls of tarragon and mint, teetered atop thick hunks of Armenian bread. Pork kebabs, marinated in oil and lemon, sizzled on the grill. Andrei's blotched and stained sweater appeared to have been marinated as well. It hung off him as if off a coat hanger.

In 1991 – when Russia's assets were up for grabs – Andrei had traded a VCR for a forty-nine-year-lease on the local cooperative's orchard. On it he had built the holiday dacha by hand, scavenging materials from an abandoned Pioneer camp. He'd turned a broken-down bus into his barn, repurposed its tyres as flower beds. He'd made an outhouse from an old phone booth. Empty wine and beer bottles were used as bricks, laid horizontally and cemented to make a glassy kitchen wall. At the end of each summer day, he'd biked Katja – then a child – to the seashore to play in the rock pools. When she was in her teens, father and daughter had tombstoned – jumped feet first – off the high rocks at Cimiez into the sea.

'People were so happy in those days,' he reminisced with such sincerity that at first I took him at his word, '… when we lived in the world's largest open-air prison.'

Katja helped to prepare the meal, curling her arm around him from time to time. Over the appetisers I learned that he had moved to Moscow to study history at university, an especially difficult subject as the past was always changing, he said. He'd then worked for Radio Moscow for over a decade, writing and presenting a weekly English-language magazine programme on Russian life, until Putin came to power. A new producer had then instructed him to replace his endearing home-grown tales with criticism of foreign countries. When he refused he was fired, like many other independent-minded journalists and presenters who wouldn't toe the line. Few of them ever worked again.

'What could I do? It's life,' he said with a shrug. 'I try to see the funny side.'

'What funny side?' railed Katja, sudden anger in her voice. 'You could have kept your pension at least. But no, you threw it all away, didn't you?'

Andrei made no reply, instead he raised his hand to silence her. It was an old argument, obviously, one that had been thrashed back and forth on many evenings. He held his glass up against the candlelight and tilted back his head to taste the wine in small mouthfuls.

'Thirty years ago Russians were gifted freedom for the first time in history,' he reflected after a short pause. 'We hadn't fought for it. Few were ready for it. No one understood that it had to be protected. So now we have lost it.'

'Tell me what we've lost, Papa?' asked his daughter, her voice softer now, yet determined to make her point. 'I do what I want. I buy what I want. I have my motorbike. I am free.'

'Free?' Andrei replied in the same strange amalgam of tenderness and cynicism. 'My child, you, me, we all are slaves. Russians have always been slaves.'

As they spoke I watched their unusual dance, Katja moving with quick little steps to fetch a plate or bowl, to shut a window or door, to guide Andrei to a chair. She looked after him, as she'd told me earlier, 'doing his cooking, cleaning and laundry like any other girl'.

At the grill he said that once, Venetian and Genoese traders had built Europe's largest slave market in Crimea. As late as the thirteenth century, tens of thousands of Slavs had been trafficked away across the peninsula to Italy, Muslim Spain and North Africa. Later the Ottomans took over the trade. Andrei even claimed the word Slav had the same root as slave.

'Humiliation,' he said, his throat tightening, his breath suddenly short. Flames leapt as fat dripped onto the coals. 'Humiliation lies at the heart of our Russian identity. It is the root of our arrogance and our insecurity. Slavs have always wanted to be part of Europe, to be treated as equal, but we feel ourselves to be its second-class citizens. That leaves us with only two choices, either we subsume our identity or inflate it through pro-Slav nationalism.'

'Drop it, Papa,' said Katja, trying to hold her tongue. She drew away from him to light a cigarette, placing herself apart from her father even though they were separated by no more than a thin partition wall.

'Why has Russia failed?' Andrei asked me, his voice again composed, uninflected. 'Because of centuries of negative selection: our strongest enslaved, our most beautiful sold, our free thinkers slaughtered and, to cap it all, Stalin's "effective management".'

'Russia hasn't failed,' called Katja from the door. 'You can't blame the country for your own blunders.'

Our conversation was punctuated by the sizzle of meat and pop of corks. After the kebabs, Andrei joined Katja for another cigarette, standing on the tiny veranda under the vines. Again she put an arm around his thin waist and rested her head on his shoulder. A cloud passed in front of the moon. Shadows brushed the orchard. An unexpected breeze ruffled the checked curtain at a half-open window. I smelt the sea.

Later at the sink, father and daughter washed the fresh raspberries, standing side by side at once joined and divided. As I refilled the teapot, I said I was glad to have caught sight of Gorbachev's villa, and come so close to Putin.

'Our leaders – our new elite – are dirt,' said Andrei in response, his face flushing from drink and conviction. 'They don't give a shit about us. They just want to fill their pockets. Their treachery has destroyed our opportunity.'

'But how could today be better?' asked Katja, concerned about his blood pressure, trying to avoid confrontation. 'Crimea is again part of great New Russia.' She used the term 'Novorossiya', an historical term dating back to the Russian Empire and encompassing much of independent Ukraine and Moldova.

'Russia is great only in its fear,' answered Andrei. 'Fear of imaginary enemies. Fear that we no longer know who we are. People fall again for simple answers.' Suddenly he was shouting, 'Be patriotic! Be loyal! *Urrah!*'

Katja hissed at him to be quiet, nodding at the open window. 'The neighbours…'

I hadn't noticed any other houses on our approach to the dacha. Certainly there were none within earshot. I remembered how – on my first visit to Eastern Europe – people had retained the habit of lowering their voice around strangers, ever fearful of being overheard by informants.

'This is your freedom, is it? The freedom to speak one's mind, as long as it doesn't contradict the leader?' cried Andrei. He then turned to me to add, 'You know, when Donald Trump won the US election, many Russians were relieved. We saw that we were no longer the only fools in the world.'

Into the night we talked of blood and money, of atomised societies and democracy hollowed out by social division and exploited by opportunists. We agreed that time and again 'the people' were kicked around like a football between elites. But the storm had gone out of the arguments. We raised our glasses to each other and drained them.

'Perhaps the world is coming to an end,' ventured Andrei drunkenly. 'Perhaps we're slipping towards a new war, or plague, and all the lights will go out. One thinks this way as one gets older,' he philosophised, his face now placid, calm, resigned. 'It was always an illusion that Russians could become part of Europe, but the rhetoric was necessary to give people hope.'

His fragile body seemed heavier than its weight, almost too leaden to move. A broken clock stood on the brick mantelpiece. Electricity cables looped above a pot of dried roses, between an open fuse box and a glass cabinet containing bug spray. He poured more wine and then – as he must have done a thousand times before – tapped the face of the broken clock.

'Once we thought we had a future, tra la la,' he said with unexpected levity. 'Thank God most of us haven't realised it is gone.' He lifted his glass and declared, '*Nostrovia!*' To your health.

I fell asleep to the sounds of their conversation, and of mice rustling in the walls. Some hours later I woke with the rain. Beyond my fretted window it shivered the vines, pearled at the tips of leaves, rolled down the trunks of plum and pear trees. I lay listening in the dim light of the cold room.

A clatter of crockery and the hiss of the coffee maker stirred me out of an inebriated dream. In the bathroom Andrei cursed when he stubbed his toe. The rain grew heavier, beating the petals off the roses, filling an old cast-iron bathtub. The chickens took shelter under a wheelbarrow in the vegetable plot.

On another day we would have hunkered indoors, resuscitated the night's conversations, gravitated seamlessly from caffeine to spirits. But it was not to be. It was time for me to move on.

The first draft of a new post-totalitarian society was being written in Crimea. Its main author – the man now in Dacha No. 3 – had co-opted soldiers and bikers, orchestrated a sham election and installed a compliant, hybrid regime. Here – as in the rest of Russia – he used the tentacles of state to silence individuals who did not support his story. He worked to rewrite the post-war order that had brought years of peace and stability to the continent.

Katja ran me to the airport, her waterproof whipping against my leg. After I'd checked in for my flight, she said, '*Balkon, dacha, pomoika.*' Balcony, dacha, rubbish bin.

I didn't understand.

'It's a Soviet expression about never throwing anything away, even if we don't need it. We put broken stuff out on the balcony, then shift it to dacha, then finally dump it into the garbage. That's my dear father.' Then she added, 'Dinner's an extra fifty dollars. Cash.'

10

Under the Skin

Underground there is no horizon. Underground the people move in halting steps, move as one, move four abreast deep down beneath the city. The earth has swallowed them, corralled them, imprisoned them. Above ground the world has been reduced to rubble. Humanity is all but extinct. The last survivors of nuclear war live on in the largest air-raid shelter ever built, moving through the deafening silence, fearful of the Dark Ones and carnivorous rats, at the end of it all.

Artyom is an orphan, living at VDNKh, the last inhabited station on the Kaluzhsko-Rizhskaya line. He is the protagonist in the post-apocalyptic science-fiction novel *Metro 2033*. He is also an avatar in the first-person shooter video game of the same name. Author Dmitry Glukhovsky created the book as an interactive experiment, drawing suggestions from thousands of Russian readers, letting them shape his text. His book mirrors their nightmares: dystopian life, mankind threatened by an evil race, small groups waging war on each other. At the end of an epic journey Artyom obliterates the mutant race, only to realise that appearances lie. The Dark Ones were not evil. Under the skin they were mankind's only hope. But with their annihilation, the promise of salvation is lost. The world becomes as empty as a derelict metro tunnel.

Three million people read the bleak collaboration online. A further million bought the print edition. Its spin-off survival game sold over two million units and a movie is in the works.

'I was twelve years old when the Soviet Union collapsed,' said Moscow-born Glukhovsky. 'Everything we knew about the history, politics, culture, all our system of values, our entire empire (that seemed eternal, as all empires do), it all was just cancelled by a TV announcement. Overnight. We woke up on the ruins of an empire, on the ruins of our own civilisation,' he said.

His idea of a dead megalopolis, and beneath it warring metro stations, rose out of the turmoil.

'We humans never learn from the mistakes of our past,' said Glukhovsky. Thirty years on, free speech and journalism have again been 'replaced by blunt propaganda and primitive brainwashing'. Fear has been channelled into chauvinism and xenophobia. Uncertainty has been assuaged by the promise of strong leadership. 'People in Russia say that they're happy with Putin, but then they're being brainwashed day and night by all channels of TV,' he said. '*Metro 2033* was just an attempt to sum up my thoughts and feelings of our life in Russia…'

Under the skin. On the skin. For millennia men and women have brought onto their skin that which lies beneath it. To uncover more of the secrets that lie in the Russian heart and soul, I decided to meet an artist who drew out the inner visions and loyalties.

'Tattoos can tell the history of a life,' said Pavel Angel, the country's most celebrated tattooist. 'Memories, turning points and rites of passage are marked on the body with a point of pain.'

I'd travelled from the bright light of late summer Crimea back to Moscow, drawn to Angel's dark basement parlour by Dmitri Denisovich's howling wolf tattoo. 'In old days if tattooist did bad job, his fingers were broken one by one,' my chicken tsar had told me a few weeks earlier. 'Is lucky for Pavel Angel that he did mine perfect.'

Angel was born in Voronezh, an industrial city some 300 miles south of Moscow. His father had been a building engineer. His mother was an art teacher who taught him 'to see beauty, to distinguish the bright side of the world from the dark'.

She also taught him to draw.

'I started to cut myself so as to remember the important points in my life,' he told me when we met. Dark tattoos emerged from the neck and cuffs of his black T-shirt, marked his oesophagus, ran along his arms and vanished down his backside. He was fit and muscular with a large, close-cropped head and mutton-chop sideburns. Yet beneath the forbidding exterior his cornflower-blue eyes hinted at a good-humoured kindness.

'I cut myself to show others who I once was, and who I am now. Here I recorded my leaving home with my first tattoo,' he said, stroking the bold, full sleeve pattern on his forearm '… with a Nazi eagle and the letters LAH. Leibstandarte Adolf Hitler.'

In the last months of the Soviet empire, Angel had been conscripted into the Red Army, one of the million soldiers who kept Central Europe under Moscow's thumb. At the end of the Cold War, and before their repatriation, these Russians had almost nothing to do. Angel filled his time with drawing, and his skill attracted the attention of fellow recruits who asked him to tattoo them.

'I did small designs with a simple needle: unit number, blood type, a bat for guys in intelligence, a lightning bolt for communications units.'

In Soviet times tattoos were found only on soldiers and criminals. As a conscript, Angel had chosen to mark himself with Nazi iconography to demonstrate his disdain for communism. 'Leibstandarte Adolf Hitler' had been the Führer's personal bodyguard, its soldiers executing thousands of Russians during the Second World War.

Criminals also chose Nazi death heads and bloody Soviet medals to denote disdain, rank or – if imprisoned – to set themselves apart from political prisoners. Stars on the shoulders or knees meant 'I kneel to no man'. Onion-domed churches acted as a talisman, the number of cupolas indicating the number of crimes or convictions. Some camp inmates even had Lenin or Stalin cut into their chests, in the belief that no firing squad would shoot the venerated portraits.

Female convicts tended to be marked with magic numbers, the thieves' cross or an erect penis and knife with the words, 'Betray me and I'll cut off your balls'. A bracelet signified a five-year sentence. Manacles indicated a decade in a gulag. Bleeding dots boasted of survival 'between four walls' in solitary confinement. A spider showed that the prisoner would walk for ever along a criminal path. Camp tattooists – known as *kol'shchiki* or prickers – were respected for their deft handling of handmade 'bee sting' *shilo* needles.

After the army Angel returned to Voronezh, tattooing friends in exchange for 'respect and a bottle of vodka'. But 'local bandits' made life dangerous – as they did all over the country – so he made tracks for the capital. He served his apprenticeship at an Italian-owned studio and then opened his own parlour near the Dinamo metro station.

'In Moscow I caught the wave of self-expression,' he said, lighting an unfiltered cigarette. A manikin wearing an Apache crest of used needles sat beside us at the table. Behind it, glass display cases were filled with miniature skulls, three-headed plastic dogs and Xenomorph, the extraterrestrial chest-buster from *Alien*. 'Democracy brought us the chance to show our true attitudes, to show what we felt. But as tattooing has become mainstream, it's lost its foundation. In the past a tattoo denoted rank and experience. It had to be earned. Today you buy it like patriotism. Both are for sale.'

At least half of Angel's time was spent reworking – or disguising – old tattoos. Politicians and businessmen like Dmitri came to him with crude spiders or crucified nudes, saying, 'Now I drive a Bentley and wear a gold Rolex but I still have this shit on my shoulder. If the minister invites me to the sauna, I'll look like a fool.' Angel subsumed the past into a new design, as he did with his own first swastika.

'In the boardroom and in the Duma, a man has to behave in a certain civilised way. But under his suit, he isn't all buttoned up. He is someone else, something wilder. He is filled with passion and fury and desire. I talk to my clients about this duality. I try to find what is inside them.'

I thought of Dmitri of course, and the wildness – or at least ritzy rebellion – that seemed to beat under his skin. I wondered aloud about the split between inner truth and that which is drawn across the surface. The choices of Angel's powerful clients fascinated me, and I asked if they tended to be tattooed with personal or traditional patriotic symbols: the Romanov coat of arms, Russian wolves or bears, the hammer and sickle rising over the Reichstag.

Angel pushed back a flop of blond hair and said: 'Most just want something "beautiful".' His enthusiasm deflated like a balloon. 'They change the old message for decoration without a message,' he replied in a flat voice.

'Dollar signs?' I asked with an eyebrow raised.

'The tattoo business is now like paid sex,' he replied with cynicism.

In Britain I know a film director who climbs mountains. He had the route of his greatest climb – Siula Grande in the Peruvian Andes – tattooed up his right leg with base camp, bivouac stops and altitudes marked on his skin. Footballer David Beckham's forty tattoos are said to remind him of 'the important people' in his life, as well as of motivational maxims rendered in Chinese and Hindi script. On his upper left arm, Canada's Justin Trudeau sports the planet Earth inside a Haida raven. Yet most modern tattoos tend to be no more than fashion accessories.

'When your body is marked, it is for life, not for a single day. It sends a message,' volunteered Angel. 'But many younger people come in and want a tattoo in five minutes. They don't have memories. They haven't even lived yet. They say that they want a tattoo to show their love, but for whom? For a woman? A child? Life? God? I work with them. I try to enhance their vision. I don't impose my ideas on them. Often I send them away because they believe that a tattoo will change them.' He snuffed out the cigarette and continued: 'In Russian we say "*Chelovek cheloveku volk*". A man is a wolf to another man. Every time Russia faces a crisis people want wolf tattoos, because life is hard and they feel under attack. I tell them to come back when times are better.'

Homo homini lupus est.

'If the economy – or the world – continues to collapse then we may return to more genuine traditions, and tattoos will come to be earned again.'

Next door, Angel's workshop was as brightly lit as a dentist's surgery. Half a dozen tattooists – all male – bent over their clients, shaving off body hair, disinfecting skin, cutting patterns and swabbing away blood. Full-length mirrors were bolted to every surface. Loud music pounded from hidden speakers. In an adjoining room female clients were marked with roses, dragons, mandalas and rising flames.

'For them a tattoo is different,' explained Angel. 'It is like a last lingerie, the last thing to be exposed to a lover. For women tattoos are a secret.'

I warmed to him, to his cornflower eyes, to the compassion that he failed to hide away. After our talk I sat for a time in the workshop, writing up my notes, thinking of Dmitry Glukhovsky. In *Metro 2033*, the protagonist Artyom spots a tattoo on the elbow of a subterranean soldier. It depicts a radiation-deformed bird with two heads, spread wings and hooked talons. In Glukhovsky's dark future, real birds no longer exist.

At the end of my visit I asked Pavel Angel if he had ever tattooed such a creature on a client.

'Dozens of times,' he answered with a laugh. 'It's the Romanov eagle, although not deformed, yet.'

11

Lies Lies Lies

I wasn't spending my last day in Moscow with Dmitri Denisovich, no matter how much I fancied another sliver of Putin's Pecker. I needed to keep my clarity, with feet on the ground and pen on the page, and his story was finished – or so I thought – unlike that of the Great Patriotic War.

It was Saturday and the museum was deserted. Not a soul idled in its Hall of Glory, beneath the towering 'Soldier of Victory' bronze. No one lingered in the Hall of Remembrance and Sorrow, under the vast web of glass beads that symbolised the tears shed for the dead. On weekdays ranks of schoolchildren were marched between dioramas of the Siege of Leningrad and Battle of Kursk, blinded by laser blasts and deafened by high-volume wartime effects. Teachers urged their charges to ponder the Nazi death camp displays. Born-again patriots donned Red Army uniforms to be photographed in front of the shattered Reichstag. Day-tripping pensioners picked up paired souvenir busts of Stalin and Putin in the basement gift shop. But come the weekend, the public chose to stay away and so the escalators were turned off and the canteen shut down.

After the shoot-'em-up popularity of Patriot Park, I'd expected the official war museum to be packed with punters. But as my footsteps echoed through the empty galleries, I realised that most ordinary Russians wanted to forget the Second World War, if only their leaders would let them.

For rather than come clean about the manifold distortions, the Kremlin rehashed the old communist myths: fascism had served Western capitalism, its leaders had been the tools of big business, the Red Army had repelled the invaders with little help from the Allies. It also worked to exploit the conflict for a new generation, as memories faded along with the last of its veterans. At every Victory Day parade since 2012, for example, younger Russians had been encouraged to carry wartime photographs of their forebears. Those who did not have their own could pick one up – conveniently mounted on a placard – at local supermarkets. Some twelve million Russians – including Putin himself – participated in the last March of the (so-called) Immortal Regiment, keeping alive the idea that Russia remained under threat. It was a cynical propaganda coup dressed up as patriotism, calculated to inflame old fears and animosities.

After ten minutes in the deserted cinema, where archive footage was freely intercut with modern re-enactments, I'd had enough. I went for a beer.

I found a neighbourhood pub in an alley between two blocks of apartments. On the screen behind the bar, CSKA Moskva battled Bayer Leverkusen in a Championships League match. A clutch of young men – in hoodies or black T-shirts, with hair shaved or worn short on back and sides – punched the air every time the home team took a shot on goal. At first glance they were not so different from supporters of Man United or Real Madrid. But as I watched I reflected on their tragic history, as victims of their own rulers more often than their neighbours. Lenin and Stalin had killed almost as many Russians as Hitler (naturally the figures are disputed). Nevertheless, their most recent successor has schemed to darken another generation's ideals, preparing them for more sacrifice and loss, selling them the lie that conflict was inevitable.

I noticed the waitress only because of the time she took to clean the adjoining table. She was watching the barman, waiting for the football match to distract him. When the Moscow team was awarded a free kick, she turned to me and started to chat. She had recognised me as a foreigner of course. When I complimented her on her English, she volunteered, 'I also speak Russian, Turkish and some Korean.'

'You should work as a translator or interpreter,' I said, 'not in a bar.'

'Only Russians can get such high-qualification jobs. We Uzbeks must take, how do you say, menial work.'

'But what if you see an ad in the newspaper?'

'It will specify that a Russian passport is necessary. Or that will be the first question in the interview.'

Uzbekistan has spent most of the past two centuries tied to Russia. Its citizens don't need a visa to enter the country, the waitress told me. A migration permit gives them the right to work and more than two million Uzbeks live in Russia, according to the Federal Migration Service. At home there are no jobs for them.

'No Uzbek comes to Russia to stay,' she said. She had almond-shaped eyes, a round wide head and a small but kindly mouth. 'Here I make about ten thousand roubles a month. If I could make three thousand roubles a month at home, I would not come. Even if I could make only one thousand, I would stay.' Three thousand roubles was about $45, which she sent home to pay for her brother's education. 'I would like to earn something more, if you understand me.' She glanced over her shoulder and added, 'Russians do not like Asians. They call us *zverki*. Meaning little beasts. Dumb beasts.'

CSKA Moskva scored the equaliser, the supporters leapt to their feet and the barman caught sight of the waitress. A sudden stiffness infused her movements as she started to wipe down my table.

'I would like to have a better life,' she said.

'Abandon intelligence all ye who enter here' should be inscribed above the gates of Moscow, wrote Pushkin, paraphrasing Dante. It was the Day of the City, a Soviet-era celebration when Moscow feted itself. There were concerts on Poklonnaya Hill and along Tsvetnoy Boulevard. At Patriarch's Ponds fans of Mikhail Bulgakov's *The Master and Margarita* dressed up as Pontius Pilate, the devil or talking cats. Revolution Square descended into a bacchanalian 'Slavic feast'. Near Barrikadnaya metro stop a sanitised version of the city's history unfolded in a parade of classic vehicles: horse-drawn tsarist carriages, Bolshevik armoured cars and – most extraordinarily – Stalinist Black Raven vans into which actors dressed as KGB thugs herded weeping civilians. Meanwhile, in keeping with tradition, Putin met the capital's newest brides on Red Square. The young women glowed with modesty for the assembled cameras. Only later did it transpire that the brides were models, hired for the day by the Kremlin press office.

Thirty years ago Christopher Hope, the South African novelist and poet, was drawn to Russia by 'the quality of the lies'. In *Moscow! Moscow!* he wrote of 'lies so lush, so many, sprouting overnight among the mossy, rooted feet of official spokesmen'. For Hope, the lies had created 'a society steadily falling apart: run your fingers over it and you'd feel the widening stitches. In the night they snapped one by one.'

I walked home through the drunken crowds, beneath a dark sky lit by grand firework displays, overcome by emotion. Russians had hungered for a classless society, for a proletariat Utopia, and so surrendered themselves to those who promised it. How could their moving story have ended in so many lies and so much misery?

In the tiny ground-floor bedsit I packed my bag for St Petersburg, and surveyed the reality of my surroundings. I was alone in a room crammed with unread books, old television sets (without leads) and a piano that no one played. The single sofa unfolded into the only bed. In the pale pink tiled bathroom, a swivelling spout served both sink and tub. Neither had a plug. My landlord – who'd lost his job some years ago and survived on sporadic Airbnb rentals – slept on a mattress on the kitchen floor whenever he had guests. On his kitchen table was a single set of cutlery and a bust of Putin.

Around midnight I heard the knocking. At first I thought it was the sound of fireworks, or a drunken Day of the City reveller, but the tapping was too controlled, too insistent, too good a beat. I looked through the grille and came face to face with familiar dark brown eyes.

'Sami!'

I opened the padded security doors to let him in. As he stepped over the threshold he let out a gasp of relief, like a hunted animal returning to its lair. I hadn't imagined that he could be any thinner, but he was. In a couple of weeks his slender face had become almost skeletal.

'You look exhausted,' I said.

There was no spring in his step, no cocky moonwalk. I grabbed him by the arm. He was shaking. He crumpled out of my grip and onto the floor.

The noise flushed my landlord out of the kitchen. I pressed money into his hand, told him that Sami was a friend and asked to use the cooker. I always travel with a small reserve of oatmeal – in case I arrive in a place after the shops and restaurants have closed – and quickly boiled it into porridge. I borrowed the only spoon.

Sami sat cross-legged on the floor and ate. Then he told me what had happened. After our parting he'd travelled to Minsk and bought passage to Europe. The smugglers had locked him and eight others in a refrigerated lorry, promising to drive them over the Belarusian border into Poland. In the lorry there was room only for them to sit down – no one could stand or stretch out – so all were thankful that the one woman was quite small. Pallets of potatoes had been loaded against a false partition. In the pitch black the refugees tried not to touch each other on the drive to the border.

Sami never discovered how the air vent became blocked, or how long it was until they began to suffocate. Fear had risen in the metallic air and in his throat. He'd pushed at the door as the walls had seemed to contract around him. Others, it was impossible to tell who in the darkness, had uncurled their limbs and started to kick at the partition, crying out for help.

The driver had heard the calls and turned off into the forest. He'd unlocked the steel door and told the survivors that they were in Europe. In the thick forest, at night, Sami was disorientated. The driver had pointed to a path and said: 'Poland'. The dead woman was dumped in a ditch.

Sami had run west, outrun the others despite his limp, jogged into Poland, he'd thought. But the driver had lied. On hearing the refugees' cries he had panicked and abandoned them inside Belarus. They had not crossed the border. They had not made it to Europe.

'All I hope for is to be safe,' he said to me.

Every year an estimated 800,000 people are smuggled into Europe in a trade more profitable than drug trafficking. Most choose to leave home in a desperate attempt to improve their lives. Some fifty gangs handle the bulk of the world's human traffic, earning millions of dollars in executing their heinous trade.

Sami had evaded arrest and made it back to Moscow, tracking me down again to a place of relative safety, on my last night in the city. In the sad little room he refused to take the sofa so I made him a bed of spare cushions. When I turned out the light, the moon cast the pattern of the security grille across the floor.

As we drifted towards sleep, Sami asked in a soft voice about Britain, bookkeepers' salaries and Tottenham Hotspur. He added, 'Michael Jackson played for Princess Diana. You know he dreamed of living in London.'

His hope – his faith – lifted me out of the broken day and the terrible story. I remembered Fyodor Tyutchev, the nineteenth-century poet, had warned that it was not possible to make sense of Russia, that the country was not amenable to reason, that to survive it one simply had to believe.

'I will help you to reach England,' I told Sami, in belief.

12

Sunday in St Petersburg

Autumn's rains arrived as a sigh, stealing into the night, hissing into the warm earth, all but unheard by the city's sleepers. By the million they shifted in their beds, rolled away from the window as if from the seasons, as if from the inevitable. Outside, the whispers turned to rattles, unbinding papery samara and drumming desiccated leaves down to earth. Startled birds shook their feathers, darted between drooping branches and tree tops. Seed heads and whirligigs twirled onto the pavement, washed into crevices and cracks, clogged the drains.

At dawn the showers stopped, leaving the streets carpeted with debris. The sleepers now pulled up their shutters, lit first cigarettes, walked dogs and cycled over the dappled curl of leaves, seed pods popping beneath their glistening tyres. Prams and skateboards then appeared in high-arched doorways. Young families emerged into the scrubbed air, tumbling past salmon-pink mansions and alongside grey canals. Elderly couples sauntered arm in arm around golden cupolas glazed with the slick of rain. In the Mikhailovsky Gardens, children rode docile ponies, danced around street musicians, begged to be photographed with the tame raccoons and doves. Their parents idled at open-backed coffee vans, ordered double espressos, scolded fox-nosed Shibas and spoilt miniature poodles. In Mars Field, the tsar's old parade ground, teens played three-a-side frisbee near to the Eternal Flame. At trendy Bekitzer, young entrepreneurs chilled over Israeli street food or checked out the latest Co-op Garage pizzas (salmon with quail eggs, duck confit with rocket).

Russia's imperial capital had something worldly about it, a noble seat at the edge of the continent, looking west across the Baltic to Europe. Peter the Great – the first tsar to venture beyond Russia's borders – had created it in the early eighteenth century. He'd drained the swamps, raised sea walls and pressed 30,000 serfs, convicts and Swedish prisoners of war into digging hundreds of miles of canals. Italianate mansions came to line the River Neva. Baroque and neoclassical palaces rose around wide piazzas. Peter spoke French at court, banned boyars' beards and imported locksmiths, shipwrights and even a Dutch vice-admiral.

In his determination to modernise the country, he also founded the Kunstkamera, the first public museum in Russia. He crammed its glass cabinets with curiosities: pickled Siamese twins with three arms, the skeleton and heart of the world's tallest man, a unicorn horn (actually a narwhal tusk). In his hand he held a child's shrunken head embalmed in Nantes brandy, distilled with pepper and spices. Peter wanted to rid his people of their belief in 'diabolical spells through sorcery and the evil eye', to debunk their superstitious dread of monsters, to show that even the world's worst deformities were the Work of God. He wanted to banish fear. But he hadn't reckoned on the mendacity of his successors.

Today St Petersburg is to Moscow as Edinburgh to Glasgow, San Francisco to LA, Bath to Bristol. Its light is soft, its shadows cool and its residents ever willing to ponder and debate. It is a place open to ideas, for whereas Moscow is all about money and power, St Petersburg is about beauty … money and power. Where better to despatch Sami to a new life?

Our departure from Moscow had been delayed to extend his Russian visa, the process smoothed with backhanders to both the landlord and a travel agency. I'd been surprised how easy it had been. All I had to do was pay.

On the train – the Soviet-era *Krasnaya Strela* Red Arrow sleeper – Sami and I had discussed the options. Over milky breakfast coffee – he drank an apricot juice – I considered bribing him onto a freighter, but I didn't rate our chances of getting past the harbour police. Ditto the twice-weekly Helsinki ferry. I knew that daily trains and buses ran to Estonia, less than a hundred miles away, but without an EU visa he'd be turned back at the border. I wasn't belittling the challenge ahead, or his need. Chekhov once wrote that a writer should not provide solutions but rather describe a situation so clearly that the reader cannot evade its truth. As a would-be person smuggler I needed to find an answer.

Two reasons had brought me to St Petersburg – cyberwarfare and President Putin – as the city was the home of both of them. After dropping our bags at the hotel, Sami and I caught the metro to Mayakovskaya and walked to a three-storey grey and yellow building near to Nevsky Prospekt. Behind the open gates of its courtyard, a young mother in pink pyjamas and rabbit-eared dressing gown smoked a cigarette. A passing drunk – gone to seed like the flower beds – confirmed that we had the right address. Vladimir Vladimirovich Putin had been born here at the Snegiryov maternity home in 1952 (the drunk actually said 1917 and then asked me for five dollars).

Ten minutes further along Ulitsa Mayakovskogo, beyond the Liverpool Bar and Pub Corleone (decked out respectively with Beatles and mafia memorabilia), we turned into drab Baskov Pereulok, a dead-straight street lined by rough, geometric, workers' tenements. Putin had grown up at No. 12, in a shared apartment with no hot water, no bathtub and plenty of rodents.

'I used to chase them around with sticks,' he wrote in his quasi autobiography *First Person*. 'I spotted a huge rat and pursued it down the hall until I drove it into a corner. It had nowhere to run. Suddenly it lashed around and threw itself at me. I was surprised and frightened. Now the rat was chasing me.'

Some historians alleged that Putin had endured an unhappy childhood – abused by an alcoholic father, suppressing homosexual tendencies, even suffering a stroke in utero – while others portrayed him simply as an unremarkable child, of average intelligence living in typical Soviet conditions. Many of the assertions had little basis in fact, unlike the certain knowledge that the incident with the rat had taught him that a cornered prey is unpredictable.

Putin's father, Vladimir Spiridonovich, had served in both the Red Army and an NKVD destruction battalion. His mother, Maria Ivanovna, had collapsed from hunger during the Siege of Leningrad, and was presumed dead. Putin's birth had been preceded by the loss of two brothers, one of whom died of diphtheria. To defend himself he took up judo and *sambo*, a Soviet martial art and combat sport. While still at school, he walked into the KGB headquarters on Liteiny Prospekt and announced that he wanted to be a spy. In the reception room he was told to get a degree, preferably in law. He obliged, studying at Leningrad State University and joined the organisation on graduation. He worked both in counter-intelligence and at the First Chief Directorate, where he was groomed for service abroad.

In 1985 he was transferred to Dresden and again accounts differ as to his actions. One biographer, Masha Gessen, wrote that in the East German backwater 'Putin and his colleagues were reduced mainly to collecting press clippings, thus contributing to the mountains of useless information produced by the KGB.' In contrast his official biography records that, on the night of the fall of the Wall, he heroically fed top-secret KGB files into a furnace.

On the long drive home to the crumbling empire, Putin was haunted by the loss of purpose and pride. The political and ideological system to which he and his parents had dedicated their lives had been shattered. Once back in St Petersburg, he was filled with redemptive purpose, and determined to restore Russia's power. At first he was a 'careful, unenthusiastic, diminutive' apparatchik, remembered former US Ambassador Michael McFaul. Yet during the course of the 1990s, by hook and by crook, he rose to become the city's deputy mayor and then – thanks to powerful friends – a Kremlin aide, intelligence chief and finally the anointed successor to Boris Yeltsin.

As president he oversaw Russia's transformation into an audacious and ambitious kleptocracy. He boosted his authority by destroying challengers and then grabbing the institutions and resources that they had plundered. Yet even as he amassed unimaginable wealth, again according to McFaul, he grew vindictive, grudging and obsessed with respect. After the trial of billionaire Mikhail Khodorkovsky, and the death of kingmaker Boris Berezovsky (found hanged in his ex-wife's Berkshire home), Putin called the other oligarchs to the Kremlin and told them to support him, or else.

'It is time for Russia to get off its knees,' he declared and set about spinning false narratives. He nurtured the old chestnut that enemies still surrounded the country. To substantiate the lie, he triggered or manipulated wars in Chechnya, Georgia, Ukraine and Syria. He worked to fuel angry insecurities and nationalist resentment, calculating that enemies were more valuable to him than friends.

Putin placed his trust in one key group alone, reviving the KGB and making it subordinate to no one. Its – and his – objective remained unchanged from Soviet days, to project Russian power and to undermine open society. More than thirty independent journalists have been murdered on his watch. Politicians rash enough to challenge him tend to either drop off the ballot paper or drop dead. Pro-democracy demonstrations – such as those that outraged him in Dresden in 1989 and Kiev in 2004 – are repressed by riot police. His use of violence, though moderate by historical standards, has made it impossible to hold free elections, to try cases in court, to maintain the rule of law. Under Putin, pluralism has become seditious. He has degraded the political order, flexed his muscles from Aleppo to Pennsylvania Avenue, and become the richest man in the world.*

On Baskov Pereulok, Sami and I gazed at the unmodernised tenement, unadorned with balconies or aesthetic value. Its two

---

* No one knows the true extent of Putin's wealth but it is rumoured to top that of Amazon's Jeff Bezos and Microsoft founder Bill Gates. His huge fortune is said to be distributed across a secret web of company holdings and properties as well as in the names of friends and associates.

security cameras stared back at us. Around the doorway hung the nameplates of the business that now occupied Putin's childhood home: the Long and Happy Aid-to-the-Elderly Foundation, the St Petersburg Boxing Federation and – I kid you not – the Foundation for Future Leaders. I buzzed its intercom, the security camera tilted towards me but no one answered. Across the road the owner of East-West Antiques told us, 'The President never comes back. He lives in a nicer house now. You are the first tourists.'

Together we retraced our steps to Ulitsa Mayakovskogo, turning right towards Liteiny Prospekt and the Neva. In five minutes we reached the Big House, as locals called the massed block of granite in which a teenage Putin had offered himself to Russia.

As we gazed at the KGB headquarters, I told Sami I couldn't believe that Vladimir Putin really considered the collapse of the Soviet Union – with its history of state terror, death-camp gulags and the forced starvation of millions – to be 'the greatest geopolitical catastrophe of the twentieth century'. Or that he was motivated by wounded pride alone. Or that he had the gall to drive resurgent Russia towards armed conflict because of his encounter with a ballsy rat. Surely he had taken to heart the lessons of all the bloody years?

'Money,' replied Sami. 'For a pot of gold, people will sell their soul.' He was paraphrasing Michael Jackson again, about the impulse to lie for money, even to kill for it.

On the Neva, two pink granite Egyptian sphinxes – originally from ancient Luxor – stand on the embankment in front of the Academy of Arts. A few hundred yards upstream, a stone's throw from the Big House, crouch two other, modern sphinxes. On one side the bronzes appear to be the most beautiful creatures: feminine, pensive, full-breasted. Yet on the other side their faces are hollow-eyed skulls. The artist Mikhail Shemyakin created them to pay tribute to the victims of political repression, siting the monument at the spot where the drains from the KGB basement had poured blood into the river.

Chekhov once foresaw that in his homeland 'a type of toad and crocodile will come to power more frightful than anything that ever came out of Spain's Inquisition – a narrow-minded, self-righteous, overbearingly ambitious type, totally lacking in conscience. Charlatans and wolves in sheep's clothing will be able to lie and dissemble to their heart's content.'

Sami and I stood in silence by the river, beside the haunted sphinxes, with the smell of autumn in the air.

13

Cold War 2.0

On Monday morning I made some calls. A friend of a friend at the Home Office told me that London had a proud history of offering asylum to those in need. 'The key is that the need has to be real,' he said.

I reminded him that northern Nigeria suffers from insurgency and kidnapping as well as both drought and floods, devastating the lives of thousands of internally displaced people.

'But you say he's in Russia.'

I explained that Sami was trapped.

'The integrity of the UK's asylum system is based on fair, objective and informed assessment of conditions in the country of origin,' he replied as if reading from a screen. 'In any case, he has to get here first.'

Sami needed a visa to enter the UK but none would be forthcoming. He could not apply for refugee status from outside the country. No airline would let him board a flight without a visa. It was a catch-22 situation; only by entering the country illegally could he apply for legal residence. I left voicemails, sent emails and heard nothing in return. I didn't cast the net wider as I realised there was no legitimate way for me to help Sami.

Once again I recognised that the freedom to travel was a privilege, a First World privilege, which may be why I hit on the idea of cruise ships. Travel writers are often gifted holidays or hotel stays in exchange for a newspaper article awash with azure seas and purple prose. I know a travel editor who has a passion for cruises, and more than once he has tried to sign me up for a complimentary trip. A quick web search revealed that both Cunard and P&O ships were due to call at St Petersburg in the next few days. So I dropped the editor a line, asking if I could join the cruise … with a friend. In my desire to help, I imagined Sami and I meeting the ship's passengers during their Hermitage Museum tour. We'd slip on to the company coach and back on board without port police or immigration checks. Sami could become the first refugee to reach Southampton in a first-class cabin.

In our hotel room Sami watched me as I waited for the reply. He must have realised that optimism had got the better of me. 'You are a good man,' he said, then went out to find a solution for himself.

In the afternoon I had a meeting that couldn't be missed. It had taken months to arrange, negotiated in secret through another Russian exile. Since the fall of the Wall, Moscow had worked to develop a new weapon. Now it was among the most powerful in its arsenal and I was to meet one of its operators, a thirty-nine-year-old woman who lived alone with two cats near to the botanical gardens.

In 1989, at the end of the Cold War, Russia wasn't connected to the internet. In 1991 Relcom, the country's first commercial internet service provider, had been ordered by the KGB to print paper copies of every email carried over its network. But the early naivety was swept aside as Kremlin tacticians fathomed the huge strategic potential of the World Wide Web.

In 2007 Moscow began to flex its cyber muscles by attacking Putin's least favourite Baltic state, crashing Estonia's national computer network. A few months later its hackers broke into Georgian government websites to manipulate public opinion during the Russian-Georgian war. In 2014 similar attacks were launched before the seizure of Crimea. Next, in 2015, Russian hackers shut down Ukraine's power grid and France's TV5Monde. In the same year an assault on the Bundestag – so stealthy that it went undetected for six months – succeeded in 'comprehensive strategic data gathering' according to the German intelligence agency. Another foreign cyber attack – similar to the first Estonian DDoS (distributed denial of service) offensive – is believed to have caused the collapse of the British government's voter registration website in the run-up to the 2016 EU Brexit referendum, thereby disenfranchising tens of thousands of people. In the same year seasoned operatives from the GRU – the armed forces' military intelligence agency – hacked the US presidential election, penetrating both Democratic and Republican Party computer networks, weaponising data and pinpointing infrastructure vulnerabilities 'for use at a later date', reported the Senate Intelligence Committee. Russia also secreted malware into the Twitter accounts of more than 10,000 Pentagon employees. One click – to an intriguing sports story or kitten lover's website – allowed the hackers to take control of the victim's account, as well as his or her mobile phone and computer. 'Cyber weapons can affect a huge amount of people as can nuclear weapons,' General Vladimir Sherstyuk, a member of Russia's National Security Council, told the *MIT Technology Review*. 'But there is one big difference between them. Cyber weapons are very cheap. Almost free of charge.'

As I waited at the botanical gardens (by the giant water-lilies pool, as arranged), I thought of how the KGB's 'Active Measures Department' has continued to subvert free thought. Its disinformation is calculated to undermine trust and shift the balance of power. Its tactics haven't much changed since Lenin and Stalin first manipulated truth at home and abroad, aiming to control people's minds by limiting the scope of their thinking.

After an hour I realised that my 'operator' wouldn't show and went in search of the St Petersburg troll factory. A red-and-white tram dropped me off on leafy Savushkina Street and I walked under the trees towards the unremarkable four-storey Olgino office building.

'Internet operators wanted! Job at chic office in Olgino!!!' the job adverts had exclaimed. 'Task: posting comments at profile sites in the internet, writing thematic posts, blogs, social networks. Payments every week and free meals!!!'

For the last decade the so-called Internet Research Agency – a particularly mendacious division of Russia's virtual arsenal – has waged war by hacking emotions. Its employees each work six Facebook or ten Twitter accounts: linking pornography to Russian opposition politicians on VKontakte, slamming democrats on Breitbart, dissing writers who criticised the Kremlin on Amazon, championing Brexit on *Daily Mail* Online. Bots, short for robots, then forward their 'personal' comments to countless fake accounts, making them trend by manipulating Google's algorithms. *Migrants rape thirteen-year-old Russian girl in Berlin! EU to ban baptism! The Queen warns of World War Three! Florida school shooter shouts Arabic phrases before killing spree! Stop the Islamisation of Texas!*

The Agency's success was breathtaking (despite the occasional tell-tale grammatical error like 'Rabid Squirrels Is Terrorising Florida'). Heart of Texas – just one of its thousands of fake accounts – garnered a quarter of a million followers (and almost started a riot outside Houston's Islamic Da'wah Center). Its YouTube videos and Instagram messages have reached more than twenty million people. Its 80,000 Facebook posts, replete with inflammatory images, were seen by 126 million Americans during the presidential election.

The Agency also targeted Britain. The 'proud TEXAN and AMERICAN patriot' @SouthLoneStar – in fact another Russian account – tweeted to its thousands of British followers: 'I hope UK after #BrexitVote will start to clean their land from Muslim invasion!' Another bellowed: 'UK vote to leave future European Caliphate!' On the day of the EU referendum, 3,800 fake accounts were mobilised tweeting 1,102 posts with the hashtag #ReasonsToLeaveEU. Every post, meme, video and deepfake photograph was designed to sow distrust, to exacerbate division, to exploit fear and to discredit truth.

Critics were ravaged by vicious retaliatory attacks. After exposing the 'troll army', the Finnish whistle-blower, Jessikka Aro, was vilified as a drug dealer on social media and mocked as a delusional bimbo in a YouTube music video. In the UK, after the publication of her articles on the manipulation of the Brexit campaign, the investigative journalist Carole Cadwalladr was Photoshopped into a clip from the film *Airplane!* In the video – which was promoted online by the registered political organisation Leave.EU – an 'hysterical' Cadwalladr was told to calm down and then hit, repeatedly, around the head. As the Russian national anthem played, a line of people queued up to take their turn. The last person in the line had a gun.

I'd arrived at the factory in time for the afternoon shift and watched people entering and leaving the building. I didn't kid myself that I was a thrusting journalist. I was no Aro, Cadwalladr, Woodward or Bernstein. No Pulitzer Prize would be forthcoming as no one stopped to talk to me. I simply wanted to look into the faces of the men and women who worked at the Agency.

Unsurprisingly only the security guard met my eyes and, although he didn't speak English, I caught his drift. I recognised the word *'ob'yekt'*. In Russian *'ob'yekt'* means 'government building', often property of the military, administration or the FSB. When he picked up the phone, I beat a hasty retreat.

On the tram ride back to town I looked over my shoulder. No one appeared to be following me. My mobile didn't start playing 'The Internationale'. And that made me worry. I'd grown up in an era when the enemy was known. He or she had a face (albeit distorted by our own propagandists). But today we don't know our enemy. We are approached with an enticing tweet, a Facebook friend request or irresistible holiday bargain. We click the link and, in an instant, our own account may be enslaved, to be used to distribute false information at some point in the future.

When I stepped off the tram my head was full of worries of anonymous power, electoral fraud and big data. I crossed the street to reach the hotel and a passing policeman collared me. He told me, in no uncertain terms, that jaywalking was illegal in Russia. A minor infringement and I was in the wrong. I'd have to pay.

I was flustered and on edge. Had I been followed? In my anxiety I reached for my passport, and didn't feel it in my breast pocket. It wasn't in my jeans. The policeman saw the blood drain from my face. He saw my real distress, and he empathised with me.

'Check pocket again,' he said in English, now sincerely concerned. 'Maybe you leave in hotel?'

He didn't march me off to the Big House. He didn't search my phone or ask for my Facebook profile. Instead he tried to help, even to reassure me that it would be wise to carry a photocopy. He seemed to forget about the jaywalking.

When I found my passport, tucked into the back of my satchel, I laughed out loud. The policeman shook his head in relief. Now we could resume the bribery game, and not confront any real transgression.

'Go back to hotel and not be stopped again,' he advised me as I slipped him $20.

In the room, Sami was waiting with the television tuned to a programme on polar bears. Appropriately, as it would turn out.

'I have found a way,' he said.

Aboard the *Queen Elizabeth*? In a rubber dinghy across the Barents Sea?

'I'm heading north.'

'North?' I said, collapsing on my bed. 'But there are only submarine bases and old gulags in the north.'

'I'm going to the Arctic.'

At midnight my phone pinged me awake. Most Russians use WhatsApp, favouring the security of its end-to-end encryption. But even though no one could read our messages, the suggested meeting place seemed to be a joke.

On Tuesday morning I pushed open the door at the appointed hour. In the shadow of the Church of the Spilled Blood, near to the spot where a tsar was most unkindly murdered, groups of young men in baseballs caps pored over black-and-white screens. A father and son sniped at croaking 8-bit ducks in *Ni Pukha, Ni Pera* (*No Fluff, No Feathers*). Primary school kids battled with virtual armour on the clunky *Tank-o-drom*. Teens crashed and burned their blinking fighter jets in *Interceptor*.

In 1975 the USSR's Ministry of Culture had set about cloning American and Japanese arcade machines. Over the coming years

millions of copycats were built in military factories. But with
the fall of the Wall, and the influx of Sony PlayStations and
the Microsoft Xbox, the old arcade games had been scrapped.
Twenty years later three collectors had hit on the idea of saving
the remaining digital relics. Around me in the Museum of Soviet
Arcade Machines, retro-loving hipsters and nostalgic retirees
dropped 15-kopek coins into slots to launch torpedoes at enemy
ships, to shoot toy shotguns at flickering targets and to travel back
to a simpler time.

'My father's favourite is *Morskoi Boi*,' murmured the woman
who appeared at my side.

Morskoi Boi, or *Sea Battle*, was a pirated version of Midway's
1976 *Sea Wolf*, produced in a military factory that became part of
Almaz-Antey, today the world's twelfth largest arms contractor and
best known for its Buk missile system.

'I bring him here, now that we have time.'

We found a table at the back of the ping-ponging alternative
universe and ordered tarragon sodas. I thanked her for her midnight
message.

'People are becoming silent again,' she volunteered in a voice so
faint as to be almost a whisper. 'That's why I decided to meet you
after all.'

Adina was of delicate build with quiet grey eyes, a small mouth
and a scar on her left temple. She wore neither jewellery nor
make-up. Her fingernails were brushed with colourless lacquer.

'Also my blood is not Russian. I am Jewish.'

Adina then told me her story: she was an only child, her engineer
father had moved to St Petersburg in the early 1980s in search of the
better life, he'd met her mother by chance, she had come from the
same small Belarus town.

'It was like a fairy tale come true,' sighed Adina.

But the fairy tale turned to tragedy. With the collapse of the
Soviet economy, thousands of firms had shut down and millions
were cast adrift. Both her parents had lost their jobs.

'I hated being hungry. I hated standing in queues for bread,
wearing hand-me-downs. I didn't get new dresses like my friends,'

she said, almost under her breath. She stroked her nails in an absent-minded manner. 'It made me feel so' – she paused to find the words – 'second rate.'

Shame and disappointment aged her parents, bringing on grey hair and brittle bones.

'Life had always been predictable for them. They liked that others made decisions, that they were relieved of responsibility. Do your job, be respectful, abide by the rules, and everything will be fine. But it wasn't.'

Yet as her parents withered, Adina blossomed into 'a special time, a time of no limits'. She trained to be an IT engineer and took advantage of the open borders, spending all her earnings on long-distance bus journeys, visiting Berlin and Paris, sleeping on new friends' sofas in Belgrade and Tel Aviv. To fund her travel bug she answered the ambiguous Internet Research Agency advert. Her good school English helped her to land a job. Her technical knowledge led to her assignment on the pensioner and employee message boards of UK telecoms companies. At the start of each shift she and her fellow 'content managers' – about eighty English speakers – were given the day's topics, advocating for groups perceived as useful to polarise British politics, championing the left-wing Momentum movement while at the same time, through different personas, praising right-wingers in the Conservative and anti-immigrant UK 'independence' parties.*

'No one liked the work but nobody quit because the money – a thousand dollars a month – was so good.'

'You were helping to change the world, post by post, person by person,' I said, shaken by her collusion.

'I didn't want to change it,' she insisted, raising her faint voice in defence. 'I wanted to see it.'

---

* Russia did not act alone, of course. The West had – and has – its own virtual disrupters and digital kleptocracies, working solo or in concert, targeting and manipulating behaviour either to make a buck or to turn a country against itself.

Adina wasn't naive so I wondered aloud about her readiness to subvert truth for a pay cheque, and about the tug of morality. Had she agreed to meet me because of regret?

'We were told to never apologise,' she replied with a flash of defiance. 'Facts are white noise and emotions rule.' Then she fell quiet, turned her glass in her hand and added, 'None of us realised that we were at war.'

She explained that she had been laid off after a year, when the Agency began to favour younger, hungrier, non-Jewish freelancers

'You see, I've become too old for Russia. I am almost forty and no one wants to hire old people like me. I want to move to a country where forty is not a terrible age but now I can't leave.'

In summers past, Adina could have applied for an Israeli passport, as so many did, but she never had the heart to abandon her parents.

'They beg me to visit them every weekend. I got Skype for them in the hope that it would excuse me. Now my mother calls me every night.'

Her father never again found employment. Her mother – who had worked in the aerospace industry – took a job making motorway noise barriers. Adina was desperate to break free of her parents, yet she was unable to let go of them. And there was more.

'Away from them I used to speak my mind, do what I wanted to do. But the situation goes backwards in Russia. Like I said, people are again becoming used to being silent, to accepting rules. My friends tell me not to worry, that we'll be in a queue for the rest of our lives. And now there are restrictions on foreign travel for soldiers, judges and former Internet Research Agency employees like me.' She laughed at the irony, her work in support of Russia now denying her the chance to leave the country. 'When I used to return from abroad it felt like coming back to prison. Now it is my prison.'

Adina wanted to show me *Morskoi Boi* again so we moved back into the arcade. She stared into a large periscope and aimed at ships moving across a virtual sea. With a press of the thumb she sank a dozen 8-bit boats.

'You know, Soviet arcade machines were supposed to be different, to have "real" value: no fantasies, no adrenaline rushes, no *Pac-Man*. We were told that they had to align with Marxist ideology. It was such a lie.'

Adina turned to leave. On the walk to the door she told me that she survived on both 'black and white pay', working as a barmaid and on the odd small IT contract. In the courtyard, in the shadow of the Church of the Spilled Blood, she said, 'I don't know why I am the way I am, why I made the choices that I did. Does anyone know?'

On my journeys I've always had the freedom to choose. I can accept or refuse an offer. I can fly out of a country to escape compromise, corruption and fear, unlike the many individuals who have entrusted me with their stories. Yet in my cold curiosity to fathom her acquiescence, and despite an attempt to empathise, I felt sudden anger towards Adina. Yes, she had been used, even abused, but she had also had a choice. And she'd become a willing saboteur.

I asked her, was she afraid?

'We have a saying that Russia is famous for its bad roads, crooks and stupid women,' she answered. She looked down at the ground for a moment and then in an unexpected gesture lifted her hand to touch my cheek.

Then she walked away.

In Soviet times, survival often meant lying. Only by spouting dogma could a child excel at school, a student win a place at university, a worker secure a good job. Ideology was used, not believed. The regime itself had to lie to survive, falsifying the past, pretending that no honest citizen needed to fear it.

Today the troll state's lies target the West. Many of us – lacking the bitter Soviet experience – gobble up its *dezinformatsiya* as truth. In our gullibility we allow Adina and her former co-workers to propagate a toxic nihilism, undermining objectivity, deepening splits in our societies and even changing the way we think. Democracy may well be brought down from within, for the cost of a few free lunches.

14

Party Party (Like It's 1969)

What makes a leader? What forces drive a young man or woman to reach for the top, to go with the flow and then to forge ahead of it? And where does their journey begin? In imaginary childhood games? In redemptive fantasies? In the thrill of beating the shit out of an opponent at a martial arts tournament? Many factors determine the course of a life, but for Vladimir Putin there was one key moment, one brilliant flash of light when as a restless fifteen-year-old he saw his future.

In 1968, Russia was captivated by *The Shield and the Sword*, a four-part black-and-white blockbuster set during the Second World War in which a Soviet agent – armed with steel nerves, a cool demeanour and perfect German – infiltrated SS headquarters in Berlin to steal the Nazis' war plans. In the dark, the teenage Putin gazed in awe at the dashing figure, his eyes fixed on the screen, his palms sweaty with excitement. At that moment he decided that he wanted to be a Soviet James Bond, subduing enemies, filled with glory. It was within days of seeing the movie – in the same week that real Russian tanks rolled into Czechoslovakia – that he walked into the Big House on Liteiny Prospekt.

Five years later, by which time he was a law student and fluent German speaker, Putin was again transfixed by a celluloid hero, along with 80 million other Russians. The twelve-part television series *Seventeen Moments of Spring* spun a similar tale, of another handsome Russian altering the course of history. In it a KGB agent uncovered a Nazi plot to negotiate peace with the Western allies behind the back of the Soviet Union. No matter that no such spy or plot existed,* the series – in which wartime newsreels mutated into fiction – was perceived as historical fact. Almost every viewer came to believe that Russia had been betrayed and that Stalin had divined the foreign trickery.

Seventeen Moments of Spring – Russia's most popular television programme, ever – was no independent production. It was conceived and commissioned by Yuri Andropov, then the chairman of the KGB. The series' director was 'assisted' by Andropov's deputy and two KGB operatives brought in as 'technical advisers'. As well as unifying the nation by reinforcing suspicion of the West, its purpose was to encourage young, educated recruits to join the security agency. With its annual rebroadcast on the anniversary of the end of the Second World War, *Seventeen Moments* remains one of the KGB's most influential operations, eclipsed only by Russian intelligence's *diversiya* – subversion – of the 2016 US presidential election.

Tobin knew movies. He knew about their power and paradoxes, about their ability to move hearts and minds, about their production costs and distribution deals. He knew that Lenin had considered movies to be the most important of all the arts and that Stalin had called them 'the greatest medium of mass agitation'. He was a London lad – fit, tough and independent-minded – who'd come to Russia on a whim, because of his passion for Sergei Eisenstein and Dostoevsky.

'I thought I'd learn Russian in a year, read *Crime and Punishment* in the original, then move on,' he said when we met at his top-floor apartment. 'That was in 1993.'

---

* For all its avowed realism, *Seventeen Moments of Spring* strayed well beyond the facts. In the last months of the war, a German general did meet the Americans in Switzerland to discuss the surrender of troops on the Italian front – but the Soviets were told about those meetings. No talks were ever held either on a complete German surrender or on a political settlement, as is claimed in the film.

At first Tobin worked as a translator and then a librarian, living in a squat, earning $100 a month.

'One hundred dollars was a fortune back then. I lived for nothing, drank for almost nothing. You could try anything, do anything. I had a dozen careers. And the women…' he recalled, his eyes widening at the memories. 'In the West, Russian women were thought to be either babushkas or Olympic shot-putters. The reality was very, very different. I developed serious neck ache watching girls.'

Tobin fell in love, married, fathered two kids and adopted a further four. He thrived and prospered as editor of the English-language *St Petersburg Times* and then of a bilingual lifestyle magazine. After the break-up of his marriage, he scooped up a vast Petrograd-side bachelor pad, installed underfloor heating and double door-locks and waxed lyrical on his long, west-facing balcony about life in the Wild East.

Tobin fell into the film business by recording English voice-overs and playing bit parts like the bearded, Kalashnikov-wielding Chechen rebel in *War*.

'I'm the one holding down a Russian prisoner's hand as his fingers were cut off,' he told me on a mellow evening as the sun set behind the spire of the Peter and Paul Fortress (where Dostoevsky had been imprisoned in 1849).

He worked as an assistant director as well. All the exterior scenes of *Downfall*, Oliver Hirschbiegel's film of the last days in Hitler's Berlin bunker, were filmed in St Petersburg. 'The production designer was beside himself with excitement,' said Tobin, not immune to the irony. 'His German special effects team were thrilled to blow up derelict Russian factories for camera.' Tobin himself managed the film's hundreds of extras, all hired locally and all dressed in full Wehrmacht battle uniforms. More than once he had to plead through his megaphone: 'Would SS officers *please* stop going to bars to drink vodka between takes?' He even caught two minor actors – carrying heavy replica machine guns and flamethrowers – popping into town to buy cigarettes.

Tobin also crewed HBO's *Rasputin* and Bernard Rose's *Anna Karenina*. Both productions were plagued by corruption and theft, as were all international films at the time. On one occasion a Russian fixer sourced a steam locomotive for Anna to throw herself under for 'the very cheapest price' of $70,000, enough money then to buy four or five St Petersburg apartments. When Tobin – translating for the producers – told him that there was only $18,000 in the budget for the whole scene, the fixer shrugged and replied, 'Okay, call it eighteen thousand dollars.'

Later, in the middle of a night shoot, the locomotive needed to be refilled with water. The same fixer commandeered a street-cleaning tanker, telling Tobin to pay him $2,000 for its rental. But at the end of the night, Tobin asked the driver directly what he was owed.

'One bottle of vodka as agreed,' the driver answered.

Foreign producers began to cancel films, scared off by audacious thieves and mafia threats. Tobin found himself working more on Russian pictures, including the sequel to Aleksei Balabanov's *Brother*, a cult gangster thriller said to be Putin's third favourite movie (after the series *The Shield and the Sword* and *Seventeen Moments of Spring*). In time he took more regular work as editor-in-chief of the English division of the Russian Travel Guide documentary television channel, becoming one of the few thousand Brits* who call Russia home, who don't want to leave, and not only because of the parties.

Russians are renowned for their great parties. Recent revelries have been more reminiscent of the age of Louis XIV than any time in the last century. In St Petersburg two oligarchs staged *Midsummer Night's Dream* bashes in a Versailles-like palace. An oil mogul commandeered the national aquarium for a pool orgy, complete with dolphins and mermaid-finned prostitutes. An

---

* According to the *Guardian*, the number of British citizens living in Russia fell from 180,000 to 30,000 between 2014 and 2016. Numbers fell further in the collapse in UK–Russia relations after the Salisbury nerve-agent attack. In 2019 the *Telegraph* estimated that there were 1,688 British expats in Russia. 'Did an audit,' one British former resident told the *Guardian*. 'Everyone's basically left.'

aerospace billionaire drafted in a dozen 'dwarfs', attached them to helium balloons and let them fly. Mikhail Gutseriev, the Kazakh tycoon, bankrolled his son's wedding to the staggering tune of $10 million. Six hundred guests were chauffeured to Moscow's Safisa club in a fleet of Rolls-Royces, entertained by J Lo, Sting and Enrique Iglesias, then flown to London for a second private concert with Beyoncé and Elton John. Some hosts balance such profligacy with humour. To mark his company's birthday, Eugene Kaspersky – the stocky and garrulous founder of the global computer security company – hired a whole train to take hundreds of his employees to Uryupinsk, a remote town some 400 miles south-east of Moscow whose name signifies 'the middle of nowhere'.

Hence a movie's end-of-shoot wrap party promised to be an unforgettable extravaganza. At the very least I expected the producers to lay on vintage champagne, dancers and a high-tech circus act or two.

Tobin also loved parties. On our walk to the venue, he reminded me that during the communist years most Russian revelries had taken place in kitchens. The kitchen had been the family's living room, guest room and debating chamber, he explained. It was the place where Soviet citizens had felt safest; amongst friends, drinking tea, sharing jokes ('A communist is someone who's read Marx, an anti-communist is someone who's understood him'). It was also where people hunkered around the radio to listen to banned BBC and Voice of America broadcasts. Sometimes food was even cooked in kitchens. But those days were long gone, said Tobin. No one had the time any more to argue late into the night about the meaning of life or the political subtext of Czechoslovak pop songs. Nowadays people struggled to make ends meet. Almost everyone needed to get up early the next morning for work.

As the elevator was under repair we climbed three flights of stairs, pushed open a heavy door and stepped into … 1969. The apartment – in which cast and crew were assembled – was still dressed for their low-budget period drama. It had been the movie's main location for a simple Brezhnev-era love story.

On the wall Lenin and Marx, their retouched complexions as flawless as their vision, looked down on the revellers. Around them on the bare white walls hung red balloons and red flags. Red carnations were tied in bunches with long ribbons of the Soviet colours. Clothes lines were suspended across the kitchen and onions sprouted in old mayonnaise jars on the windowsills. Cabbage soup and beetroot borsch simmered on the cooker.

More guests arrived, dressed as Pioneers in crisp white shirts and red neckties. The women wore no make-up and the men's hair was greased. No one kissed, instead they shook hands with serious demeanour.

To kick off the party, the host – the film's producer – sang 'Whirlwinds of Danger' ('Whirlwinds of danger are raging around us…'). Others joined in for a spirited rendition of 'May There Always Be Sunshine', raising their right arms in salute. A chant followed, 'Glory! Glory! Glory!' We all took up the cry. 'Glory! Glory! Glory!' Outside, astonished passers-by stopped and stared from the pavement.

When the wardrobe woman giggled, she was hushed into silence. Levity did not befit the seriousness of the occasion. Someone – I think it was one of the scriptwriters – started to sing, her voice crackling with emotion:

> We're merrily dancing
> Around a big tree.
> In our Motherland,
> We are happy and free.
> In our Motherland,
> We're singing our song,
> For Comrade Stalin, the Great One.

But the partygoers were not as one in their love for Comrade Stalin. A clutching couple – sunk in the battered sofa – stopped spilling secrets to throw pickled mushrooms at the singer. Others retaliated from the kitchen with a barrage of sprouting onions. The film's composer braved the hail of projectiles to reach the piano and play 'Where Begins Our Motherland?', the theme from *The Shield and the Sword*. In response someone started banging pots and slamming cupboards out of time with the music.

As our tea glasses were refilled with vodka for the third or fourth time, the party split into two camps. Some of the crew members put their hearts into the play-acting, roaring across the room 'Red banners advance!' Others pulled off their Pioneer kerchiefs and taunted their colleagues with 'Bury your Lenin'. The sound recordist and his boom man shoved at each other, only half in jest. Ill-advised alliances began to fall apart. The script girl burst into tears. A couple of performers tried to bridge the gap by starting to dance but they only managed to mash crisps and discarded articles of clothing into the avocado rug.

The evening had an uncanny resonance for me, taking me back to a similar party on my original journey. Then, as now, I started to feel quite mad. Where was I? What year was it? Was that an actor dressed as Vladimir Putin at the door?

Thirty years ago in Warsaw, London and Washington, we had danced on the grave of communism, in an act of defiance, in celebration of the resilience of the human spirit. Europe – especially Eastern Europe – had survived the rages of the demigods and their hateful executioners. The continent had emerged, scarred but whole, into a better world, or so it had seemed.

But with the passing decades the old grew older, the young stopped listening and new demigods stepped forward, twisting the past to suit their present. Perhaps it was ever thus, perhaps our common desire to better ourselves had always been hobbled by individual greed and arrogance, and the thought of it wrenched my heart.

To recharge my spirits and glass, I retreated into the kitchen where the film's young camera assistant – who had been born after the fall of the Wall – told me in slurred and broken English that he didn't want to eat socialist salami but he did want to live in a country where, in his own words, 'people are treated like human beings'.

In time the wrap party was wrapped and guests went home to their beds and overdue bills. Tobin and I walked away along streets slick and shiny with rain.

In Alexandrovskiy Park, near to the Gorkovskaya metro station, we paused to stare at a pre-revolution monument. At the centre of a massive bronze cross, two Russian sailors opened the sea cocks to flood and scuttle their ship so as to prevent it from falling into enemy hands. The sculpture commemorated the 1904 sinking of the torpedo boat *Steregushchiy* (*Valiant*) during the Russo-Japanese War. But its heroic story – like the ones that had shaped Putin – was a fiction. In reality a Japanese naval squadron had captured the *Steregushchiy*. Almost all the Russian officers and crew had been killed in the battle. Sometime later the torpedo boat sank, due to human error. But the tsar wanted to propagate another version of history, and so the truth was twisted, and the monument erected in honour of the sailors' imagined bravery and sacrifice.

Glory. Glory to the victorious people.

15

Beauty and the Beast

Beauty can even save the world, wrote Dostoevsky, and I wondered if spending four years in a Siberian gulag had done in his head. Beauty never closed a single prison nor halted the Blitzkrieg. Beauty stopped neither assassins nor suicide bombers. How on earth could beauty save the world?

Aleksandr Solzhenitsyn – who had also been banished to the camps, poisoned by the KGB and deported from the Soviet Union – knew the answer. In the essence of beauty, he said, was a certain peculiarity, a peculiarity in the status of art. He believed that art 'scoops up the truth' and presents it to us as a living force. Such true works take hold of us, compel us and ennoble us. Their convincingness (his word) 'forces even an opposing heart to surrender' so that 'nobody ever, not even in ages to come, will appear to refute them'.

'A work of art bears within itself its own verification,' he said. 'Conceptions which are devised or stretched do not stand being portrayed in images, they all come crashing down, appear sickly and pale, convince no one.'

Every one of us has an ear for a false note, a nose for a lie. We are innately wary of artifice and quacks. We know that true beauty is not skin deep. But as a mass, as a collective, we can lose our common sense.

Hence despots and their like want as little as possible to do with the individual. In both communist and fascist ideology – as in modern populism – a leader rises out of the masses as if by the force of nature. He is portrayed as a visionary who binds individuals together, making them capable of deeds that they could not otherwise achieve. He offers them an ideal, and to grasp it they – we – surrender to him. Our emotions are manipulated. We stop thinking critically. We are coerced into accepting his truth as our own. Nothing can stand in his way, or save the world, except the individual, and beauty.

'Here lived Lydia Evgenevna Bogdanova, homemaker, born in 1911, arrested 02.06.1937, executed 15.09.1937,' read the text on the passport-sized, rectangular steel plaque. On its left-hand side was an open square, a hole symbolising a missing photograph.

'To me the physical effort is important,' Alexa called to me from the top of the stepladder, shifting her weight to drive the drill bit deeper into the building's brick wall. 'I want to sweat – not just talk – to return our nation's memory.'

Ten years ago the political journalist and civic campaigner Sergey Parkhomenko set out to remember the victims of Soviet treachery. His project 'Last Address' aimed to commemorate individuals at their last place of residence.* Almost immediately the authorities in St Petersburg and Moscow set about crippling his work. Minister of Justice Alexander Konovalov even designated Memorial – the civil rights society that administered 'Last Address' – a 'foreign agent' which 'undermines the foundations of the constitutional order of the Russian Federation'. He called for its liquidation.

---

* Parkhomenko was inspired by *Stolperstein*, the brass-capped 'stumble stones' that have been planted among the cobbles of 500 German towns and cities, engraved with the names of individuals murdered by the Nazis. But in contrast with the Germans, few Russians accept that past atrocities must be unearthed and confessed for the psychic health of a society. Hence, whereas 75,000 *Stolpersteine* have to date been laid across Western Europe, only 750 'Last Address' plaques had been put up in Russia, by a few brave, individual volunteers like Alexa.

'I think I know every plaque in St Petersburg,' Alexa said while descending the ladder. She was in her early twenties, dressed in denim dungarees with her hair tied back in a ponytail. She had intense brown eyes, their seriousness lightened by the softness of youth. She was studying psychology at university. 'There are three at Pushkinskaya ulitsa 19, five at Fontanka Embankment 129, two at the Fountain House, and these on Bolshaya Pushkarskaya,' she told me, taking each one to heart. 'In 1937 Lydia Bogdanova and her husband were arrested here as Polish spies,' she explained, tilting her head towards the front door of the building, climbing back up the ladder with hammer and rawl plugs. 'Why? Because they'd received a package of children's clothes from a relative in Warsaw. Their six-year-old son was dressed in them when his parents were taken away. He never saw them again.'

As she spoke, I passed up to her the simple steel plate: one sign, one name, one life out of the millions killed during the Great Terror. While signing a long execution list, Stalin was reported to have muttered: 'Who's going to remember all this riff-raff in ten or twenty years time? No one.'

But Alexa – alongside other student activists, independent journalists and historians – was encouraging the act of remembrance. So I asked her, as she bolted Lydia Bogdanova's plaque onto the wall, why so many of her countrymen preferred to forget?

'Russians do not forget but they have chosen not to remember,' she replied, her voice echoing down the street where the deceased had once walked, talked and wept. 'Do you know about the "mother" of the gulag?' she asked me.

I did. Stalin's first 'corrective' labour camp had been a repurposed monastery 600 miles north of St Petersburg on the Solovetsky Islands. Tens of thousands of his victims had been incarcerated there.

'It's become a museum of political repression, hasn't it?' I said.

'It *was* for a while,' she replied. 'Now old camp guards get together there to celebrate the founding of the gulag system.'

I had first learned about Solovetsky, and the work of 'Last Address', in Moscow. In a nondescript block off the Garden Ring, I'd been moved to tears in a basement archive to victims of the camps. In filing cabinets and on open shelves were millions of items donated by their families: hundreds of children's letters begging Stalin for their parents' release, notes thrown from sealed railway carriages, pine-needle dolls made by inmates for deserted daughters, threadbare prison jackets and spent bullets. During the Terror few people knew why they'd been arrested. Most assumed that it was an administrative cock-up, a matter of mistaken identity. Few comprehended that their lives could be for ever changed because of a flippant remark or postcard from abroad. No one knew where they were to be taken; loaded onto cattle trucks, shipped hundreds or thousands of miles to the railhead, forced to walk into the wilderness and – on arrival – even build their own prisons.

After the archive, I'd gone to Lubyanka. In Soviet times the KGB's headquarters had been called the tallest building in Moscow, because Siberia could be seen from its basement. For decades its founder, Felix Dzerzhinsky, had dominated the central Moscow square, both in the iniquitous organisation and with his statue. In 1991 a crowd of protesters had torn him down but his mendacious KGB meat grinder remained, the ochre facade and terracotta cornices of its palace glowering across the city.

I'd sat in the sunshine listening to the traffic sigh around the square, watching its clerks and secretaries settle on park benches during their lunch break. One woman had tripped on her heels and fallen, grazing her knee. She'd grumbled to friends about her ruined stocking, paying no heed to the Solovetsky Stone. The massive granite rock had been hewn from the White Sea island and mounted in the square at a canted angle as if about to fall; inert yet laden with poignancy.

Every autumn hundreds of mourners queued beside it to read out loud the name, age, profession and execution date of Stalin's victims. Some years the queue was so long that people had to wait an hour for their turn at the microphone. The ceremony was known as the 'Return of the Names' and, at the present rate, it will take more than a century to read out the names of all the dead.

As the clerks had finished their lunch and returned to their desks, to an afternoon of filing surveillance requests or operating security cameras, I'd decided to travel to Solovetsky, to a holy and haunted place so remote that 'a scream from here would never be heard' according to Solzhenitsyn. It would be my last stop in Russia.

Back in St Petersburg, Alexa packed her tool box and loaded it into an ageing grey minivan. Together we lashed the ladder to its roof rack.

'Our terrible history is almost too much to bear. Shame and complicity is modern Russia, as is this,' she said, gesturing at the plaque. '"Last Address" is our response to the amnesia, to the guilt and sorrow, to the lie that Stalin created a great country.'

Beyond her a street sweeper broomed autumn leaves into piles along Bolshaya Pushkarskaya. A sudden gust of wind caught them, spinning them in a vortex around the hapless man. He picked up his broom again and, like a long-suffering Sisyphus, swept them back into piles.

16

Angels

She was an angel, glowing in the setting sun. As the aircraft turned, its last rays brushed the short hairs on her forearm. Life throbbed beneath them and her woven leather bracelet, under a simple wrist tattoo, at the ends of slender fingers tipped with chipped purple nail varnish. In the golden light the young woman looked as if she'd flown out of a fifteenth-century Rostov icon or Chagall oil, apart from the black jeans and chequered blouse that hung loose around her hips. I guessed that she was returning home to Arkhangelsk from university, or about to start her first job as a teacher. In the palm of her hand she cupped an inflight sandwich as if it were a timid bird. She raised it to her lips, taking care so it did not take wing, and took a small bite.

Then the sun fell behind us and the neon cabin lights shuddered to life, revealing to me the true woman: tired eyes, dry skin, mortal. She was no student or young teacher, not any longer. She was a wage slave, or perhaps a divorcee at the end of a journey rather than the beginning, just getting by, just counting the days. She folded the waxed sandwich wrapper in half, then half again, pinching the edges hard with her nails as if fixing time in origami. She gazed down at the dusting of snow along the sea's edge. Away to the north stretched white land and grey water.

I turned away to explain the plan to Sami, again – land in Arkhangelsk, change planes for the Solovetsky Islands, spend a few days on the archipelago, then send him north to Murmansk – but he didn't hear me. As so often now he was plugged into his headphones. He'd come back to the hotel with renewed determination. His new way out, gleaned from fellow migrants, sounded so unlikely that I wondered if a rubber dinghy across the Barents Sea really would be a more sensible route. At least our trajectories were aligned for one last time, until we touched down and my arrangements crumbled.

The United Aviation Antonov couldn't make the short hop to Solovki, whether because of an oil leak, bad weather or pilot inebriation I couldn't tell, and Nordavia's flights to the islands were fully booked for the next fortnight. Our only option was to take a boat, but to reach Kem – Solovki's mainland port – we had to catch an overnight train.

In the taxi Arkhangelsk revealed itself in fuming chimneys, skeletal cranes and monstrous piers. Around them on the headland massed black cargo barges and staggering sailors. The city's last wooden neighbourhood – its ancient timbers weathered stone grey – was squeezed between overbearing concrete blocks. Our train cut through them and the late afternoon, rolling south and west past overgrown railway tracks lined with abandoned freight cars and clumps of spindly trees. Beneath the Severodvinsk Bridge the Dvina shone like burnished silver, possibly from the mercury that was pumped into it by the upstream pulp and timber mills.

The days were getting shorter and we turned in at dusk, Sami scrambling into the upper bunk. 'I talk too much,' he said without removing his headphones. 'When I play back what I've said during the day, I ask myself, "Did I say that? Was that really necessary?" I tell myself, "Don't talk so much." But come the morning I'm jabber jabbering again.'

I couldn't sleep so gazed out of the window at the mantle of forest, at nameless swamps turning to ice, at streams tinted yellow by the tundra. I caught sight of a station from time to time until the blackening sky inked away the horizon. In the rocking carriage, without lights or reference points to link me to the ground, I felt myself to be cut adrift, perched between departure and destination, yesterday and today.

I must have slept for – in that dark place – I saw the young woman from the aeroplane, the last rays of sunlight forming her halo. But instead of a sandwich I saw that she was now eating moss. Her leather bracelet had become a manacle. Her purple nail varnish had been chipped away by axe work. In the timber camp her life had been ground to the bone. In a canvas tent she built a windbreak out of corpses. Almost no one had ever escaped from Solovki, the island gulag, and no one had ever stood tall. All were bent like a million birch saplings weighed down by snow.

At dawn our train stopped at Kem. In the breaking light a geriatric bus wheezed us to the pier where a ferry waited among rusted fishing boats. We squeezed into its glass-cracked cabin with dozens of pilgrims, all women, who stared wide-eyed at Sami, a young man blacker than any they had ever seen. Only as we pulled away from the harbour for the three-hour crossing, did the women drop their eyes, don headscarves and start to pray.

Solovki is Russia's Stonehenge, Lourdes and Auschwitz. Ancient people were drawn to the White Sea archipelago as if by a magnet, winding mysterious stone labyrinths across its sacred earth, imagining it as the portal between this world and the next. Since time immemorial it has been a place of both light and darkness. Two thousand years ago, shamans chose it as a gateway to the Saivo, the land of the dead in Sámi mythology. Its monastery was founded in the fifteenth century for prayer, refuge and incarceration. Disciples and heretics were interned within its sacred walls, the devout and the damned living side by side for almost 400 years.

On the backs of the tsar's prisoners, and the salt and timber trades, the monastery became rich, the second wealthiest in the land. Two to three hundred inmates were said to have dragged each of its vast glacial foundation stones into place, building upon them the twenty-foot-thick walls. In the name of God, jailer-monks worked the condemned to death in the forests or left them to rot in coffin-like cells. At the same time pilgrims – for whom Solovki was the spiritual heart of Russia – arrived by summer steamships to kneel in its holy chapels and to light candles at the tombs of its saints.

In 1903 Nicholas II closed the prison, so horrified was he by its abuses, only for it to be reopened after his execution. In the 1920s the Bolsheviks banished the monks, stripped the monastery of its gold and made it the headquarters of the Northern Special Purposes Camps. Solovki became the first cancer cell of the tumour that would spread across Russia, wrote Solzhenitsyn. In its 'killing forests' royalists in rags, poets stripped of their pens, academics, clerks and angels felled timber by hand, dragged the wet logs to the shore, died by the thousand. In winter it was impossible to conceal the killings, wrote one survivor, for 'the naked, dead, frozen people were everywhere ... their elbows, hands, legs, heads, backs sticking out of the snow'. Another recalled that every morning guards 'armed with long sea hooks, through slightly open gates, tried to drag the dead bodies out of the cells'. At the same time the living attempted to hold on to the dead 'to serve them as mattresses'.

Inmates were lice-ridden, surviving on breadcrumbs and gruel. Those who missed their work target were punished with 'slaughter by sticks and swimming in ice holes'. Priests were stripped naked, dunked in water then staked in winter courtyards until they became living ice statues. Others were tortured until they were no longer recognisable – not as class enemies, not even as human. The luckiest prisoners were those who were shot on arrival.

The pilgrims crossed themselves with renewed fervour as Solovki's gilded domes rose on the horizon like a line of musical notes. A breeze blew up from the west, flicking frothy tufts off the wave tops. Overhead blue holes pierced the clouds and I felt the wind brush against my cheek.

Together we stepped ashore as had the prisoners, as had a Nazi delegation who came in the 1930s to glean tips on the camp's 'correctional' regime, as had Putin himself. He had come to the citadel-cemetery to mark its re-establishment as a monastery, declaring without irony that all peoples were equal before God, and that Russia had always guaranteed that equality.

Like him, Sami and I now walked on the bones of its less-than-equal citizens, drawn forward by the toll of a giant bell. We followed worshippers and bearded monks in black frocks through the massive stone walls and across a cobbled courtyard to morning liturgy. In the chapel – once a twenty-eight-cell barracks – faithful voices lifted towards the heavens. We climbed the stairs above the granary to stare into vaulted brick chambers, on the walls of which prisoners had once scratched their names. Around the perimeter, among grazing goats, we stepped over unnumbered mass graves. Sami didn't 'jabber' at all that morning, and not only because of the cold. Again and again he tightened his coat against it and the ghosts.

Then I spotted the hangar.

Inside the drafty, barn-like building there had once existed an extraordinary, ephemeral modern art gallery. Over three fleeting Arctic summers, contemporary work – remarkable in its incongruity – had tumbled into and out of it: architectural fantasies had spread across its pinewood walls, fanciful scrap-metal sculptures had marched towards its Tamarin pier, a lattice of large white crosses had reached out into the sea. Then its doors were locked and its organisers condemned as *rastliteli russkoi dushi*, molesters of the Russian soul.

'Those years were a real adventure,' said Luba Kuzovnikova, one of the so-called 'molesters'. We had arranged to meet outside her unlikely Arctic gallery, on her first return to the island in almost two decades. 'We had no website, no social networks. There was only one telephone line for the whole island.' She pushed back her mane of curly, shoulder-length hair and added, 'Yet it was a springboard for everything that happened afterwards.'

Everything.

And nothing.

Luba had grown up in Severodvinsk, the Soviet Union's great northern shipyard. Within sight of her family's apartment, the huge SEVMASH Machine-Building facility had produced as many as five new boats every year, including the world's largest nuclear submarine. Her father had been an electrical engineer, her mother a teacher and Luba's childhood one of privilege.

'In the shops we had boys' clothes and girls' clothes. We had bananas in September. Sometimes we could even buy little chocolate cheese treats. Severodvinsk was a closed town because of its military importance and I never went hungry. I didn't realise my luck.'

But then came the 1990s and 'everything disappeared'. Jobs and money vanished and Luba's father came to be paid in kind, not cash: vodka, 'Bush legs' and a thousand rolls of toilet paper for rewiring a factory. Her mother's salary went unpaid for months. As so many others, the family survived on vegetables grown at their dacha, and forest mushrooms, until Luba won a scholarship to study abroad.

At Utica College in Upstate New York and Norway's Arctic University in Tromsø, Luba studied languages, philology and art history, saving every penny, sending all that she could back to her parents. She lost herself in exhibitions at Syracuse's Munson-Williams-Proctor Arts Institute and, during a further year abroad in Denmark, gazed in wonder at Anish Kapoor and Kirstine Vaaben's sculptures at Copenhagen's museums. On her return home she was required to work as an assistant teacher in a Russian school.

'I was super-excited to be posted to Solovki,' she told me, now over mugs of tea in a guest house cafe. Her small, refined features – crinkly aquamarine eyes, petite upturned nose, high cheekbones – were offset by a laugh so large that it seemed to echo through the steamy windows and around so-called Prosperity Bay. 'As a schoolteacher I knew I could become a local, visiting the labyrinths, living in the monastery, studying its artefacts.'

She went on: 'In those early days every passageway was open, every door was unlocked. I explored the refectory, the bell tower, the Uspensky and Preobrazhensky cathedrals. One midnight I walked by moonlight through the half-ruined, half-restored Church of Nicholas, my footsteps crunching on the snow in the nave.' She paused, an infectious warmth spreading around her, and added, 'That first winter was magical.'

But in 2000, the year of her arrival, Solovki was caught in a power struggle, like all of Russia. As the monastery was re-consecrated,

Luba – along with two artist partners – decided to create an art centre in the abandoned aircraft hangar.

'Our objective was to place Solovki into the contemporary cultural context, and to search for new solutions to Russia's economic and social problems,' she told me, never suspecting that the decision would put her at odds with the Russian Orthodox Church.

Together she and her partners cleared the building of rotted fishing nets, stapled plastic sheeting to the walls and built a larchwood bar, bookshop and moveable Tracey Emin-type bed. With 'wild youthfulness' they created a venue for dialogue, inviting Russian and international artists as well as organising dance and bookbinding classes for islanders.

'We were the gallery's curators, its guides, bar staff and nightwatchmen. Every time it rained the roof leaked and we had to move the bed and our borrowed computer. How we managed to organise that first summer season, on a budget of a few hundred dollars, I still cannot understand.'

As well as tens of thousands of pilgrims, Solovki draws to its shores artists and intellectuals escaping city life. Along its unpaved lanes the incomers live amongst the archipelago's 800 or so permanent residents: fishermen, monastery gardeners, guesthouse staff, and the sons and daughters of former camp guards.

'On the island there was no meeting place so at the end of every day visitors and locals came to the gallery. We'd grab anyone interesting – a visiting biologist, historians, an astrophysicist – and persuade them to give a talk. I'd bicycle to the pier, post office and village water pump, sticking up posters announcing the event. Sometimes only ten people would show. Sometimes there'd be as many as one hundred. But every night we'd be in the hangar until three or four in the morning, talking, debating and drinking port wine. We became friends with the local community, and enemies of the monastery.'

The first summer show featured architectural caprices from Moscow, Novosibirsk and Ljubljana. In the second summer, local children – guided by professional artists – reimagined the island's vast junk yard into a fanciful 'Zoo Park'; an abandoned guardhouse became *The Penguin*, scrap metal pipes and white paint made the *Dachshund-Zebra*, the rusted cab of a camp lorry mutated into *The Kind Giant*. In its third season Luba and her partners curated *Metamorphoses*, transforming the function and meaning of a dozen abandoned structures.

'It was a time when everything felt possible,' recalled Luba.

Every day ArtHangar's wide doors were thrown open to the world. Every night its inviting light gleamed through the chevron-patterned boards and across the water. Yet with each new summer less and less became possible.

In the village a chilling exhibition had been mounted on the tragic gulag years: cat-o'-nine-tails whips, prison-cell doors, orders of execution, photographs of twisted corpses strewn across a field and skulls stacked amongst the alder trees. It was the first exhibition of its kind in the country, and it troubled the powerful Patriarch of Moscow and all Rus', primate of the Russian Orthodox Church. He was determined to control Solovki and its history. He ordered that the exhibition be closed and that all traces of the labour camp be expunged. Then he turned on the gallery, denouncing contemporary art as 'imported pseudo-culture'. He damned the Zoo Park as a Disneyland, speculating that, if left unchecked, its sacrilege would soon overwhelm the monastery itself.

Luba argued that ArtHangar was on the outskirts of the village. She reminded her critics that the building had never served any religious purpose. It had been built in 1925 to house the gulag's Grigorovich M-24 flying boat. In fact, the hangar was one of the few places on the island where, to use the local expression, 'no blood had been shed'.

'Solovki is in all senses a frontier,' she reasoned, explaining that in common with Christianity, contemporary art was concerned with man's quest. 'It is a border place, a marginal place, a place of intricate and subtle entwinement of land and water, of past and present, of positive and negative experience. Artists need such places for their search, and Solovki needs art to encourage reflection.'

Luba showed the Patriarch's secretariat the gallery's guest book, filled as it was with enthusiastic comments. She related the story of a bereaved mother who'd made a pilgrimage to the islands after the death of her two children in a car accident. On seeing the wacky Zoo Park creatures the woman had laughed out loud for the first time in five years.

But Luba's arguments fell on deaf ears. The Church wanted no multiple meanings, no laughter. It wanted control. Russian pilgrims who came to Solovki on a quest were to be given answers, not to find them individually through art. Local villagers – who feared eviction from their homes and expulsion from the Church – fell silent and the building was padlocked shut.

Over that last summer, dancers performed around it in the open air but soon afterwards Luba left the island, unwilling to return for many years.

'I couldn't face it,' she admitted. 'The joy had leached away during the fight with the monastery. In Russia, State and Church have been good friends since Byzantine times.'

Later that day Sami and I looked through the gaps between the planks. The promise of the Patriarch – another former KGB man, according to Forbes Media's research in the Soviet Archives – to transform the hangar into an information centre had come to nothing. No work had been done since Luba had been banished from it. In fact it appeared that no one had even been inside it for more than a decade. Beams and roof timbers lay on the ground, faded artworks dangled off the walls and the original ArtHangar sign – fashioned in appropriate constructivist style – was hidden out of sight. The historic building was simply rotting away.

'Art gives us insight into something we do not see at first glance,' Luba told me. She had moved on to curate projects and festivals across the north including Norway's Barents Spektakel. 'Artists have a capacity for insight, perhaps even an ability to look into the future. My role is as a kind of facilitator, introducing artists to special places that are going through change.' She paused and looked around herself. 'It all began here in Solovki.'

·

* * *

Sami and I walked away from hangar and monastery, away from the faithful and the dilapidated village, into the forest. He was quiet again, steeling himself for the journey ahead. Among the spruce and pine, in the cold dappled sunlight, we found a small lake skimmed with wafer-thin ice. Across it skated water beetles like minute balls of mercury. Columns of vapour rose out of the woods like the smoke from bonfires. A crow's caw echoed from the far shore. Within a few weeks the water would be frozen solid and the ice reach as far as the Barents Sea.

Solitude had brought the first Russians to Solovki for religious retreat, then in exile, then under arrest. Today most came and went as they pleased. Few were in danger of being imprisoned or worked to death. Nevertheless they were trapped, by their unwillingness to face the past, by a deceitful and disingenuous national narrative. The Russian Revolution had enslaved generations. When it collapsed, an inner circle of trusted St Petersburg friends had refashioned its lies to empower and enrich themselves.

Memorial – the organisation behind 'Last Address' – had once built the only monument to political prisoners executed on Solovki. But within days its stone slabs had vanished.

So too did the telephone of the wind.

Last year an elderly visitor to the archipelago – no one had asked his name – set an old rotary telephone on a tree stump on a rise of wooded land to the east of the monastery. No wires connected it to a network. The handset was cracked and broken. Yet every morning the man left his timber-frame hotel and trekked out to the woods to talk on it. After three days he began to invite other visitors to use the phone, offering them the chance to speak with old friends. One or two put the receiver to their ears and heard nothing. Most chose to ignore him, tightening their scarves around their heads and hurrying back to the safety of the monastery. Then he told a monk, who had joined him on the rise of land, that he was speaking to angels. That night the phone vanished. In the morning the old man also left the island, never to return.

17

London Road

'There's something I need to say, like to get it out,' said Sami.

We were back on the mainland at Kem. We were parting again. Sami was heading north on the 'Arktika' to Murmansk. My southbound train was due an hour later, bound for St Petersburg and out of Russia. Around us on the platform hawkers sold smoked fish from wooden flats, boiled potatoes and bottles of beer. Yawning rail travellers shuffled between them in their slippers, stretching legs and stiff backs, opening their purses to buy punnets of late season *chernika* berries and home-made cabbage pies.

There's an old Russian custom of sitting together in silence for a minute before starting a journey, but we had no time. 'You should get on board and find a seat,' I said. The train only stopped for ten minutes and it was packed. In a window I saw half a dozen African faces, looking out of place at this end of the world. Sami had met them in St Petersburg, linking up as travellers do, and heard about the Arctic route. He'd arranged to travel with them on the so-called London Road. After the twelve-hour ride to Murmansk, another train would take them to the Norwegian frontier. Rumour had it that the Russian border guards there were letting migrants pass through without checking for visas, in effect dumping them on Europe.

'It's another loan, yeah?' he insisted as he pocketed the notes.

I nodded. 'Go on, Sami,' I said as the locomotive sounded its warning whistle.

'Rightfully so. Rightfully so,' he muttered but he could neither step off the platform nor let go of the train. He gripped the carriage door handle and tried to speak. I'd rarely seen him at a loss for words. I wondered how many partings he'd had to face; from his mother then father, from fellow travellers with whom he'd shared a night, a ride, a hope. All had been left behind, all apart from hope.

'What did you want to say, Sami?' I asked.

'It's … whatever,' he finally replied. 'You are the word man. You say it.'

In his hesitation, Sami had blocked the carriage door. A grumbling passenger tried to push past him. When Sami stepped out of his way, the man, who was drunk, took a swing at him but slipped and fell onto the platform. Somehow his leg ended up under the train and an officious despatcher stormed towards us.

'Get on. Get on,' I hissed then turned my attention to the drunk. By the time the despatcher reached us, Sami was gone.

The whistle sounded again as we pulled the drunk back onto his feet. He wheeled around, pointed up at the Africans and demanded – as far as I could tell – their arrest. Now a policeman appeared and the hawkers crowded around to see if he would club the man or at least drag him away. But the slamming carriage doors shook the drunk to his senses. His manner shifted from open hostility to sheepish submission. He begged his pardon and hauled himself up the steps as the train began to move. Both despatcher and policeman left him to be someone else's problem. I watched the 'Arktika' until the red tail lights vanished beyond a glade of stunted birches on its long journey to the Arctic Circle.

The 875-mile Murmansk railroad line had been built over twenty months by tens of thousands of labourers, navvies and POWs. Along it thousands of political prisoners were sent north to the camps and – during the Second World War – millions of tons of Allied supplies transported south from the Barents Sea railhead. To this day Murmansk remains the largest transit point in the Arctic but, as I later learned, Sami never reached it.

Across the world refugee routes are ever-shifting, traffickers and opportunists exploiting need and inequality for profit, even for political ends. Russia's 1,300-mile-long northern frontier with Norway and Finland is among the country's most strategic, guarded by the army, the KGB and the Border Service. Along its length nothing happens without Moscow's approval. The Kremlin alone decides which roads to open and close in the heavily militarised region.

On the train Sami learned from the other Africans that Norway had closed its crossing points to foot travellers. In response some 5,500 Afghans, Iranians and Pakistanis had cycled into Kirkenes, until bicycles too were banned. So instead of heading to Murmansk, and freewheeling a Raleigh into the passport-free Schengen zone, he and the other Africans got off in Kandalaksha, a place best known for its fish plants and while-you-wait deportation orders. In that city local officials, hotel owners and drivers worked together with criminal gangs to manage the migration business. Package deals cost between $500 and $2,000, depending on individual need. Payment was in cash only. No proof existed of the involvement of the Russian state, yet – immediately after Helsinki had voiced support for NATO – some 1,500 refugees were despatched across its border as a warning. The Kremlin wanted to remind the Finns that over eleven million foreigners lived on Russian territory, a vast pool of potential migrants who could be used to flood Europe.

Neither Sami nor I had expected him to become a geopolitical pawn. In Kandalaksha, he and the other Africans sank their money into a decrepit beige Lada and joined a convoy of rust-buckets for the 120-mile drive to Finland. Twice on the journey the Soviet-era wreck stalled and had to be push-started by the five men with the single Gambian woman at the wheel. Once, Sami caught sight of a deer herd cantering across the red and brown tundra.

As the cars neared the border his breath quickened. He knew that he mustn't panic. He knew that he had to be invisible at the last frontier. But with so much at stake, fear threatened to overwhelm him. He thought he didn't stand a chance.

He shouldn't have worried. Moscow was again sending a message and the convoy was allowed to breeze – or at least judder – through the three Russian checkpoints to reach the frontier.

At the Salla border post Sami dropped to his knees to touch the ground. The Finnish officials questioned and fingerprinted him, then gave him a paper that recognised him as an 'irregular migrant'. His unroadworthy vehicle was confiscated and dumped in a scrapyard beyond the customs hall, along with as many as a thousand other Ladas and Volgas rusting away beneath the trees. He told a medical officer that he felt 'so tired'. He named me as his next of kin. He was surprised that no one asked him for money; not during the interview, not in the sleeping hall, not in the minivan to Kemijärvi and Helsinki.

The flow of migrants and refugees on the Arctic route was tiny compared to the hundreds of thousands who have fled through Turkey and the Balkans over the last years. Yet both flows were used – to a greater or lesser extent – as weapons, funnelled into Europe to stoke the continent's migration crisis and to undermine its unity, to tear apart the EU.

Moscow has always striven to control its 'near abroad', the tsars' cavalries, Red Army tanks, cyber warriors and now migrants sent forth to ravage its adversaries. Its strategy has been to attack (or counter-attack) as a means of defence. So it was that Sami – a bereaved, moonwalking, almost-ever-talking African – became one of its unwitting foot-soldiers, a human time bomb calculated to spark an explosion, somewhere, someday in Europe.

Estonia

18

Home

'Welcome to the front line,' said Kristjan, unfolding his arms to embrace a gusty sweep of shoreline. 'Welcome to my home.'

I had stepped out of the largest country in the world into one of the smallest, from a land with a million men at arms to a pocket-handkerchief-sized state with 6,000 soldiers. An arrow straight rail line had carried me out of Russia towards the ferry port, slicing through dense conifer forests washed by salty sea air. Dilapidated wooden villages had given way to neat thatched-roof farmhouses, solid medieval castles and busy towns with teeming high streets. Copses of birch trees had stepped down to the Baltic. Across the water, islets were scattered like plump cushions trimmed with jetties and boats.

I felt elated, my spirits lifted in the borderland, thrilled to see Kristjan again. We'd first met ten years earlier in Berlin when he was the Estonian defence attaché to Germany. Now we gazed together across the ferry's bow towards the tufted pines and emerald grass of his low-lying island home.

'No soldier wants to fight a war on home turf,' he said, the wind snatching away parts of every sentence. 'We Estonians have no choice.'

Kristjan's military career spanned the three dramatic decades: drafted into the Soviet Army, booting them out as part of the Estonian Defence Forces, lecturing on leadership for NATO,

serving on peacekeeping missions around the world. Over the years –
on the journey from collectivism to free economy, dictatorship to
democracy – he had helped to build the now-independent nation.

'My island – Saaremaa – was the last part of the country to fall to
Knights of the Sword in 1227,' Kristjan said, his high forehead, long
straight nose and strong chin giving him a natural air of authority.
'It may be the last place to fall to Russians in twenty-first century,
when they attack.'

'*When* they attack…' I repeated, his certainty startling me.
'Not *if*?'

'The Russian threat is nothing new to us,' he replied as our ferry
pushed through the sea spray. 'What is new is that we are now
an ideological threat to them. Our economic and social success
shames them.'

I'd never thought that shame could spark an invasion but then
I'd never spent a weekend with a lieutenant-colonel.

'Russians are proud, a trait which most Europeans have put
behind them,' he explained. His short dark hair was peppered with
grey but his light blue eyes and elastic, boyish demeanour made
him appear younger than his fifty-four years, younger than a man
who carried the weight of so much history within him. 'To sustain
their sense of superiority, they work to weaken their neighbours.
They also dress up their failures as successes, as you've seen. Like
I said, the threat is nothing new to us.'

Estonia is less than half the size of Portugal but as strategic as
Gibraltar. Its people – one of Europe's earliest indigenous tribes –
have been shaped by seven centuries of occupation under Danes,
Teutonic knights, Swedish kings and the tsars. Russia governed
the country until 1917 when – for neither the first nor last
time – the Estonians drove them away. But the country's location,
at the head of the Baltic, able to defend or lay siege to nearby St
Petersburg, doomed their fragile independence. With the hated
Molotov–Ribbentrop Pact, the dictators' dirty deal that divvied up
Eastern Europe in 1939, the Soviets enslaved Estonia for another
half century, plus three war years when the Nazis nabbed it for
themselves.

'We've learned a thing or two about invaders over time,' said Kristjan, his smile sharper than a bayonet.

At Saaremaa, the largest of Estonia's 1,500 islands, our ferry dropped its ramp to disgorge bearded woodsmen, a vanload of folk dancers in long red skirts and a newly-wed couple on a Ural motorbike (with sidecar and bridal flower crown). Kristjan and I motored inland behind them and scruffy family hatchbacks, past waterside cottages and yellow-painted homesteads ringed by pines. In the old-growth forests lived wolves, moose and red deer. In the swamps were beaver, and mosquitos 'as big as moths'. Overhead, high mares' tail clouds brushed the heavens like a gauze of egg white.

Every mile or two an overloaded Skoda or a battered SUV peeled off onto a dirt track, kicking up clouds of dust. I watched them vanish between trees. Estonians – like most Russians – still have roots in the countryside, returning to their 'summer houses' as often as possible, Kristjan among them. But the link is not simply a holiday convenience, he told me, rather it's central to their identity.

'The secret of our success is our size,' he volunteered. 'And that the Soviet occupation lasted only two generations.'

Kristjan's maternal grandparents had lived on Saaremaa until deported along with tens of thousands of others during the Second World War. The men and boys had vanished into Siberia, never to be seen again, but his grandmother and mother-to-be, aged just one at the time, managed to escape from the transit camp and return to the island.

'Their survival – and that of my paternal grandparents – meant I grew up hearing the truth. My teachers had no chance with their fake stories,' Kristjan said. 'At school we were told that such-and-such a person had been a communist hero. Then later at home my grandmother revealed that the man had been a thief or had emigrated to Canada.'

As we drove deeper into the 'island land', Kristjan recounted the tale of Mikhail Pasternak, a captain with an NKVD/KGB destruction battalion (Putin's father had served in a similar *istrebiteli* unit). In 1941 Hitler had reneged on the Molotov–Ribbentrop Pact, launching his ruinous attack on Russia through Ukraine and the

Baltic states. To cripple the German advance, the retreating Soviets destroyed everything that might be useful to their enemy, torching villages and fields as well as robbing and murdering locals (the destruction battalions' initial duty had been to undertake 'internal ethnic cleansing operations'). On the outskirts of the capital, Tallinn, a farmer named Johannes Loopere had awaited them at his dinner table. When Pasternak burst in with drawn Nagant revolver, Loopere had killed him with a single shot to the head. After the war, when the Soviets reoccupied Estonia, the KGB caught wind of the incident and unearthed the body. In an outrageous revisionist whopper, they proclaimed Pasternak to be a hero who'd died fighting the German invaders, overlooking the fact that his pockets had been full of stolen watches and jewellery. A photograph of his 'valiant' skull – with the single bullet hole in the forehead – was plastered across all of Estonia's newspapers.

'But the farmer, Johannes Loopere, was my grandmother Aliise's cousin. When she told me the truth, I – as a nine-year-old schoolboy – told my classmates. We all started to joke about Pasternak, this "people's hero". We all refused to join "his" Young Pioneers. His story and photograph soon vanished.'

It's been said that tyranny is not as terrifying as submission to it, that silence in the face of it is much more frightening. Kristjan's family did not submit. His widowed maternal grandmother Helmi raised three children alone despite the confiscation of her Saaremaa farm. His paternal grandmother kept a secret shelf of banned books by Solzhenitsyn, Orwell, Eduard Laaman and Johannes Hiiemets (which she loaned out 'one by one so we'd learn never to fall for the lies'). His grandfather, the historian Harri Moora, survived both Nazi and Soviet prisons.

In the twentieth century, Estonia had suffered 'only' two generations of occupation, Kristjan had told me. Belarus and Ukraine – borderlands I was yet to visit – had had a different experience. Because those countries were occupied for three generations, no living memory had remained of another way of life.

But no grandmother's truths could keep young Kristjan out of the Red Army. After his first year of university, he was conscripted

to serve as a tank crew commander in the Caucasus. On his return
to Tartu University, he again stood up for principles, telling his
Russian superiors that he – along with other reserve officers –
would not fight for the Soviet Union in the event of war.

'So I was forbidden to graduate,' he said with a laugh, his lively,
self-effacing humour deflating any hint of self-importance. 'Do
you know the joke about the difference between NATO and Soviet
military fences? NATO fences point outwards to keep intruders
from entering the camp. Soviet fences point inwards to keep
soldiers from escaping it.'

At first our island tour seemed a little haphazard, and lacking a
single destination. We visited medieval Kuressaare Castle. We
followed noble beech avenues to ruined German manor houses.
We pulled up the weeds around his grandmother's grave in her old
village of Saikla. With sure-footed military stride, Kristjan marched
me around Valjala hill fort, one of the last places in Europe to be
Christianised.* Finally at sunset, on a dry rise of land, he showed
me a sacred boulder chiselled with palm-sized pockets. Into them
islanders ancient and modern had poured prayers and coins, the
kopecks, kroons and Euros lying undisturbed for decades.

'And this was my command post,' Kristjan said over a bachelor-
like supper of breaded herring, *rosolje* beetroot salad and coal-black
rye bread. Our night was spent in the Valjala clergy house, a long,
austere wooden building in the shadow of Estonia's oldest surviving
country church. 'My duty was to prepare the island for war.'

During tsarist times, Saaremaa had served as a sea fortress to
protect the Russian shipping lanes. Germans took the island
during both world wars. Soviets then turned it into a vast missile
base, denying access to all but local residents. After the collapse
of communism (and his belated graduation), Kristjan joined the

---

* In the thirteenth century, crusaders had breached the fort's ramparts, destroyed the
statues of the hammer-wielding god Tharapita and subjected the pagan Saarlanders to a
mass baptism. Legend has it that afterwards those independent souls had scurried away
to the nearest river to wash off the foreigners' Christianity.

Defence Forces' Baltic battalion because 'Estonia had changed and
I had to change with it.' For four years he commanded the island's
volunteer defenders: establishing protective positions, stockpiling
food, upgrading medical facilities and planning for the arrival of
up to 100,000 mainlanders.

'I asked the local council how the hospitals would cope, where
to house refugees, and where to bury the bodies of enemy and
Estonian combatants,' he said, adding with a wry grin, 'If you can't
start at the beginning then start at the end.'

In the lamplight as he spoke I noticed the slight downward slope
of the left side of his face. His left eye barely lifted when he smiled.
He wore a collared shirt and woollen polo-neck sweater buttoned
at the throat.

'Saaremaa is Estonia's "strategic rear", separated from the
mainland by the strait with an open air corridor to the west,' he
told me. 'It will be our last front line, our last line of defence.'

I slept poorly, perhaps unnerved by Kristjan's certainty of imminent
war, perhaps because – as I later learned – the Bolsheviks had
once used the clergy house for their interrogations. All manner of
historical figures – Northern Crusaders, Knights of the Sword, SS
Einsatzgruppen death squads and political commissars – stomped
across my dreams, making such a racket that I woke with a start.
I could hardly keep track of the waves of invaders.

In the soft morning light, beneath furrowed banks of high Baltic
cloud, I wandered across the lane to St Martin's church. Its massive
walls and lofty, narrow windows had been built to serve as a refuge
in yet another time of trouble. Above its vaults was a secret safe
room that could be reached only by a ladder, which could be pulled
up during an attack. Its tower – said Kristjan – had been built in
part from archaic pre-Christian tombstone fragments. Likewise,
almost all of the old Soviet radar stations and coastal installations
had been reduced to rubble after the withdrawal of the Red Army.

Kristjan knew of one surviving missile base, a few miles to the
south of the hill fort. We drove from Valjala to Kallemäe, then
followed a leafy track through the woods into an open clearing

encircled by oak and birch. Nothing remained of the base's three barracks, save a foundation or two overgrown with brambles. Yet beyond them, across a marsh and hence inaccessible to the government grinders, spread the rusted relics of empire.

Together we picked our way around ugly concrete storerooms, built without skill or care, and marked with faded Cyrillic warning signs: Chemical Weapons, Do Not Smoke, Crush the Fascist Vipers! Two or three bunkers were open to the elements, their bombproof doors having been removed and sold as scrap metal. Saplings had taken root in the shells of missile truck garages, cracking their tarpaper roofs, dislodging and distorting brick walls so that their tops were wildly uneven like broken teeth in a child's drawing.

During the Cold War, dozens of S-75 Dvina and S-125 Neva surface-to-air missiles had been sited at Kallemäe. Beyond the mouldering guardhouse, a gaping, horizontal steel tube thrust into the burnt earth. The camouflaged fifty-metre missile silo appeared to have been built to house a heavy mobile launch vehicle, perhaps an SS-1 Scud or even a nuclear weapon.

'And the Russians claim that they brought us culture,' said Kristjan as we stepped around the snaking cables and rusted spirals of barbed wire. 'They claim to be insulted because we aren't thankful.'

We perched for a moment on the remnants of a makeshift crane, fashioned from missile casings. In the tainted glade, it was impossible not to think of the invader's return, not least because small groups of Russian 'tourists' have started visiting Saaremaa in military-style four-wheel-drives, camping along the coast and surveying the island in secret. Moscow's latest war games also demonstrate that Estonia's fears are no fantasy. In recent years Russia's armed forces have twice rehearsed an attack on the Baltics, with a simulated nuclear strike on Warsaw to deter Western attempts to interfere with the invasion. Russian aircraft have also practised nuclear assaults on both Sweden and Denmark, the latter timed to coincide with the annual Bornholm festival (where a single real bombing raid could annihilate the entire Danish leadership as well as 90,000 guests).

Once again I couldn't help but wonder why the Kremlin remained so unwilling to live in peace with its neighbours, flexing its military and virtual muscles, giving oxygen to radical thinkers such as Aleksandr 'Rasputin' Dugin, the ultra-nationalist who wants to hasten the 'end of times' with all-out war. Of course the origins of Russian delusion lie in its history, in Moscow's enduring messianic belief that it alone can save mankind; as the last bastion of true Orthodox Christianity,* through the divine right of the tsars, with international communism and now in the theory – put forth by firebrand Sergey Kurginyan – that it will be the world's saviour from capitalism.

'Russia wants to return to a mythical place of power and glory, not to help to build a more stable world,' said Kristjan. 'Nations – especially insecure nations – dream up such wishful fictions.'

Estonia could never win a conventional war, so it will not fight one. Since 1918 the volunteer Estonian Defence League, the Kaitseliit, has helped to preserve the state, maintaining order during the Russian Revolution, preventing a communist coup in 1924, surviving undercover through both the Nazi and Soviet years. Now, as then, its part-time soldiers train to be insurgents: bivouacking in the winter woods, improvising explosives in the field, learning to fight far behind enemy lines, preparing for the inevitable.

In front of us paraded uniformed harbourmasters with small Estonian flags fluttering from their bayonets. Fresh-faced policewomen in battledress trooped by with sub-machine guns clamped to their chests. Retired nurses rode in a hand-me-down Swedish armoured personnel carrier. Four beefy butchers sucked in

---

* Russia's sense of messianic mission was magnified further by the 2018 split of the Ukrainian Orthodox Church from the Moscow Patriarchate. The schism was called the most significant rift in Eastern Christendom since 1054, when Eastern Orthodoxy separated itself from what is now the Roman Catholic Church. But the break had less to do with faith than with power, and Putin's use of the Church to legitimise many of his actions.

their stomachs to sit tall in a venerable Willys jeep. After a cat had ambled across the road came two ranks of Young Eagles, boys and teenagers not yet old enough to be issued with their own weapons. Next three dozen housewives, librarians and council workers marched by in the crisp dress uniforms and blue boater hats of the Naiskodukaitse Women's Home Defence corps.

After Saaremaa, Kristjan and I had returned to the mainland and made for Rakvere, a pretty town no more than a grenade-toss from the Russian border. Nearby, thousands of tons of unexploded ordnance rusted in the Tapa forests, once a Red Army artillery range. Thirty years after their withdrawal the region's tap water is still said to be inflammable – *Tapa põlev vesi* – as so much Soviet aviation fuel was dumped at its military airfield.

In the shadow of hills, alongside the parade route, Leclerc battle tanks of the 1er Régiment de Chasseurs idled alongside a Challenger II of the Queen's Royal Hussars. A dozen British squaddies handed brochures to locals then quick-marched behind the Estonians. Overhead buzzed a couple of American Apache and Black Hawk helicopters from the US 10th Combat Aviation Brigade. Their symbolic presence in Estonia – along with a handful of other NATO troops – had motivated Putin to order Russians to prepare for 'a time of war'.

'Partisan war is our way,' said Kristjan, explaining how an 'imaginative insurgency' evened the odds against a powerful army, as Americans had learned to their cost in Iraq and Afghanistan. 'We can't touch the Russians' armour but we can damage their supply convoys and terrify their soldiers. Usually.'

With a quick laugh he recalled an operation that hadn't gone as intended.

'Once, during the war, a plan was hatched to commandeer a Russian supply train,' he told me. 'Three Kaitseliit volunteers agreed to stop the train by pretending to be Russians. All went well, the Estonians sharing cigarettes and winning over the guards, until suddenly one of them lashed out and punched a Russian to the ground. As the Estonians ran away, their plan in ruins, they asked their friend why he had hit the guard. '"Because that Bolshie had such an ugly face," he replied.'

As well as by deep-rooted independence, many Kaitseliit volunteers had been inspired by the Forest Brothers. These wartime partisans (or 'enemies of the people' according to Moscow's propagandists) had hidden in Estonia's woods for years, harrying the occupation forces. By 1947 some 15,000 of them had been arrested and executed. Two years later the Brothers' support base was destroyed by the deportation of a further 20,000 Estonian men, women and children. In spite of – or perhaps because of – these devastating losses, the Forest Brothers fought on for three more decades, living and working in groups of six or ten, acting without a central line of command that could be broken by arrests and torture. In 1978 one of the last of their number, August Sabe, was caught by two KGB agents posing as fishermen. When ordered to surrender, Sabe jumped into a lake and drowned himself. He wanted to end his life as a free man.

After the parade, border policewomen mingled with Latvian Volunteers and American GIs chatted up Finnish Reservists. Kaitseliit lieutenants kissed partners, held babies and retouched their lipstick. Stalls had been set up to entice recruits to join the police or the regular Estonian army. Schoolkids collected posters on medicinal forest herbs and Russian armoured vehicles. Families took horse-carriage rides around the lanes. Food carts served sausages and beer. A Rifles Regiment band started to perform classic pop hits including – not inappropriately – the Who's 'Won't Get Fooled Again'. At a town square cafe, I ordered coffee and, while we waited for it to arrive, asked Kristjan about home.

'Home?' he said, his look direct and enquiring. 'What do you mean?'

'I mean *Heimat* or homeland,' I said. 'I mean the individual identifying with the nation. For me it's a dated, dreamy concept: Ulysses' homecoming, Coriolanus back from the wars, the Hollywood hero returning to the family farm and marrying his childhood sweetheart as if life were inevitably a cyclical journey.'

'National identity is the myth that built the modern world,' he replied.

'Exactly, and in larger nations it's mostly made up.'

Nation builders invent a mythology to bond together individuals who may share nothing other than inhabiting the same piece of land. Americans claim to have always been united by their exceptionalism. Russians stick together as if they're surrounded by enemies. Brits tell themselves that they're all plucky islanders.

These myths lie at the root of the concept of home. There is some geographical or historical basis to them but their main purpose is as glue. People – the *bydlo* – need to be convinced to support their country, even to fight and to die for it. Hence the Nazis' Nuremberg rallies and Soviet May Day parades. Hence Putin's Immortal Regiment and Patriot Park. Hence the romancing of the French Resistance and the exploitation of the heroism of the Battle of Britain. The myth of a nation bonds us while it deludes us, priming us for patriotism yet also for racism, xenophobia and even genocide.

'People are conditioned to see their country as an extension of themselves.'

'That doesn't make it true,' I said to Kristjan. 'But is it different for a small country?' Estonia seemed to have survived – and thrived – because of the years of occupation, rather than in spite of them.

'We have seen many empires come and go,' he said as the coffee arrived at our table. 'We have learned that the better our preparation, the longer the battle can be postponed. But we do not kid ourselves. We know war is coming.'

Estonians' engagement with history has taught them bitter lessons: defend yourself, fight for independence and expect no mercy from a conqueror. If you surrender, the nation will lose much more than its battle casualties.

Some twenty-five years ago, when the West still imagined Russia to be an honest and responsible partner, Lennart Meri, the first president of post-Soviet Estonia (whose books Kristjan had read from his grandmother's secret shelf), had warned of Moscow's enduring imperialist appetite.

In a prophetic speech he'd pointed out that Solzhenitsyn's call for Russians 'to bid farewell to the empire and ... solve their own economic, social and also intellectual problems' had been ignored. He'd drawn attention to the Kremlin's declaration that Russia had a 'special role' as *primus inter pares* – the first among equals – in the lands of the former Soviet empire. He'd reminded his audience of the Ministry of Foreign Affairs' belligerent assertion that the 'protection' of ethnic Russian groups in neighbouring countries 'could not be solved by diplomatic means alone'.

'Because we are a people belonging to Western European society and since, unfortunately, we live in a land which is geo-strategically very vulnerable, we have developed a stronger instinct than many a European for discerning the problems and threats that loom in our vicinity,' Meri had said, warning of 'forces in Russia' who believe 'they can solve their country's immense problems by outward expansion and by threatening their neighbours'.

'Whoever really wants to help Russia and the Russian people today must make it emphatically clear to the Russian leadership that another imperialist expansion will not stand a chance,' Meri had concluded. 'Whoever fails to do so will actually help the enemies of democracy in Russia and other post-communist states.'

Too few in the West listened to him.

19

Soviet Secret Barbecue Society

I decided to linger in Estonia, writing up notes, gathering thoughts, walking where Danish knights, Dominican friars and Danzig merchants had walked. On Tallinn's zigzagging medieval lanes I tried to picture them alongside the capital's more recent residents: Skype geeks, Ukrainian sex workers and party people heading off to DM Baar, 'the world's Number One Depeche Mode-themed nightclub' (are there any others?). In my mind's eye fur traders from Novgorod strode beside high-booted tsarist cavalrymen. War widows fled with their children beneath the devil's masks on the portals of St Catherine's friary. I watched starving men resist the call to serve 'under the flag of fame' in Hitler's Wehrmacht and then – after Red Army tanks retook the city – to follow Stalin's 'true path'. I heard tailgates slam shut, and pictured crammed military trucks driving away beneath the lime trees and onion domes. Some 30 per cent of Estonians exiled to Siberia in the 1940s were less than sixteen years old. On Castle Square, in the Danish King's Garden and along the Lower Town battlements, their voices still hung in the air. On two dozen afternoons, after my writing mornings, I moved among them and across the centuries, stretching my legs and imagination, listening to their laughter, their cries, the barked orders and gunshots.

Tallinn was built on salt, say the locals, on salt and tears. Trade made the vassal city rich while war and pestilence racked it. In

1343 ethnic Estonians rose up against the then ruling Teutonic
Order, burning a Cistercian abbey and slaying dozens of monks
as well as 'virgins, women, servants, maidservants, noblemen and
commoners, young and old; all who were of German blood'. In
retaliation, the Aryan overlords hacked to death the country's last
pagan chiefs at Paide Castle. Later, half of the Estonian population
perished in the two-generation-long Livonian War. Eight plagues
next ravaged the city. Then at the end of the seventeenth century,
famine killed off 80,000 more citizens in two years.

Yet for centuries Tallinn thrived as part of the Hanseatic League,
contributing men and money to the thousand-ship trading union.
Its German guilds and merchants sent herring, hops, cloth and salt
to Russia, brought furs, beeswax and seal fat to the West. In the
Old Town they built themselves noble meeting halls and elegant
high-gabled houses with ochre and peach facades, encircling them
with formidable walls and more than five dozen defence towers.
Their St Olaf's church, with its slender Gothic spire, was once the
tallest building in the world.

Come the nineteeth century, after the collapse of the League and
the first Russian invasion (nine of Ivan the Terrible's cannonballs
remain embedded in the walls of the Kiek in de Kök fortress), Tallinn
dozed as 'a quiet provincial town, a piece of petrified Middle Ages
... pure and genuine', according to traveller Eduard von Ungern-
Sternberg. On Sunday mornings in the twenty-first century it
seemed to sleep on, the chimes of church bells ringing back and
forth across the pitched terracotta roofs as if in casual conversation.
Atop craggy Toompea hill, the resting place of a mythical giant,
taxi tyres thrummed on cobblestones, waitresses skipped puddles
on their way to work and big-boned Viking tourists yawned over
coffee. Gangs of English lads nursed hangovers after all-night
bachelor parties while more sober holidaymakers filed between
St Mary's Lutheran Cathedral – girdled with the coats of arms of
banished Teutonic families – and its nemesis, the Alexander Nevsky
Orthodox Cathedral, a symbol of Russian oppression.

My plan was to head south, arcing through the borderlands
that Moscow continued to claim as its own, but before leaving the

relaxed and open city I needed to make a pilgrimage – to a traffic island.

In the last months of the Second World War, the remains of a dozen Soviet soldiers had been buried at Tõnismägi. The Russian occupiers renamed the gravesite Liberators' Square and built on it a one-metre-high wooden pyramid crowned with a tinny red star. Two Estonian girls – fourteen-year-old Aili Jürgenson and fifteen-year-old Ageeda Paavel – then destroyed it.

'How long should we watch this red star, a memorial for Russian looters, at the time when all our statues are being destroyed?' asked Jürgenson later. 'We just couldn't get our heads around it. We decided that if such robbers are raging in Estonia, they should see how one of their memorials gets blown up. We could have just doused the wooden thing with petrol and set fire to it, but we wanted it to go with a bang!'

Over the previous months, Soviet occupation forces – in another effort to rewrite history – had indeed smashed hundreds of Estonian monuments. A communist committee in Võrumaa reported: 'In order to carry out demolition works, fifteen Party activists and 275 persons from the Destruction Battalion must be mobilised. Fifteen workers are needed for the execution of each demolition and ten people are needed for protection … as well as 225 kg of TNT, 150 metres of fuse and 100 primers plus eleven lorries to carry away the ruins.' The Russians had set about eradicating all memory of the earlier, anti-Soviet Estonian War of Independence. In their fervour, they'd even torn up Estonian military gravestones and buried their own dead on top of fallen locals.

'There was nothing really difficult about it,' recalled schoolgirl Paavel. 'The important thing was that the fuse was long enough to give us a safe distance for running away. We put in place the materials for the blast. We had no supporters. The fact that a militia officer who was on duty was flirting with a girl at a distance and did not notice us made it easier for us. Although this girl did not belong to our group, she was also later arrested.'

After the blast Jürgenson and Paavel were branded as 'juvenile terrorists' and deported to the gulag. The Soviets then replaced the wooden pyramid with a bronze statue of a Red Army soldier, adding later an eternal flame.

To most Estonians the memorial remained another symbol of Russian repression and, with the collapse of the Soviet Union, the government decided to move the Bronze Soldier and the human remains to Tallinn's military cemetery. But for the many Russians who'd been settled in Estonia after the war, in a concerted effort to dilute its ethnic homogeneity, the statue symbolised their claim on the republic. Local agitators were paid by persons unknown to inflame emotions, sparking two nights of rioting. A so-called 'Army of Russian Resistance' circulated a declaration calling for 'all Russian men living in Estonia' to take up arms against the government. A Russian State Duma delegation flew into town, warning that moving the statue would be a grave offence to history and 'disastrous for Estonians'.

Moscow's tactics were nothing new, as Kristjan had told me. As Russia TV cameramen waited in vain for Estonian troops to emerge from their barracks, hoping to film military intervention, the police plucked from the crowd the key agitators, each of whom had a crisp €500 note in his pocket. They drove them far out into the countryside and dumped them unharmed by the roadside. The statue's removal went ahead as planned and the Russian delegation – which had demanded the whole government's resignation – was asked politely to desist from intervening in Estonia's internal affairs.

Within hours of the so-called 2007 Bronze Night riots, Russia launched its first vengeful cyber attack, shutting down the websites of the Estonian parliament, banks, ministries, newspapers and broadcasters.

In the cool afternoon sunshine I walked around the Tõnismägi traffic island, thinking of Jürgenson and Paavel, of the destroyed lives and desecrated graves. On a park bench a young mother watched her toddler playing in the huge flowerbed that spread over the former site of the Bronze Soldier of Tallinn. We fell into conversation and I asked her if she knew the history of Tõnismägi. She looked at me as if I were mad.

'Every Estonian knows it,' she said. 'But we prefer to enjoy the flowers instead.'

Estonians revere their land, as I'd learned on Kristjan's seemingly haphazard tour. On Saaremaa I'd seen coins deposited on the mysterious offertory stone. He'd spoken of ancient 'energy paths' that linked megaliths, ridge tops and river fords. I'd read about magic springs, holy lakes and sacred groves where trees were wrapped in ribbons. So it was no surprise that Nature – or at least the threat to it – had emboldened Estonians to stand up against Russia.

In 1986, before the fall of the Wall, Moscow had hatched a plan to dig a vast, open-pit phosphorite mine in the Virumaa region south-east of the capital. The intended excavation would unearth radioactive materials near to the source of the Emajõgi, literally Mother River, and so risked contaminating up to 40 per cent of the country's water supply. Estonians also feared that the mine would spur another wave of Russian migrants.

In response, students at Tartu University paraded through the streets holding hands and wearing yellow 'Phosphorite – No Thanks' T-shirts. Copycat protests ignited across the country and a 'fact-finding' mission arrived from Moscow's Ministry of Fertiliser Industries to push through the plan. But in an ingenious piece of theatre, the Russians were encouraged to pick up lumps of the unearthed mineral from a test hole. Once exposed to the air, rock phosphate warms to the touch and the Russians – fearing radioactive contamination – dropped the stones like hot potatoes.

'Now you are dead,' the Estonian geologists coolly told them.

Two weeks later Moscow cancelled the Virumaa project.

The success of the protest became a catalyst for further anti-Soviet action. In 1989 over two million people joined hands to create a 420-mile human chain across all three Baltic states. Two years later Estonians again joined hands to form human shields around their parliament and TV towers, stopping Soviet tanks and paratroopers from seizing them.

As Estonians had occupied the same tract of land for more than
five millennia, Kristjan suggested that I occupy it too, although for a
somewhat shorter period of time. He sent me south to Lake Võrtsjärv,
the source of the 'Mother River'. Around it, the forest smelt of resin
and blueberry leaves. Tapering trunks glowed luminous red in the
evening light. Fresh breezes whispered through the treetops, tracing
audible paths through the pines, while underfoot billowy green
hummocks of sphagnum moss cushioned the forest floor.

Over the next week I walked through dappled light and around
copses of slender silver birch. Again and again I paused beside a
stream or peaty pond to catch a moment in notes, or to map my
journey as the long shadows mapped the pine-needle earth. On
Võrtsjärv's northern shore I even stood by a mystical healing stone
beneath which music was said to be heard at night.

Once again I wasn't alone, both because the Forest Brothers
had survived in these woods and because Kristjan – from whom
I'd parted in Tallinn – had instructed the locals to look after me.
Every evening I was invited to eat with neighbours, to drink beside
bonfires on pebbled beaches, to sweat like a swine in their saunas.
And it was there, at 175°F, that I came to meet the captain of the
Soviet Secret Barbecue Society.

Jaan Habicht was sixty-two years old. Or seventy-two. As a young
man growing up in Soviet Estonia he had been told that he could
never travel abroad because his father had been a banker. Or a
property developer. He had been found guilty by association, he
told me, but had refused to accept 'state-sponsored incarceration'.
Instead at Turku University he'd trained as a molecular biologist so
that he could – somehow – live a travelling life.

'I was stuck like the proverbial pig in a sty,' he told me as he
poured water on the hot stones. 'Until I heard about Ireland.'

In 1989 Jaan learned that the Irish Peace Institute sponsored
Estonians to visit the republic. To land himself an invitation, he
went to Moscow with two large bottles of Old Tallinn, a high-
octane rum-based liqueur said to be so powerful that, in a cocktail
called the Hammer and Sickle, it hits the head and cuts off the

legs. At the Irish embassy, Jaan proceeded to intoxicate a senior diplomat (or junior attaché) to such an extent that his name was added to the official list. Both a visa and a ticket were issued on the spot and, before Soviet officialdom spotted the offence, Jaan was en route to Dublin. Or Limerick. Or so he said.

To be honest the facts seemed shaky, perhaps because of the sauna's heat, or the dark Põhjala beer, or simply because Jaan was a storyteller par excellence. When he'd opened the spruce door and waved me inside – a high-spirited, rotund figure with bushy eyebrows, ruffled blond hair and not a stitch of clothing – the flames flared around the stove and the temperature jumped at least ten degrees.

'Ireland was my epiphany,' he declared with a sweep of his plump arms, stirring both the aromatic alder-wood smoke and the excitement inside his head. 'It made me the barbecue king of Estonia.'

The Irish Peace Institute had been founded to promote peace and reconciliation in Northern Ireland. With the easing of the Troubles, it had widened its focus to offer international courses on conflict resolution. For some unfathomable reason, Jaan's course included a cookery competition.

'None of the other Estonians realised that we had to create a dish,' recalled Jaan, pointing out that the IPI's chairman Pat O'Sullivan had been a leading spirit in the Irish Barbecue Association. 'I stepped forward and changed my life.'

Jaan claimed that his success was due to his biochemical knowledge, and sprats. To save money while abroad, he had brought with him to Ireland tins of the silvery, herring-like Baltic fish. In a flash of inspiration – and scientific ingenuity – he'd barbecued them on a schnitzel, and won second prize.

In the sauna the temperature rose again with the wild improbability of his story, especially when he told me that the KGB had caught wind of his win (and perhaps the toasted sprats). As he ladled more water onto the hot stones, he went on: 'The local KGB goon came to arrest me. He marched into the hotel and barked, "Jaan Habicht, you are ordered to return immediately to the Estonian Soviet Socialist Republic." Luckily I had brought with me an emergency supply of Old Tallinn and I persuaded him to join me in a farewell toast, and then another, and another. At the end of the night I dumped him on the steps of the Soviet embassy, totally legless.'

Conveniently the Soviet Union then collapsed and Jaan – like Estonia itself – was free. Over the coming years his Irish success led to invitations to dozens of international barbecue competitions, enabling him to refine his repertoire: grilled ribs with apple-cowberry salad, barbecued salmon with vegetable tagliatelle and racy ginger-chilli sauce, chicken roll filled with Parmesan cheese, and pasta in a raspberry beet vinaigrette.

'In Cape Town I served bullock fillet with fruit lasagne. In Memphis I smoked meat loaf doused in grated chocolate. But my greatest, *greatest* moment was in Kansas City.'

As the sauna grew hotter and hotter, I heard that Jaan's reputation had brought him to the attention of the world champion Kansas City Barbecue Society. His full-blown eccentricity – cooking in a black jumpsuit, calling himself a Glasnost Cowboy, travelling with a collapsible two-level smoker that brought to mind a drum of enriched plutonium – made him a celebrity on the barbecue circuit. To prove the point the Kansas City organisers rented him a longer limousine than Mick Jagger, who happened to be in town for a Rolling Stones concert.

'They told me that Jagger came to Kansas every other year but the presence of the Glasnost Cowboy was a once-in-a-lifetime event,' he added, tears of laughter welling in his eyes. 'All I needed was meat and a match.'

His ribs basted in blackberry-cherry-tomato sauce won first prize and a Midwestern entrepreneur asked to market him, coining the Soviet Secret Barbecue Society brand, despite Jaan being neither Soviet nor secretive.

'We designed a special jar in the shape of an SS-32 nuclear missile. I was on the way to becoming a millionaire, except for one missing ingredient.' He shook his head in mock gravity. 'The basis of my secret sauce was tomatoes crushed by the unwashed feet of Tartu virgins. As soon as the Americans heard that, the FDA banned its import.'

In the blinding heat it no longer seemed to matter what was fact or not. Jaan kept both stories and coals rolling, stoking the fire, moving on to the European Championships in Milan where, in an act of sweet revenge, he told the judges that the barbecue hadn't been invented in the United States but rather in an Estonian smoke sauna.

'Naturally I won because the Italians hate the Americans.'

Over the years the thrill of the grill took Jaan to the Calgary Cowboy Cook-Off and the Clarence Oinktoberfest in New York State. At home he masterminded pig-outs at Tallinn's Golden Grill Fiesta and – earlier that very day – hosted a party at the new National Museum, serving a celebratory meal of pork basted with paprika and Estonian cheeses aged in Old Tallinn and dyed with the national colours.

'All pure and natural,' he insisted in spite of Estonia's colours being an unnatural blue, black and white.

'It's not all spin, you know,' he insisted with a theatrical wink. 'The secret…' he whispered, leaning forward as the beads of sweat rolled down his face, '… is knowing how to get to the molecular level to tenderise pork tissues.' With hand on heart he declared that he was happiest when wielding a spatula, but I was relieved to learn that he had not given up his day job. He told me that he continued to teach at Tartu University, his 'Molecular Biology and the Barbecue' course being particularly popular with carnivorous undergrads.

As Jaan shared more overcooked tips – dry the meat before seasoning and cooking it, leave it undisturbed on the grill for the first sixty seconds, rest it for twenty minutes before serving – I managed to summon enough clarity to reflect that native Estonians had often gone hungry over the seven centuries of occupation. If a piece of bread was dropped on the floor, the custom had been to pick it up, to kiss it respectfully, and to eat it.

'Slow roasting really did originate in Nordic smoke saunas where meat – in a traditional baking oven – tenderises over two days,'

Jaan said before limbering up for a bout of mutual 'whisking' with a *viht* of birch branches to exfoliate and cleanse. But I could take no more of his fire. I was already burnt to a crisp. I was also very thirsty.

'Drink before the barbecue,' he declared with another wild laugh. 'Drink during it and drink after it!'

Together Jaan and I stepped out of the sauna's sharp heat and into the soft dusk, streaking down the bank and into Lake Võrtsjärv. Once the shock of cold water had receded, we floated on our backs, gazing up at the stars. In Estonia, as elsewhere in the north, the sauna was a place for physical and spiritual cleansing, for getting bare in all senses of the word, and even – it must be said – for blowing smoke.

'It's a barbecue world,' said Jaan, the king of the grill. 'It's our world.'

Kaliningrad

20

The Others

The Baltic states are as unalike as England, Scotland and Ireland. Language, religion and temperament differ in the three countries. Estonians see themselves as Nordic Vikings. Lithuania – 'the Baltic Italy' – is peopled with devout Catholics. Latvians are rather laissez-faire about God and most Estonians don't think He exists at all (how else to explain so many centuries of hardship?). Latvians believe that Estonians are slow-witted while Estonians claim that their southern neighbours lack coordination because they are born with extra toes. I'd asked Kristjan if the Estonians are one people. In truth, all three countries have been shaped by incomers.

Under communism, Estonians were the 'Others' in their own country. Russian settlers were trucked in, treated as superior, until they made up almost 30 per cent of the population. In Tallinn, taxi drivers – most of whom had come from the Urals – wouldn't give rides to Estonian speakers. Shop assistants – a privileged position in a country where everything was in short supply – always served ethnic Russians first. But with independence, the roles were reversed. The incomers became the Others, and an unwelcome reminder of Soviet rule. The new government in Tallinn told them to make a choice: either apply to be an Estonian citizen or be classed as stateless. It was the same situation across the Baltics, except in one conquered corner of them.

A true and sincere traveller needs to read the runes, to seize opportunities and to change plans. Spontaneous decisions can

open new doors, or lead to a dead end that wastes a week. On the
southbound metallic grey Lux Express coach (with red go-faster
stripe) I opened my passport for the third time to check my double-
entry Russian visa. I'd decided to visit a place where the Others had
taken control, after wiping out the original inhabitants.

For 700 years Königsberg had been German: a university town
founded by Teutonic Knights, the coronation city of Prussian
monarchs and the birthplace of Immanuel Kant. On its broad
and leafy avenues had risen gothic towers, the Schlosskirche palace
church and the Moscowiter-Saal, one of the largest ceremonial
halls in the Reich. The city's fabric and families had been enriched
through the wheat, timber, hemp and fur trades. Its flourishing
port had been the last known location of an 'Eighth Wonder of the
World'.

In 1945, after devastating raids by hundreds of RAF Lancaster
bombers, the city fell to the Red Army. Along its rubble-strewn
streets Soviet soldiers exacted a brutal revenge for Nazi aggression.
Survivors were tortured, women raped and naked bodies nailed to
doors. The few residents who remained alive in the ruins were then
starved to death or forced into slave labour. Whereas in Estonia
the Soviets had set out to weaken the indigenous population, in
Königsberg they eradicated it.

For the next fifty years Kaliningrad, as it was renamed, was closed
to the West. Russians, Ukrainians and Belarusians filled the vacated
city and set to work for the military: servicing Moscow's 100,000-
man garrison, overhauling its Baltic fleet at Baltiysk, teaching at the
cadet school, managing the stockpiles of conventional and nuclear
weapons.

Kaliningrad has no common border with Russia, which lies
almost 300 miles to the east, so to visit the territory I had to catch
a train from Vilnius. Beyond the carriage window, overnight snow
dusted the abandoned orchards and fields on either side of the rail
line. A cement statue of a heroic farmworker guarded the entrance
to a deserted collective farm. An old woman towed a churn of
well water on a sleigh. Some 300 of the enclave's villages remain
abandoned to this day.

Soon the low lines of drab houses gave way to Khrushchyovka apartment blocks. In the spreading shadows every building looked colder than a Siberian icebox. Every third person seemed to be wearing a uniform. Across from the central station – built by Germans in 1929 – I found a hotel, dropped my bag and set out to explore.

Under hissing quartz street lamps, Kaliningrad revealed itself as one of the world's ugliest cities: a chaos of shabby roads, glinting neon and crumbling estates. Electrical cables dangled across dirty avenues. Shards of broken vodka bottles splintered underfoot. Drunks and feral dogs roamed the ghostly parks where the old town had once stood. Atop the site of medieval Königsberg Castle – the remains of which were demolished on the orders of Leonid Brezhnev – rose the monstrous House of Soviets, declared unsafe as soon as it was built, its foundations collapsing into the tunnels and moat of the old fortress. Locals called the eyesore the 'Revenge of the Prussians'.

I took in the Eternal Flame in Victory Park and a couple of the city's 'Euro' malls. Late-night locals wandered in and out of them, staring at plasma screens, buying nothing. I was reminded that Kaliningrad's residents are sixty-five times poorer than the average EU citizen, yet both the city's former mayor and its governor own second homes on the Côte d'Azur.

At the Planet Entertainment mall, the Beer Club was a low-rent dive with blacked-out windows and surly waiters. I sat alone at a table writing up the day's sparse notes. On the walls around me hung posters for Disco Boom dance parties and the Tet-a-Tet strip club. The upcoming Fashion Girls Night seemed to have little to do with wearing clothes.

To Western observers during the Cold War, Kaliningrad had been simply another chunk of stolen real estate in the Soviet empire. But with the enlargement of the European Union, the military fiefdom found itself in the heart of the continent, wedged between Poland and Lithuania, nearer to Berlin than to Moscow. Its sudden strategic importance was matched only by its alarming social collapse: 30 per cent unemployment, Russia's highest crime

rate, widespread prostitution and heroin use.* Baltic Tobacco was
the town's largest civilian employer, its cigarettes – especially its
Jin Ling brand – smuggled by the *billion* into Western Europe.
A single shipping container, filled with some 10 million cigarettes,
could be bought for about $100,000 at its eight-acre port complex.
But once secreted into Sweden or Germany, the shipment could
be sold on for $3 million. If it reached the UK or Norway, where
cigarette taxes are higher, the same shipment would be worth nearly
$6 million.

I walked back to the hotel through a thick sea mist that tasted
of burnt toast, generated by the raw sewage that's pumped from
the town's failing pre-war treatment plant. When I turned off the
bedside lamp, sulphurous yellow street light fell across the floor.
Next door I heard throaty whispers and then the sound of sudden
swift lovemaking. No other noise emerged through the paper-thin
walls for the rest of the night. Around dawn I woke to the crack of
gunfire and thump of explosions. At breakfast I was told that I'd
heard a weekly live-fire exercise.

I knew no one in Moscow's armed bastion, and it showed in the
blank pages of my notebook. The door I'd opened seemed to lead
to a dead end. In the restaurant I had a second cup of coffee. In my
room I turned on the TV, then turned it off. At the reception desk
I asked about city tours, clutching at straws. I bought a ticket for
an afternoon visit to the Kaliningrad Amber Museum.

'If you buy a second tour, it's half price,' said the receptionist.

I chose the Sobranie casino evening.

In the first years after the fall of the Wall, the Kremlin had
toyed with the idea of liberalising Kaliningrad, spinning it as a
Baltic Hong Kong. But when the elite realised that their survival
was best assured by bigging up Russia's military mission, the tune
changed. Patriarch Kirill of Moscow was called upon to assert
that Kaliningrad was the new 'ideological battlefield between the

---

* All Kaliningrad's public toilets are illuminated with blue light that makes veins
undetectable and so prevents local users from injecting themselves.

West and Russia' and a 'beacon of the Russian World in Europe'. Tentative ties with the rest of the continent were severed and the most respected NGO in the oblast, the German-Russian House, was labelled a 'foreign agent'. Both the local government and the Russian Orthodox Church then declared war on history, the Patriarch himself referred to the German heritage as a series of 'old stones that should not be revered or given predominance over the legacy of Russian national culture'.

At the same time Kaliningrad started to build casinos. First up was the Sobranie, said to be among the largest in Europe. Over the next decade fourteen more cash cows – along with twenty-one hotels, three concert halls, a stadium and a water park – had begun to take shape in the 'Amberland' gambling zone.

In the hotel foyer our guide wore a cowboy hat, if you can believe it, and introduced himself as Lucky Lev. He had a boy's face dotted with freckles and a thin-lipped smile. Our small group consisted of two middle-aged Americans, a Yorkshireman on a World Cup rebound visit and the young French couple from the adjoining room.

On the drive to the Sobranie we passed a military convoy en route to Baltiysk, home port of Russia's Special Purpose Squadron (its mini-sub host ships are designed to tap and cut undersea internet cables). Lev explained about the house rules and warned us about forged Euro notes and prostitutes (one in three of Kaliningrad's sex workers were said to be HIV positive). I tried to draw him out, on the off-chance that I could pen a portrait of him, but he said of his background only that he'd attended the local cadet school, as had all the region's children, to learn 'how to defend Russia from enemy incursions'.

Our taxi rattled off the potholed street and onto a Monaco-slick paving stone drive. A doorman stepped forward to open the rusty door and – with a flourish – ushered us into a turreted, mock-Louis XV chateau.

Under a mirrored ceiling, tuxedo-suited flunkies relieved us of our coats and more Euros, motioning forward attendants in fishnet stockings with silver trays of Crimean champagne. Together we strode across the marble foyer, through a golden yellow passageway and into the vast gaming hall. Starlights and cut-glass chandeliers glittered over red baize tables. A clutch of serious men in black turtlenecks and jackets leaned forward to place bets. Around us video lottery terminals pinged, ice rattled in cocktail shakers and decks of cards were shuffled.

Lev guided us to the blackjack and six-card poker tables. He hovered for a time at a roulette wheel, studying its spin. In an adjoining room, where banks of pulsating slots coiled around a raised mirror-glass bar, he told us that there were already more than a thousand of the machines in Amberland.

'This place makes me feel good, it does,' he said as he set to work drawing us 'into the zone'.

I am not a party animal. I prefer to go to bed long before midnight. I like to wake early and put pen to paper. I didn't want another intoxicated Slavic evening, dropping my notes in a strawberry vodka punchbowl. I wasn't going to risk my book advance at the baccarat table. Instead I settled down to watch Lev earn his cut by helping the others to buy chips, place bets and lose their shirts.

As the evening advanced a slightly mesmeric compulsion seemed to possess him. He started to move faster, to speak in half-sentences, to call for more champagne. He encouraged the Yorkshireman to play two tables at once. He flirted with the French woman until her partner sauntered back from the toilet. He failed to convince the Americans that he owned a ranch in Montana. He pressed another glass into my hand with the words, 'Go on, partner. Give the wheel a spin. The night is young.'

I didn't and, around eleven, I decided not to write about Kaliningrad. On the road, a travel writer meets people, makes observations and collects stories. A parallel journey, equally real, is then made at his or her desk. There, experience and memories are distilled in a process that is inevitably partial and impressionistic. But I'd stumbled on no promising material, sensed no moment that needed to be infused with meaning and value. I would cut both my losses and the chapter, and move on in the morning.

To pass the last hour of the tour, I made my way to the in-house theatre to watch the Tomsk Baby 'Twerk' Dance Team. In essence, the twerk – or booty – dance obliged performers to shove their rumps in the audience's face, while jiggling other bits of their anatomy. It was a primitive and sexist display, choreographed to a grinding beat, and – in one of those coincidences common to both life and art – the dancers were dressed as cowgirls. As they shook their tasselled butts and whipped back their long hair, Lev sat down beside me.

'You're not going to play tonight?' he asked.

I shook my head.

'So why come to Kaliningrad?'

I gave him half an answer, explaining my interest in history.

'Then you know about Baltic gold?' he guessed.

His so-called 'Baltic gold' was amber, fossilised tree resin that sold for more than its weight in real gold. Ninety per cent of the world's supply was found in and around Kaliningrad.

'China is the biggest buyer. Germans are also good. They pay five or six times more for an insect in the stone. Why else would this be called Amberland?' Lev was engaging and likeable but he was looking for an angle, scheming how to lighten my wallet. A sudden thought – or was it dollar signs? – sparked in his eyes and he bent forward to whisper, 'You say you're interested in history?'

I nodded.

'Sir, let me tell you there is nothing, nothing like the Amber Room.'

'The lost Amber Room?'

'Lost? Who says it's lost?' said Lev, pushing back his hat and tapping his temple. 'A man only needs to know where to look, and to be willing to pay.'

At the start of the eighteenth century the Amber Room was gifted by Prussia's Frederick William I to Peter the Great. Russian artisans then enhanced the work until it contained over six tonnes of amber, backed with gold leaf and mirrors. During the Second World War, the Germans looted it from the Catherine Palace near St Petersburg and brought it to Königsberg, after which the 'Eighth

Wonder of the World' vanished. Some eyewitnesses claimed it was loaded onto the MV *Wilhelm Gustloff*, the German evacuation ship that was sunk by a Soviet submarine with the loss of 10,000 lives. Others reported that it was destroyed during the RAF bombing. In any event, for more than seventy years its whereabouts had been a mystery to all. Except it seemed to Lucky Lev.

At midnight he scooped us up. He sat with the Yorkshireman in the taxi's front seat. I squeezed into the back with the French couple. The Americans went home as they wouldn't pay the extra fee.

Kaliningrad's streets were deserted now, swept clear of ancient buses and military convoys. Fewer than half the city's street lights – and none of the street signs – were illuminated and soon I was as lost as the Amber Room, until the taxi swung over Kant Island – once called *Kneiphof* from the Old Prussian word for swamp – and I recognised the House of Soviets.

In the moonlight the brutalist building brought to mind a giant robot buried up to its shoulders. Lev led us to a gap in the corrugated hoarding, ushering us into the closed site with a torch he'd bought from the driver. Underfoot the ground was wet with melted snow and the French woman slipped in her heels.

Beyond a cracked concrete fountain, Lev found a flight of steps. He led us down into a decaying hall of crumbling walls and sodden mattresses. The lift shaft had no doors. The ceiling was as cracked as crazy paving. In the light of our mobile phones the building looked post-apocalyptic, empty, dead.

'Do you know the way?' I asked Lev as he made for a metal door.

'I am risk taker,' he replied and I wondered if he'd ever been there before.

The House of Soviets was meant to be Kaliningrad's showcase. But as the concrete colossus had risen above the skyline its heavy foundations had sunk into the marshy earth, even after the building's height was scaled back to twenty-one floors. Lev seemed to believe that if he could reach the castle's surviving underground passageways – uncovered by recent digs and said to be as much as four storeys deep – he would find the secret hiding place of the Amber Room.

We dropped down another flight of stairs, deeper into the ground, along dank and dripping passageways with earthen floors. In the subterranean labyrinth I wondered if we should have unravelled a ball of thread, as Theseus did when he went to slay the Minotaur.

The Yorkshireman's iPhone was the first to lose power and, after another few minutes, my low battery icon began to flash. In its dimming light I reached out to touch the wall for reassurance and Lev, seeing my hesitation, gave me the torch. The warmth of the air surprised me but not my creeping claustrophobia. As I imagined the weight of earth – and dodgy Soviet concrete – massing on my shoulders, my sense of adventure began to desert me.

'Come on, sir,' he chided.

I was ready to turn back. There was nothing for me to write about. But then Lev turned another dank corner and met an old wall. He whooped, reaching out to touch its interlocking face stones. It was the work of masons, almost certainly German, definitely not Soviet. Lev felt his way along the cut stones until he felt a rough opening. A hole had been hacked through the skin of the old wall and into a surviving castle tunnel.

'Almost there,' he cheered, lifting himself up to scramble through the hole. Again the peculiar mesmeric compulsion seemed to possess him. 'Almost there.'

But we were nowhere near anywhere. Obviously the passage had already been discovered and explored by official archaeologists as well as amateur treasure hunters. In all likelihood they'd found nothing. Certainly they had been better prepared than our intoxicated troupe. As I expressed my reservations, Lev's feet vanished into the hole. There was a splash and then an almighty roar.

'My phone. My fucking phone.'

The deeper castle tunnel was flooded, as it must have been since the end of the war. In it Lev thrashed about, dunking down into the inky water in the hope of finding his mobile. He felt nothing, and now we had only one torch.

'*Da gde zhe on, tvoyu mat'!*' he shouted, speaking Russian now, abandoning his cowboy affectation. 'Where is it? Give me some light. What the fuck…?'

In the dark tunnel – or at least along a ledge on its wall – Lev
had sensed movement. He had swatted at it, swearing in sudden
fear. We heard another splash, a high-pitched hiss and then a tight,
terrified figure bowled out of the hole towards us.

'*C'est un chat*,' cried the woman. 'A cat.'

The cat was a kitten: small, sodden and malnourished. God
knows how it had found its way into the ruined tunnel, except
through another unknown entrance. The woman swept it up in her
arms and howled, perhaps in part because the poor animal stank
of sewage.

'Lev, let's get out of here,' I called.

He appeared in the hole, cursing our faint-heartedness, damning
our failure to go 'the last few metres'. He stank too.

I led the way back through the Soviet passageways, following
my imaginary line of thread, praying that the torch batteries didn't
give out before we reached the surface. Lev brought up the rear,
comforting the others, talking up the adventure, telling us 'I'm a
midnight cowboy' until we could only laugh.

Outside in the cold blue dawn the air smelt again of burnt
toast. We slipped back through the metal hoarding and cut across
Moscow Prospect to reach the Ibis. Lev found a taxi to take us back
to our hotel. The French couple sank into a corner of its back seat,
their arms wrapped around the stinking animal.

I left Kaliningrad later that morning, well aware that *pipiska
putina* still coursed through my veins.

Transnistria

21

Back in the USSR

Sunlight sparkled off the broad Dniester River. Smugglers' tracks wound across the virgin snow. Patriotic oligarchs in Adidas tracksuits hunted wild boar with AK-47s. Snowflakes settled on the broad shoulders of Russian 'peacekeepers', guarding yet more old Soviet munitions dumps.

It wasn't my first trip to Transnistria, a breakaway republic of a breakaway republic of the old Soviet Union. A decade ago I spent a month in the banana-shaped, sliver-thin nowhereland. In its capital, Tiraspol, I'd watched young activists train for 'spontaneous actions' at the Che Guevara High School of Political Leadership. I'd met geriatric KGB colonels and retired Red Army generals. I'd drunk coffee with the president's lover, who also served as the country's foreign minister. I'd even come to know the fate of the 'father of the republic' after he'd bought a couple too many S-Class Mercedes.

'If you get into trouble, we can't get you out,' a British diplomat had warned me at the time. Nevertheless I flew back across the continent to return to a place recognised by no country in the world.

I started as I'd begun my first visit, at the headquarters of the Communist Party of Transnistria. A concrete Lenin surveyed the front hall of the two-up-two-down conversion. 'Iron Felix' Dzerzhinsky, first chairman of the Cheka and KGB, glowered from his portrait behind the Lavazza coffee machine.

'The Soviet Union is the place where I was born. It is my Motherland,' declared chairman Oleg Khorzhan, embracing me like a long-lost brother in arms. Things seemed to be looking up since our last meeting, a new silver Breitling Chronomat sparkling on his wrist. 'My job as party leader is to preserve – and to carry forward – the positive attributes of the USSR: its power, its social guarantees, its absence of borders and, above all, its belief in tomorrow.'

Since time immemorial (that is, about 200 years) little Transnistria had been part of Greater Russia. But during the Second World War, Stalin had reached west across the Dniester to seize neighbouring Romanian Moldova. He'd tacked it on to Slav Transnistria, creating the Moldavian Soviet Socialist Republic. Thousands of retiring Red Army officers then transformed it into a Bolshevik Costa del Sol, building their dachas along its riverbanks, savouring the balmy southern climate and – as old soldiers everywhere – dreaming of further glories.

Their chance came with the fall of the Berlin Wall. As the Soviet Union splintered, Western-looking Moldova turned its back on its Slavic side. It declared Romanian to be its official language and joined both NATO's Partnership for Peace and the Council of Europe. In response the Kremlin stepped in 'to protect Russian minorities' on the Dniester's eastern bank, ensuring that the nostalgic military men (and a few wily oligarchs) could retain their links with Moscow.

'In the upheaval, I saw ordinary civilians shot on the Dubăsari Bridge,' Khorzhan told me with feeling, naming the river crossing where three 'rebel' Transnistrians had been killed by Moldovan troops, thereby inflaming the so-called War of Independence. 'I was fourteen years old at the time. I saw how nationalistic feeling was being cultivated in Moldova, and how Moldovans turned against their brothers. I realised then that I could not live in such a place. As soon as I finished high school I became a communist.'

He signed up to the breakaway territory, hoping that party membership would wipe away his real sense of rootlessness. In those tumultuous days he didn't dwell on communism's flaws or fragility. Like millions of others in fractured Eastern Europe, he simply felt lost.

'I believed – and still believe – that all the former Soviet republics will one day join together again, not as a single state but as an economic union. This is not a dream, it's a reality for me.'

Behind Khorzhan hung a wall map of the old USSR, its socialist republics united in fraternal brotherhood. Since the Union's dissolution, splintered parts – like Transnistria, and Kaliningrad – have been used to jab the West.

'People with such strong historical and economic connections are meant to live together for eternity,' he declared, striking his chest with his fist, condemning the 'nonsense of the fascists in Ukraine' (that is, democratic protesters). He added, 'I rejoice in President Putin's desire to unite Russian soil.'

Then, not for the last time, he began to wax lyrical about the Russian soul. 'As a Westerner you will not understand the importance of the land, of the soul to us. The Western soul is like a fenced garden: well nurtured, well maintained, with a sensible structure. Our soul, our Slav *duscha*, is totally different. It is wild. It is open. It has no limit. It is like a vast steppe from which we get all that nourishes us, but in which we can become lost.'

Khorzhan unfolded his podgy fingers and rose from both his soliloquy and his melamine desk to open a cupboard. With great ceremony, he presented me with a red communist rain shell, thousands of which had been handed out to supporters, and friends of supporters, and friends of friends of supporters who couldn't resist freebies. He also gave me a party pen, noting with pride, 'It's made in Germany.'

His passion struck me, as did his commitment to a political fiction, and it brought on a potent sense of unreality. It wasn't simply a reaction to his incoherent doublethink, although that was part of it, rather it was an awareness of the seductiveness of nonsense over verifiable truth.

'I don't understand,' I said.

'Around the world young people wear the hammer and sickle on their T-shirts. Communist symbols are graffitied on walls. This is not nostalgia. Youngsters realise what is good for the planet. They understand that selfishness guarantees them no future,' he explained, emotion rising in his voice as he mingled Marxist–Leninism with anti-globalisation Newspeak. 'Soviet leaders understood the importance of selflessness,' he shouted, spit flying in my face. 'Did Stalin lead an independent Georgia or the united Soviet Union? Was Nikita Khrushchev a Ukrainian politician or a great Soviet leader?'

As I wrestled with the subtleties of his argument, he puckered his lips and calmed himself to recall how after Transnistria's War of Independence – which had claimed to be preserving communism – the communists had been elbowed out of power.

'They stole our property,' he grumbled, a frown now troubling his boyish looks. 'My comrades and I were arrested for organising a meeting and sentenced to one and a half years in prison. But communist parties from around the world – even from Great Britain – sent telegrams of support and the sentence was commuted.'

The Communist Party's office had once occupied the biggest building in the land. Every state employee had been a party member. Marxism–Leninism had been the most powerful ideological weapon in the struggle against imperialism. But now Khorzhan's HQ had been relocated at the end of an alley.

'It wasn't fair,' he sighed.

Nonetheless since his release from prison (he was locked up for only thirty-six hours), he and the authorities had found a way to work together, to square fantasy and reality if you like, or so it seemed judging from his weight gain (and new watch).

'We modern communists have left behind the old stereotypes,' he told me. 'We have accepted the market economy and the ownership of private property. At the same time, we have kept our historical symbols alive. Lenin still stands in most of our town squares. Tiraspol's main street is named after the October Revolution.'

In the years since my first visit communism had remained 'the pride and future', he assured me. He called it 'the glue of the people'. The hammer and sickle still 'rose like the sun in the republic's crest and flag'.

'These symbols enable us to respect history, and to avoid repeating errors, and so will help our Motherland to find its way towards the future.'

With those stirring words the last communist deputy in the last Supreme Soviet smiled sweetly, offered me his plump hand, then opened the door to usher me back into the real world.

In truth, Transnistria was no joke. On the cold next morning, snow flurries danced in the air, caught the slipstream of a shivering trolley bus, whipped into the faces of the flat-capped men towing wooden carts towards the market. At a bus stop thick-set commuters waited in battle fatigues. Young women, their faces haloed in deep, fur-lined hoods, stamped the winter out of their high-heeled boots. The ancient trolley shuddered to a halt, its contacts sparking and crackling on the iced overhead wires. The driver swung down from his cab, hoisted himself up onto the roof and – with raw hands soon blackened with grease – hacked the ice off the contacts with a broken bayonet. He eased the arms back onto the lines, ignored the passengers and continued on his way, past babushkas selling tangerines frozen as hard as orange rocks and billboards celebrating the victory of the latest president. Beyond the billboards a graphite Porsche with tinted windscreen jumped the traffic lights. Two militiamen – there are no police in Transnistria – looked the other way.

On that bitter morning Vladimir Nikoluk wasn't working. It was his fifty-eighth birthday and he and his pretty, petite third wife, Alexandra, had invited me to join the celebrations.

'Welcome, comrade,' Nikoluk roared, pouring tumblers of Ukrainian Khlebnaya Sleza. On the tongue the cool, clean vodka tasted of freshly baked white bread. 'In my house your glass will never be empty.'

News of my return had spread quickly among Tiraspol's in-crowd. As the daft dreamland had lost half its population in a decade, even the most popular host was hard-pressed to find fresh blood for parties, or so I guessed from the number of invitations on my voicemail.

Nikoluk was a big, generous man with salt-and-pepper goatee beard, fist-flattened nose and immense hands. He called himself a 'maximalist': buying the best food, cooking the largest quantities, snatching the most beautiful women in the country (and – when necessary – marrying them). 'No one calls me a minimalist,' he warned in a voice loud enough to shake snow off the roof. He was an engineer, head of the Union of Builders, and surely the least cautious man in Transnistria.

In an icy parking lot, he loaded an oil drum barbecue with charcoal and set it alight with a blowtorch.

'We will eat *kostitza*,' he declared, flourishing two platters of home-cured pork cut as thick as his thumbs. When he threw them on the grill one could almost hear the pig squeal. 'No T-bone steak ever tasted as good.'

Nikoluk was born near the source of the Dniester in the western Ukraine. The region had been part of the Austro-Hungarian empire until the First World War, then Polish until the start of the Second, then German, Soviet and finally an independent state. Despite the changes, its people had retained characteristic Polish (and German) industriousness. At technical college in Lviv, Nikoluk and his classmates were taught that they would become the best engineers in the USSR.

'"You are the leaders, the Jews of the Jews,"* they told us. "Nothing can stand in your way." That wasn't the usual communist approach,' he assured me, rubbing the last lustre off the old Soviet archetypes.

On graduation Nikoluk had been posted downriver in Soviet Moldova. The young crane mechanic liked the republic with its southern women and heady local wine. At the first Builders' Day festival he drank too much of it and told the factory boss that he'd take his job within two years. And he did.

'Success was the religion of the Lviv Technical Institute,' he said, lighting a Cuban cigar. As its smoke mingled with the aroma of

---

* Meaning hard-working and ambitious; a paradox, as the Jews of Lviv – which until 1939 had been a city of 'blurred borders' and clashing colours, the 'red-white, blue-yellow and a touch of black-gold' of Poland, Ukraine and Austria, according to the writer Joseph Roth – were wiped out in the war.

scorched meat he added, 'I buy them on the Uruguayan market. They are cheaper that way.'

In 1990 Nikoluk directed similar ambition into the War of Independence, becoming vice-director of the Strike Committee for an Independent Transnistria.

'In Moldova people chanted "Moldova for ethnic Moldovans" and called me an incomer,' he recalled, refilling my glass, lobbing the first empty bottle into the snow. 'Where could I go? I joined the comrades who wanted to maintain links with Russia. I rang Gorbachev himself and met Deputy Premier Ryzhkov. I told them, "The Soviet Union is falling apart." They assured me that it would never happen. But it did.'

He sucked on his cigar.

'For the next half a year I wore a flak jacket. I carried a gun. I had my special missions. I fought to preserve our Motherland.'

As Nikoluk raised his glass to Motherlands, his wife Alexandra emerged from their ground-floor apartment, tottering on her heels between the snowdrifts, carrying plates of pickled watermelon and *salo*, salt-cured slabs of fatback pork. Nikoluk wiped away his tears to fetch a steaming jug of *ukha* fish broth, concocted from freshwater perch and vodka and reputed to prevent hangovers (it didn't).

Behind them the patched, five-storey block was criss-crossed by gas and drain pipes, its balconies boxed in and curtained against the cold. At an upper window a housewife had broken off from her morning chores. She leaned out of her window to smoke a cigarette, tapping the ash onto the frozen garden below.

'Vodka is best drunk in threes,' cheered Nikoluk, turning back to me as he cracked open another bottle. 'If you drink alone, you are an alcoholic. If two people drink, a man and a woman for example, they are interested in something else. But with three drinkers, you have the perfect number of companions.' He refilled the glasses and added, 'Try the blood sausage.'

With independence Nikoluk became a big fish in a very small pond. He grasped the chance to rebuild Transnistria's war-damaged infrastructure, winning the contracts to repair the Dniester bridges. He went on to supply the steel for all of the republic's petrol stations.

'I benefited from the situation,' he confessed, crunching the tension out of his neck. 'Also Transnistria – lying between Western Europe and Ukraine – has more than two hundred miles of open border. What else do I need to say? All the big money has come to us because of our unrecognised status, through contraband of one sort or other, like in the USA during Prohibition.' He paused to assure me, 'But I did no smuggling. I tolerated no corruption. I paid my taxes, unlike Big Brother.'

'Tell me about Big Brother,' I asked on cue.

'Big Brother has a buy-and-sell ideology. They are interested only in profit. They make money. I make things.'

He laid down his cigar, scraped the charcoal off the steaks then sprayed the grill with spirit. Flames leapt into the air, almost singeing my eyebrows and melting snow around the barbecue.

'In the Soviet years people had stability, social guarantees and their own apartment,' he reminisced, warming to his theme. 'I still have those things, plus a new Lexus, only now I must work thirty-six hours every day.'

In time more glasses were raised and emptied and the steaks were done. We wove our way indoors – heads buzzing, fighting for focus – and Nikoluk twisted his broad shoulders through the doorways between bedroom suites and fitness room, showing off the newly fitted kitchen and sauna converted from an old bomb shelter. On a huge widescreen TV in the living room his four-year-old daughter Maria watched Ukrainian cartoons at top volume. I asked Nikoluk how he had found the apartment on central Karl Marx Street.

'I was just lucky,' he said and laughed, delighted by the choices he had made, his expansive spirit filling the room with crackling energy. Behind him the icemaker clinked in a stainless steel American fridge-freezer.

Nikoluk's table groaned under the weight of yet more food: platters of charcuterie, plates of marinated tomatoes, three varieties of potato, half a dozen cheeses as well as the remaining butter-tender *kostitza* pork. In Eastern Europe it's said that guests are welcomed with everything on the table, while in the West the best food was kept in the cupboard. There were also more bottles. Every time a new vodka was opened and the glasses filled, little Maria tried to recap it.

We ate, drank then debated historical materialism and business synergy. I asked him about the utopian ideals of developed socialism and he quizzed me on Apple Inc.'s share price. Maria lay on a toy tiger rug and turned up the television again.

Around nightfall Nikoluk barked at her, an edge of unpredictability flashing in his eyes. Alexandra noticed it and slipped out of her chair to nestle in his lap like a small and delicate bird. He was twice her size, and twice her age.

'I found her working at the Domsoviet,' he said as if discussing the netting of a rare specimen for a collection. 'Every time I passed the city hall I'd call by her office and say, "Your uncle is back to see you again."'

'I didn't notice him at first,' chirped Alexandra in mischievous English, her smile revealing new dental braces. 'But he was very persistent, and very sly.'

Nikoluk bellowed with delight, wrapping her in his beefy arms. The short sleeves of his black T-shirt emphasised his biceps. Her proximity mellowed him and in a surprisingly wistful voice he said to me, 'It was always my dream to travel. But I can't, even with my two passports.'

All Transnistrians had a Transnistrian passport, which was useless for foreign travel. All wanted a Moldovan passport, which was rarely forthcoming. Most were stuck with a Russian or Ukrainian document.

'Why are we just a forgotten island between Moldova and Ukraine?' slurred Nikoluk in lament, overlooking the fact that its fuzziness had enabled him to prosper. 'No one is happy with the present status. If Europe really wants to end our isolation, they should simply welcome us as brothers.'

I suggested that Transnistria would never be allowed to join the EU as it was run by criminals (present company excepted). But by then it was too late for such discussions. As she stroked his beard, Alexandra chirped, 'I'd like my name to be on a European passport.'

With another glass-cracking laugh, Nikoluk pulled himself upright in his chair. Pretending to be a border guard, he inspected her document and welcomed her into an imaginary, expanded European Union. 'Nikoluk, Alexandra...' he read aloud, swaying, then hesitated. He had forgotten her middle name. 'What is your patronymic again?' he asked his young wife.

For the first two decades of Transnistria's existence, its leader, Russian-born Igor Smirnov, had maintained the guise of a working man. His suits had been tailored with peculiar, short, rolled-up sleeves. A Lenin goatee beard had enhanced his presidential looks. None of his four election victories was recognised by the outside world yet when he fell from power he smashed his office, wailing at his aides, 'You said that I would win. You said that I was the winner.' His election slogan had been 'The Motherland is not for sale', a truth for the simple reason that it had already been sold. Soon after the election Smirnov went missing. And so did 90 per cent of the central bank's gold reserves. There is no evidence that the disappearances were linked, but the incoming president claimed to have found only $49,000 in the national kitty. Nevertheless, five years later the 'father of the republic' was back, and on the board of Nikoluk's 'Big Brother'.

The next morning I went in search of him – or rather it. Beyond wretched little shops, gloomy apartment blocks and broken-down garages, I recognised the sweeping blue arch crowned with a sheriff's yellow star. Beneath it, a uniformed security guard checked my passport then waved me into the landscaped oasis of the Sheriff Sports Complex.

Sheriff – a state within a non-state – was the country's most powerful corporation. Its three vast stadiums and football clubs were its brashest holding, built up over the last decades at a cost of more than $200 million. When filled to capacity the three FIFA-approved arenas could seat one-tenth of Transnistria's entire population.

'Why football?' enthused Pyotr Lyalyuk, director of the complex, when we met on a manicured training pitch. 'Because football is the ambassador of peace. After the collapse of the Soviet Union, we at Sheriff decided to invest our money in the ambassador of peace.'

In flawless English, Lyalyuk introduced himself as Transnistria's former criminal police chief. Like the company's founders, all of Sheriff's executives had first worked as intelligence officers or in law enforcement during Smirnov's regency.

'I oversaw the project from the very start,' recalled Lyalyuk while adjusting his Dolce & Gabbana jacket. 'I remember when there was nothing here but a simple field. Now we have built a kingdom for football.'

In a vast, heated indoor hall, half a dozen teams of different ages practised at the nets. As we circled it, Lyalyuk explained with smooth self-esteem how Sheriff sponsors sports clubs in dozens of local kindergartens. Once a year the children and their families are invited to the complex. Company coaches then select the best players and offer them places at the Sheriff football academy. Over 400 boys are schooled there without charge. Boys from out-of-town are given room and board. Boots and kit are also free.

As a result of its programme and investment, FC Sheriff Tiraspol has come to dominate football on both banks of the Dniester, twice winning the Commonwealth of Independent States Cup and determined to top the UEFA Champions League. Graduates of the academy had been sold to European and Russian clubs.

Nikoluk had told me that football was good business. 'Young players are sold abroad for millions. No one does the business better than Sheriff,' he'd boasted.

I wondered how such a costly sports complex could be afforded in a country with an average monthly income of $150, so I asked Lyalyuk where the money came from.

'Business,' he replied smoothly with a charming smile, before inviting me to his private dining room for cake and coffee. 'Or perhaps you'd prefer champagne?'

***

Sheriff had been founded by Viktor Gushan and Ilya Kazmaly, two former KGB officers who had been Smirnov's 'sheriffs' during the so-called independence war. But unlike Wild West lawmen, these sheriffs' primary intention had not been to fight crime. As well as the football teams and sports complex, their company had come to own two banks, a chain of petrol stations, the state's mobile phone network and a couple of radio and television channels, as well as the Mercedes-Benz franchise. Its dozen supermarkets offered a huge selection – fresh mangos and raspberries in the depths of winter, salted Russian salmon, black caviar from the company farm at $1,500 per kilo – despite the moans of local people that they could find nothing affordable on its shelves.

Of course Sheriff wasn't the only party to have benefited from Transnistria's non-existence. As Nikoluk had suggested, alcohol, cigarettes and humans had been slipped across its porous borders. So many trailer loads of chicken had been imported duty-free, then smuggled in secret to Ukraine, that on paper every Transnistrian appeared to eat sixty kilos of the meat per year. Profit was also squeezed from the vast Cuciurgan power plant that supplies Transnistria as well as Moldova and much of Odessa. One year after its surprise sale to a Belgian shell company for a knock-down price, the plant was bought by Russia's state electricity producer RAO UES, netting the managers (some of whom were on the boards of both companies) about $100 million.

Arms traders had also been welcomed in the nowhereland. First, about half of the 40,000 tonnes of 'decommissioned' Soviet weapons and ammunition stored near Cobasna – a small town near the Ukrainian border – had turned up in the Balkans, Chechnya and the Congo. Allegations then began to circulate about secret weapons factories that manufactured mines, grenade launchers and parts for Grad missiles (not dissimilar to those fired from the SA-11 Buk that brought down Malaysia Airlines flight MH17).

To find out more I headed to Bendery, an industrial city that straddles the Dniester. The town's main employer is Moldavcabel, one of the companies alleged to be a secret weapons maker. Like many of Transnistria's enterprises, Moldavcabel's buildings looked grey and rusted, and often appeared to be abandoned, until one noticed the new surveillance cameras and busy employees' car parks.

'Here in Bendery we *have* worked, we *are* working and we *will* work,' Yunis Ragimov assured me when we met in his office. 'No financial crisis, no currency collapse, no raw-material inflation will stop us.'

Ragimov, fifty-five, was Moldavcabel's general director. A dynamic and genial man, he had been born in Armenia, educated in Azerbaijan and could crack jokes in five languages.

'Before we begin let me tell you that I served in Afghanistan,' he said with mock seriousness. He knew why I had come to Bendery. 'So be aware that the KGB may be listening to our every word,' he jested, bringing to mind Stalin's diktat that gaiety had been the most outstanding feature of the Soviet Union.

His factory had been founded in 1958. At its peak it had employed 2,500 people and supplied the electrical windings for many of the USSR's small motors: washing machines, television tubes, T-62 battle-tank starter engines. Later it began producing cable conductors for generators.

Ragimov became its director when a St Petersburg conglomerate bought the vast plant for $1.7 million, about the cost of a single Tomahawk cruise missile. He was brought in to slash employee numbers and double productivity.

'Sevcabel's acquisition has enabled us to be part of a big family, bringing us access to more markets,' he said. He had curly black hair, a wide moustache and lashes so dark that his eyes appeared to be rimmed with kohl. 'Now we need new investment. We're operating almost at zero revenue, bled white by competition and the lack of recognition. The United States and the EU want to keep us down. They want to weaken us.' He added, 'For this reason I am sure Transnistria will be reunified in ten years.'

'With Moldova?' I asked.

He shook his head. 'With Ukraine, Belarus and Kazakhstan.' He gestured towards the western border. 'Moldova is our neighbour. If you live in a block of flats and have bad neighbours you can move. We don't have that option.'

Outside it had begun to snow again, the flakes settling on backs and hats, hiding the horizon beneath a white blanket. An industrial graveyard of disused rail lines and dismembered gantry cranes loomed out of the pallid air. Idle loading areas were knee-deep in pale drifts.

Ragimov took me to see one of the three accessible warehouses. Inside it pot plants drooped around 'heritage equipment' that dated from Soviet times. A stout worker tended the machine that had produced the cable for Iran's Bushehr nuclear power station. At a wooden desk another woman in a pink woolly hat monitored quality control in a cloth-bound ledger. Next door serpents of cable snaked across the floor, around humming machines, beneath a portrait of Lenin.

At Moldavcabel I saw no sign of landmines, missile launchers or Kalashnikov ammunition production lines. Nothing apart from *draniki* potato pancakes seemed to be hidden in the staff canteen. Nor did I spot any sign of Aerocom or Jet Line, the freight airlines that had landed regularly for 'technical reasons' at nearby Tiraspol on their way to Africa. Both carriers had been controlled by Viktor Bout, the enterprising arms smuggler and convicted 'merchant of death'.

'You see, we have no secret weapons plant here,' joked Ragimov.

In recent years other enterprising Transnistrians have been arrested in Chişinău, capital of Moldova, while attempting to flog military items including weapons-grade Uranium-235. Elsewhere, Georgian black-marketeers offered ISIS, for $2.5 million, a couple of kilos of Caesium-137, the isotope of choice for dirty bombs due to its rapid absorption in the lungs. (The jihadists themselves had snatched forty kilograms of low-enriched uranium when they took Mosul University.) And Al-Qaeda once looked into buying fuel cells from dismantled Soviet nuclear submarines on the Kola Peninsula, just up the road from where Sami and I had parted. These are only four of 3,500 incidents of the theft, loss and trafficking of radioactive material since the fall of the Wall, according to the International Atomic Energy Agency.* Add in a conventional arms trade worth $400 billion per year, with Russia as the world's second largest weapons producer (and its mafia's sophisticated smuggling networks), and any intrepid entrepreneur can be part of a sure-fire money-making venture, if untroubled by morality or the sanctity of human life.

* As the former CIA director George Tenet observed, 'In the current market place if you have a hundred million dollars, you can be your own nuclear power.' A frugal terrorist shopping for Armageddon can put together a dirty bomb for substantially less outlay.

22

Fear is a Habit

Beyond the offices of the rich and powerful, fear remains a habit in Transnistria. In dirt-poor Dzerzhinsky, a village named after the founder of the KGB, collective farm workers count their $15 'Putin pension', praise the Kremlin and keep their complaints to themselves. At the Noul Neamț monastery in Chitcani, Abbot Father Pasii lowered his voice to tell me, 'It will take time to change the old ways of thinking.' And at Tashlyk Compulsory Educational School, teachers simply follow orders.

Tashlyk is half an hour's drive north of Tiraspol. Its name means 'rocky place' in Turkish, so called by the fifteenth-century settlers whose houses still squat on a low embankment above the Dniester. But the Turks are long gone, along with thousands of other villagers who've left to find work in Moscow, Odessa and Verona. Along its muddy main street a thin line of smoke rose from a single chimney. Every other building seemed deserted with windows broken and doors closed by a twist of rusty wire or twine. Two wooden planks, set at right angles to each other, overlooked the river's flood plain. Once a seat for friends, they too were now unoccupied.

On the hill above stands the school. Its water is drawn from a well, not the mains. An outside toilet block serves its 357 students and 43 teachers. Work stopped on its canteen building two decades ago. The reason for its poverty is not hard to understand despite

Tashlyk being represented in the Supreme Soviet by Sheriff's co-founder Ilya Kazmaly, the republic's richest man.

'We teach by the National Education Plan as prescribed by the Ministry: maths, history, science and languages,' explained the school's headmistress, who had gathered her fellow teachers in the staff room to meet me. 'We work as prescribed, as ordered. If we disagree with the curriculum what, in truth, can we do about it? We hope for radical change in the system.'

'Change?' I said, wondering who were the true heroes – and victims – in Transnistria. 'Look around you. You don't have running water or a canteen.'

The staff stayed silent.

'What about history?' I asked them. 'How do you teach your … glorious history?'

'Please bear in mind that this is a Moldovan school, and the majority of people in Tashlyk are Moldovan. So we are in the minority in Transnistria,' said another teacher, who also asked not to be named. 'We use Soviet-era textbooks translated into Moldovan which, for example, talk about the Great 1917 Russian Revolution. I try to update them by presenting another point of view, moving from the old utopian ideals to so-called developed socialism. But I have no material for this, only my own experience.'

'And Stalin?' I questioned.

'The accepted view is that Joseph Stalin brought Soviet victory in the Second World War. Our textbooks – or "manuals" – do not mention the deportations, the gulags, the loss of the brightest minds.' She took a deep breath, her voice full of emotion. 'I am only entitled to teach the unilateral presentation of the historical process.' She paused to consider her words. 'Anyway, I know most children will move away from Tashlyk after graduation.'

In the newest Russian-language history textbook, commissioned by Putin himself, Russia's tsars and communist leaders alike are presented as 'enlightened autocrats'. Stalin's famines, purges and mass deportations are explained away as the 'unavoidable cost of modernisation'.

In a classroom, students worked in pairs at pale blue desks beneath the words 'Science is the torch of truth'. Most girls wore their hair long, plaited or secured with plastic clips and simple bows. Many hung silver crosses around their necks. The boys sported white shirts without logos or branding. Their heroes were footballers and actors: Ronaldo, Andrey Arshavin and Arnold Schwarzenegger. Vladimir, aged fourteen, told me that when he grew up he wanted to be a businessman 'selling clothes and furniture'. The girls dreamed of being lawyers, designers or – in one case – a police officer.

'I want to join the police when I graduate,' said fifteen-year-old Varvara.

'But there is only a militia in Transnistria.'

'In Russia,' she replied, as if it was obvious. 'This is my home but what could I do here? There is no work. I have to go away.'

Non-stop emigration had reduced Tashlyk to a small community of children and babushkas. Most of these pupils lived either with their grandparents or alone in the family house, the neighbours keeping a watch on them while their parents laboured abroad. Even the headmistress's husband had moved to Moscow, in 1995. 'We don't know where all the time has gone,' she told me.

'You know, this is like a village school. The children are by nature accepting and patient. Few of them are rebellious.'

'And you?' I asked the teachers. 'Why haven't you moved away?'

'I've been trying for the last twenty years,' answered their soft-spoken colleague. 'I'm still trying.'

I felt a pang of despair for the failing village and its forgotten people. Beyond the school's dirt playground, the fields that had once belonged to the collective farm lay fallow, and neat ranks of beech trees marched alongside the Dniester, tilting towards the setting sun.

In the decade since my first visit it wasn't only teachers and students who had moved abroad. Back then I'd met Nina Shtanski, the newly appointed foreign minister under the newly elected President Yevgeny Shevchuk. Within hours of Shevchuk's victory, dozens of

craggy bureaucrats and hoary nomenklatura had been replaced
by 'Shev's chicks'. His new Minister of Justice Maria Melnik
had just marked her thirtieth birthday. Alena Shulga, Minister
for Economic Development, was then thirty-two. Both the new
Minister of Health and the new director of national television were
rosy-cheeked 28-year-olds. Apart from utilising these impeccable
young women's bright vitality and expertise, the new president's
intention had been to 'sex up' the republic's image abroad, letting
their sheen obscure the shadows of the past.

Of course fear – not gaiety – had been the most outstanding
feature of the Soviet Union. Generations of its citizens had grown
up in terror of the pre-dawn knock on the door, of exile, of the
gulag. In 1989 I'd thought that fear had been buried beneath the
rubble of the Berlin Wall. But when I sat together with Shtanski in
her office, she had disabused me of my fantasy.

'Over the last years fear has become again a habit in Pridnestrovie,'
she'd admitted, forming her response with care, using her preferred
name for the republic. 'Today our people are waiting for some sort
of settlement, for a system of international guarantees.' The fullness
of her lips and eyes had been emphasised by her dark, chestnut
fringe. Her tailored blazer and stylishly short skirt had accentuated
her height. She'd folded her hands together and ventured that the
only way to break the habit of fear was 'to find a solution to my
country's unrecognised status'. She'd added, 'It is a frozen conflict
but still it is a conflict with accumulating conflict potential. It is
dangerous.'

In those weeks following her appointment, 34-year-old
Shtanski's beauty had transformed Transnistria's image abroad.
Male diplomats from Brussels, Geneva and London had queued up
to stare at her across the ministry's broad boardroom table. At the
same time she'd launched her personal PR campaign, on Facebook.

'Good morning, friends, countries, continents! Wishing you a
great week! May the news only be good, the winter frosts only kind,
and meetings warm!' she'd written soon after her appointment.
Another of her daily posts had read: 'Watching Eurovision. Those
Swedes have really bowled me over!!!!! Cool!' Once she'd even

ventured: 'People of Tiraspol! Tell me please where is a good place to roller skate?'

Her candid, snappy posts about her love of fashion, home baking and Irish cider – alongside astute comments on trade and political negotiations – had seemed to reverse the outmoded Cold War stereotypes, making the republic appear trendily modern. She'd shared with the world her enthusiasm for Morgan Freeman, Joe Cocker, Portishead. She'd raved about Christmas trees during a Foreign Office-sponsored trip to Northern Ireland. After the Munich Security Conference she'd revealed a passion for German marzipan. Her likes had included Chanel, Esquire Russia and Vladimir Putin. She'd even posted a favourite joke about a couple's conversation after a night of lovemaking, 'She: My darling, shall we get married? He: Let's stay in touch.'

Her soft Facebook diplomacy had disseminated information about Transnistria, wrapped in an attractive package, winning her thousands of friends – a significant achievement given that the unrecognised state has no embassies and only scant resources to promote itself abroad.

Back at the ministry table, Shtanski had criticised 'black myths' spread by the West, portraying Transnistria as a source of arms and drugs smuggling as well as a conduit for human trafficking. She'd emphasised that Transnistria's people were 'bound together by a shared Soviet identity'. Over coffee she recalled a story about her daughter. One day her primary school teacher had begun a discussion about ethnic diversity, explaining to the class that Russians, Ukrainians and Moldovans lived together in harmony and in equal numbers in the republic. The teacher then asked the children to stand up and state their ethnicity. One by one the children announced with pride: 'I am Pridnestrovian.'

'Our children are like a mirror,' Shtanski had told me. 'This is national identity over ethnicity, and this fact will help us to solve common problems. Together we can build a common place.'

But her and President Shevchuk's golden age did not last. Their 'common place' was doomed to fail because they'd turned against Sheriff. One year into his term, Shevchuk accused the company of squirrelling billions of dollars away in foreign tax havens. Sheriff denied the allegation, yet as if in retaliation to it – and with the support of the vengeful 'father of the republic' Smirnov – packed the Supreme Soviet with its supporters. It wanted the fabricated homeland to remain a profitable contrivance, kept in a state of suspended animation. Shevchuk was accused of high treason and the misappropriation of $100 million. He (and his new bride Shtanski) were forced to flee the country.

Sheriff 'tells people about my millions so as to conceal information about their billions', Shevchuk complained from his new luxury apartment over the border in Chişinău. The Supreme Council had used 'blackmail, pressure and arrests to force out testimonies' against him. 'This is a well-planned scenario with a goal to retain power,' he said.

At the end of our first meeting, when she and her lover-president were still in office, I had asked Nina Shtanski about her duty – and that of her then young and sincere colleagues – towards a people who were at once fearful and hopeful, who watched their words while befriending her and the new president on Facebook.

'We feel the weight of expectation,' she had replied with a smile at once beautiful and sad. 'And we feel that the people's expectations are too high.'

What then is Transnistria? To nail down an answer I returned to a last old haunt. At the edge of the Ministry of Justice compound, in a central Tiraspol office building, was GUIN, the State Service for the Execution of Punishment. In its dismal entrance hall – above the portraits of fifteen stone-faced officers – were inscribed words attributed to Peter the Great: 'Prison is a Hell for which we need tough professionals who work with good heart and joy.'

After the foundation of the sliver-thin republic, few of its superannuated Heroes of the Soviet Union had chosen to busy themselves improving their golf swing. Instead the retired brass hats set about commandeering government ministries, forming private security firms and – in one case – building a zoo.

General Nikolai Goncharenko was a recipient of the Order of the Red Banner. In 1968 he had ridden a Red Army tank into Czechoslovakia to crush the Prague Spring. In 1991 his OMON Special Purpose Mobile Unit had rounded up Latvian freedom fighters in Riga. When the Baltic states had proclaimed their independence, he had taken shelter in Transnistria.

In the terra incognita, Goncharenko had taken charge of the prison service, organising it along military lines. He'd renovated Colony No. 1 in Glinoe where the cells had reputedly provided as little as one square metre of living space per prisoner. He'd reduced the incidence of tuberculosis at both Colony No. 2 and Colony No. 3. He'd believed in a world where 'every action against Order was an offence against the State'. Yet it wasn't humans who most benefited in a daring dictatorship.

For Goncharenko loved animals and soon, visiting delegations from Abkhazia, Artsakh, South Ossetia and other fraternal non-nations caught wind of his passion. They begun to indulge it with a turtle dove here, an anaconda there. In time he had dozens, and then hundreds, of creatures. In his enthusiasm for selfless collectivism, he ordered the construction of cages and corrals in GUIN's central courtyard. Beneath the ubiquitous portrait of Dzerzhinsky, Goncharenko enjoyed nothing more than petting a dove or discussing his ostrich's vitamin supplements. One bitter Transnistrian winter he even housed the Pogona desert dragon lizards in his dacha sauna, to save the poor beasts from freezing to death.

On my last day I stepped into his bestial courtyard and the rip-roaring hubbub. Around me screamed peacocks and honking Mandarin ducks. Swans hissed and pigeons cooed. Prison officers in battle fatigues used riot shields to shovel back the fallen snow and a rasp of guinea fowl. In the ring of enclosures pranced neighing Highland ponies, a barking prairie dog and Emma the ostrich, pecking at the frozen mud. A brood of chickens clucked in contentment, unaware that they existed only to be fed to the hissing, four-metre python that slithered along the ministry's long hallways when the keeper cleaned its cage. Goncharenko's zoo was their earthly paradise, or the closest they'd get to it in the nowhereland. Together in equality – if not harmony – the tamed and unthinking proletariat chirped, piped, roared and hee-hawed for the joy of living in the only place in the world never to accept the collapse of the USSR.

Ukraine

23

Theatre of Bad Dreams

NIGHTMARE NO. I

Shadows twisted and turned on the bleached surface. Deformed figures reached out, cried out, trapped in the maze. Arms wove above bent heads, kinked around white corners, felt their way forward beneath the blazing lights. The audience, as lost and as blind as the victims, wailed with them at the start of the haunted night.

Dnipro, the world's fastest-shrinking city, felt like the end of things. It was a place on the edge, a hundred miles from the Donbas battlefield, an outpost for one million souls, infamous for its missiles, maniacs and murders. Plus its edgy art scene.

In an abandoned circus building, a red-brick roundhouse buried under decades of graffiti, the performers struggled on, pushed on, still trying to escape captivity. On crutches, in wheelchairs, balanced on unsteady feet, they tested the passageways, fell into loops and closed circuits, cried out again and again for ten excruciating minutes. To make the maze, hundreds of old bed sheets had been stretched between metal poles, suspended by wires, lit from above so the scant, mixed audience could look down from their ringside seats. Around me sat students in thick sheepskin coats, shivering Israeli tourists, two New York art majors who'd taken a wrong turn in Lviv, as well as a handful of out-of-work engineers and out-of-luck veterans. In front of us one actress appeared to discover the secret of the maze. She pressed herself against its undulating right wall, sliding her hand around every turn. But her plan failed for the maze was far from perfect. The installation was nothing but dead ends.

Once Dnipro's flat and fertile steppe had been the Wild Fields at the edge of Kievan Rus', the thirteenth-century kingdom that stretched from the Carpathians to the Volga. Its history, like that of all of Ukraine, was one of heroic effort and mortifying tragedy. Turks, Tartars, Poles, Tsars and Soviets had subjugated the borderland for almost a thousand years. Seven million Ukrainians starved to death in Stalin's genocidal famine. Another seven million perished during two world wars. In 1787 Catherine the Great had named Dnipro – then called Ekaterinoslav – the administrative centre of Novorossiya. She'd chosen it as her empire's third capital city, after Moscow and St Petersburg, so as to subject it, taking its grain, making it her buffer zone. 'Ukraina' can be translated as 'on the edge'.

But long ago Dnipro had tumbled over that edge. Snow cloaked its dirty Dnieper banks. Deep drifts shrouded its deserted gatehouses and graveyards. Severed power lines fell short of its frozen office blocks. Soiled white mantles ruched against its abandoned factories and gathered around its empty dormitories.

On a cold nightmare evening I'd made tracks to the so-called circus building, following broken pipelines that brought to mind enormous serpents sleeping beneath filthy blankets.

'Theatre is a place for reliving human experience,' said Yuliya, the angry young director of the Theatre of Bad Dreams. I'd come to Dnipro to meet her and her collective of wounded souls: part installation artists, part performers, all marked by life. Some of the company had war wounds. One was an amputee. Three or four suffered from developmental disorders and birth defects – poor motor skills, cleft lip, Down's syndrome. Yuliya's head was small for her body, emphasising her dark brown eyes and elongated nose. Her forehead appeared collapsed as if in a lifelong frown. She was prone to a sudden loss of balance.

'I am interested in the events and stories that shape our lives,' she said when we met in the foyer. The bed-sheet maze was the first of the evening's three short performances. 'In the stories that a person keeps for themself, and the stories over which we have no control.'

Yuliya's father had met Yuliya's mother in a staff canteen at the Yuzhny Machine-Building Plant. Their shifts and lunch trays had collided in the queue when he knocked her liver dumpling onto the red linoleum floor. At work he'd always prided himself on the accuracy of his guidance systems. That lunchtime he felt doubly pleased to have hit his target.

In Soviet days Dnipro had been an industrial powerhouse. One of the key centres of the nuclear and space industries, its factories had built the launch vehicles for the first Sputniks, as well as entire ballistic missile systems. At Yuzhmash, Yuliya's father had played his part in the production of SS-27 'Sickle B' ICBMs. Yuliya's mother had organised the transport of the 120 nuclear missiles produced by the plant every year.

Yuliya's parents married in the Dnipro's Domsoviet, taking their honeymoon at her family's old dacha near to the headwaters of the Dnieper. When she fell pregnant in 1986, her mother returned alone to the isolated cottage with plans for a peaceful, extended pregnancy.

It wasn't to be.

On a Friday night in April the nearby Chernobyl nuclear reactor burst into flames. The cause was not so much an accident as an overdue turbine test that had gone wrong. Engineers attempted to shutdown but the control rods – which had been tipped in graphite as a cost-saving measure – superheated the core, causing a full-scale meltdown. Open-air graphite fires leapt into the air. Plumes of radioactive smoke spiralled into the atmosphere. But local party bosses hushed up the disaster, issuing no health warnings or explanations. No one let on that the fallout was worse than at Hiroshima and Nagasaki. Instead a new fairground with Ferris wheel and dodgems was opened early to distract the plant's 5,000 workers. Saturday's football matches and outdoor school gymnastic displays went ahead as planned. Kiev's May Day parade – with ranks of children waving paper flowers and military bands playing patriotic marches – took place as radioactive soot showered on the capital. Moscow made no statement for two weeks, other than to accuse the Western media of spreading 'malicious mountains of lies' about the explosion.*

Alone at the family dacha, Yuliya's mother knew nothing of the disaster, the house being outside the initial six-mile exclusion zone. She tended the garden, made meals of its fresh vegetables and took gentle walks by the black poplars that lined the riverbank. By the time Yuliya's father managed to contact her – by way of a local defence unit – she had been exposed to as much as 100 roentgens of ionised radiation. She left for Dnipro as winds carried Chernobyl's contamination across Belarus and Poland, into Sweden and Norway, as far as the Welsh mountains and the Scottish Highlands. In the autumn Yuliya was born with microcephaly.

On the stage the bed-sheet maze had been adapted for the evening's second performance. As the lights went up, an amorphous shape occupied the centre. Around it on the floor the metal poles had been laid out in a wide circle, cut through with an arrow-straight line like a slashed zero. Two actors rolled their wheelchairs round and round its rim, gazing towards the hub in suspicion. To them the shape was something unknown, something foreign and not understood. In their fear they began to shout at it, provoking it with 'Khto ty? Khto ty?' The audience – encouraged to participate – took up the call, also demanding in angry Ukrainian: 'Who are you?'

In response the shape began to stir, moving to the sound of its own eerie oscillations. Within lengths of sheeting, the hidden performers rose to their feet, moving as if a single being, calling out in strange half-heard tongues.

'Who am I? Who am I?'

---

* The Chernobyl nuclear disaster – which irradiated and led to the deaths of tens of thousands – convinced Mikhail Gorbachev of the need for radical political reforms. 'Chernobyl shed light on many of the sicknesses of our system as a whole,' he said later.

Again the rhythmic chanting lifted in volume, filling the space, aggravating both the shape and the wheelchairs that circled around it. Again there was something hypnotic, even spellbinding in the performance piece. Our raised voices agitated the shape, making it weave and rock in its place. Then in a kind of sordid wonder, it expelled – gave birth to – a body, wrapped in a single sheet as if in swaddling clothes. That body, that newborn, lay curled like a foetus on the zero's metal slash and started to whimper.

Now the other actors stole to the back of the stage and the far end of the slash. There they formed up behind the two wheelchairs to bellow together: 'Who are you? Who are you?'

Finally, in this most surreal show, they added in the sound of a train. The actors had become the wagons behind wheelchair locomotives. In the uproar they started to move forward, hobbling along the metal slash, pushing the wheelchairs into the circle and towards the whimpering foetal figure.

I thought of the trains that had taken Ukraine's victims to Siberia and Auschwitz, that had carried away its nuclear missiles, that had brought me to Dnipro. The crying, crippled troupe of players bore down on the child, on the feared unknown, intent on crushing it.

At that point the stage lights were meant to snap off and the actors disperse, to return for a curtain call. But the company's technical person   who doubled as stagehand and box-office manager – had slipped out for a cigarette, caught his mechanical hand on a door handle and missed his cue. To avoid squashing the 'baby' the wheelchairs veered off the track. In the confusion the limping players lost their footing and fell on each other. Yuliya screeched as she struggled to free herself from the swaddling clothes. Only then did the lights go out on the troubling, amateur tragicomedy.

NIGHTMARE NO. 3

Ukrainians had seen themselves as a nation without a state, until the collapse of the Soviet Union. In 1991, 90 per cent of them voted for independence, their Orange and Maidan revolutions then ousting pro-Russia politicians and deepening ties with democratic

Europe. Yet Moscow saw the new state as a source of instability, poisoned by infectious Western ideas, and set about undermining it by annexing Crimea and fomenting war on its eastern borders.

Yuliya had created her Theatre of Bad Dreams in the wake of the Maidan protests. She'd decided to form her own company after she had been barred from two local amateur dramatics groups for being too outspoken. In Dnipro she turned adversity to advantage and found no lack of takers. In the first month alone she recruited injured veterans from both the Afghan war and civil clashes, two Yuzhmash workers maimed by industrial accidents, even another Chernobyl survivor. At the Theatre of Bad Dreams she made them confront their demons.

In the same spirit of inclusion, players and audiences alike provided material. Their performances dealt with armed conflict, disabled lives, loss of identity and racism. The company made no money of course; costumes, lights, even the sheets had had to be begged or borrowed. Yuliya herself lived with friends in an abandoned rail freight station. Penury was an everyday reality.

We huddled together around the steaming samovar, drinking tea before the final play. 'Our theatre is about politics and dreams, good and bad,' she blurted, nestling the chipped glass in her hand, shivering with cold.

'And about nightmares,' I said.

To Yuliya the world was splintering, and the largest crack cut through Ukraine. In the 1990s industrious Dnipro had crumbled. Yuzhmash lost all its missile orders and many of its engineers. Its managers asked the remaining liquid-propulsion specialists and aerospace boffins (including Yuliya's father) to turn their expertise to the manufacture of trolley buses. Inflation rocketed as the country's gross domestic product halved. At the same time Moscow began to lavish thousands of passports on ethnic Russians, promising them study grants, generous pensions and the rest. Then it made the protection of their rights a pretext for invasion, sending in the tanks and little green men.*

---

* Little green men – *zelyonye chelovechki* – were masked soldiers in unmarked green army uniforms who appeared in eastern Ukraine in 2014 brandishing modern Russian military

'We have always lived with the dark, with war, deceit and ruin,' she went on at speed. 'This is part of Europe's essence, part of the nightmare. It doesn't vanish after one generation of peace.'

Our exchange unfolded in short bursts, Yuliya speaking with the same intensity as her plays, talking suddenly about Dnipro and her disillusioned parents, about the dire uncertainty of their lives, about a city built to destroy other cities.

'Now the brightest Soviet minds make tractors and don't get paid. They never wanted to do bad things but do they have any choice?'

The cold shook Yuliya onto her feet and back to the stage. Across its length the sheets now zigzagged in two parallel lines, their sides propped up by metal poles, creating the impression of opposing trenches. Into them limped and rolled the broken actors, playing the part of rival soldiers. At the start of the third play, they manned their posts, aimed cut-out weapons and took potshots at each other across no-man's-land.

'Donetsk! Popasna!' they called out, one by one, relating real stories from real front-line towns in eastern Ukraine. One player recalled weeping like a child as volleys of rockets pulverised his trench. Another read aloud text messages, sent to his phone by Russian electronic warfare systems. He was nothing but 'meat for his commanders'. His mangled body wouldn't be found 'until the snow melts'.

'Mariupol! Luhansk! Torez!'

In the audience two local men translated for me then stepped down onto the stage to join the performance. They walked between the lines, passing back and forth a handheld microphone, telling of children walking to school under fire, of old men fishing alongside minefields, of the young couple who kissed outside a Mariinka disco as it was hit by a stray shell.

---

weapons. Putin stated first that the men in green were not part of Russian Armed Forces, then that they were spontaneous 'self-defence groups' and finally that they were his Spetsnaz, special forces troops.

'Do you know why soldiers in the army have to wake up at six in the morning?' asked the player beside me. 'Because at that hour you feel like killing everybody.'

By now everyone was on the stage. In the freezing circus house, actors and audience alike imagined themselves to be on – or back on – the war's front line, among the 10,000 soldiers and civilians who had lost their lives there in the last decade. Three women gripped each other, crying without stopping, their grief stuck like a cracked record. Rebels lobbed imaginary grenades over their heads and guerrilla fighters made imaginary advances on enemy positions. A part-paralysed player relived the moment that he had been hit by shrapnel. Their pain began to transcend time and place as Yuliya clutched her poor malformed head and wailed.

'Repetition of agony is important. By facing it, problems may be truly resolved,' she said in a kind of rage, at the end of the night. 'Political theatre asks difficult questions: Who are we? Why did my sister die and I live? We face the truth.'

Outside, an icy wind howled into my bones. Twisted, skeletal cranes glistened in their icy coats under a sliver of moon. Beneath the still and frozen landscape, the earth was barren and hard. On the walk to my hotel I was unable to control my shivering.

I had a cold coming on, of that there was no doubt. When travelling I always try to keep well. Illness numbs the senses and clouds judgement. Objectivity goes for a burton, as does any sense of urgency. Time is always precious, of course, but it seems especially so when on the road: catching trains and planes, discovering new towns and cities, gathering stories and making notes. Yet even if I'd loved the place, I didn't want to spend too long in Dnipro, nursing myself back to health, within range of Russian-backed rebel (rocket-assisted) artillery.

At least I'd had the forethought to spring for a good hotel, and to slip the desk clerk a folded note to ensure my room had a bath. But I must have over-tipped him for, as I lowered myself into the steaming water, I beheld a treetop view across the city. Beyond the wide window, dawn broke over the Orthodox cathedral, its foundation stone laid by Catherine the Great and Austrian Emperor Joseph II. The yellow fumes of distant Prydniprovsk power station rose like spun gold into the lightening sky.

Once the shivering began to abate, I took another garlic pill and reflected on crippled Ukraine. Resistance to authority was its national idea, the consequence of the centuries of subjugation. Wily Ukrainians of yore defied their rulers, looked after themselves and so survived occupation, pogroms, famines and holocaust. Russia worked to wound the fledgling democracy but it was the Ukrainians themselves – propelled by their own myths – who did the most damage. Kiev's own officials, parliamentarians and businessmen plundered the state budget and stole or sold national assets (including an RD-250 ICBM engine – or at least its technology – that found its way from Dnipro to Pyongyang to power North Korea's long-range ballistic missile system). Ukrainians have made their country so ungovernable that Transparency International – which monitors corruption worldwide – rates it as 142nd in the world, alongside Uganda.

I gazed out across the broken city and wondered if I was seeing the real end of Europe – fragile, fragmented and lost in a maze. Then the hot water ran out and I sneezed again.

24

All That Glitters

I was looking for a church, although not because I felt like death. My car rose off the steppe and into the Carpathians, the arc of mountains that stretched from Ukraine through Hungary and the Czech Republic to form a natural barrier between the Slavic and Romanised worlds. It was a remote, meaningless fragment of territory cut off from everywhere, according to the historian A. J. P. Taylor.

I'd rented the car in Chernivtsi, once home to 'Jews in kaftans ... spur-jingling Romanian soldiers ... colourfully dressed peasant women with baskets of eggs on their heads and solid ethnic German burghers in wide knickerbockers and Tyrolean hats', recalled the Austrian author Gregor von Rezzori in *The Snows of Yesteryear*. To Jews the city had been טשערנאָוויץ. Its Romanian rulers had called it Cernăuţi. Under the Austrians it had been Czernowitz. To Poles it was Czerniowce and to Russians Chernovtsy. Once it had been dubbed 'Little Vienna' and 'Jerusalem upon the Prut'. But in the fury of the Second World War, its diverse culture had been ravaged and expunged. In its absence, the modern and homogeneous city didn't move me, unlike its car rental firms. I hired a not-too-ancient Skoda and, like so many before me, headed out of town.

I was on the trail of another story. I'd heard about an old church hidden high in Zakarpattia's mountains, built for an emperor who'd never visited. In an effort to set the rough wooden structure apart, local men had taken to shaking out their hair over the altar after Mass. As their region was known for its gold deposits, and most men worked in the mines, minute specs of gold dust fell from many tousled heads. Over a century of Sundays the altar and apse came to be covered with thick billows and folds of glinting gold, and the emperor caught wind of the story. Enticed by his subjects' devotion, he made plans to visit the little church, until the outbreak of the First World War doomed both his plans and his empire.

The car climbed past smoky hazelnut trees rimmed by cool morning light, its pistons hammering like my head. Snowy footpaths ran through woods above which the branches of ancient spruces hung like mourning weeds. To keep warm I'd jacked up the heat, but still I was shivering from the cold.

Wars had torn apart this 'meaningless fragment' as they had all of Ukraine. In 1914 Ukrainians found themselves conscripted into opposing armies: 3.5 million serving the tsar, a quarter-million in the Austrian army. During the Russian Revolution, much of which was fought on Ukraine's bloodlands, more than 100,000 civilians lost their lives, Kiev changing hands fourteen times in eighteen months. Ukrainians turned on each other again during the Second World War, to serve either in the Red Army or as *Hilfswillige*, the Nazis' 'willing helpers' who arrested and massacred Jews. After the war Ukrainian patriots and collaborators alike were deported en masse, condemned to be 'special settlers' in Siberia.

In its search for role models, Ukraine's latest nation-builders had decided to glorify wartime nationalists, including Stepan Bandera. Kiev wanted to use his example to rally support for its war against Moscow. Unfortunately Bandera had led the anti-Semitic 'Organisation of Ukrainian Nationalists', which had intended to liquidate the country's Jews. It had also massacred tens of thousands of Polish civilians in western Ukraine in 1943–44. The OUN's ambition had been to turn Ukraine into a one-party fascist dictatorship without minorities.

But people forget or lie or fall for the propaganda, so it was not a great surprise to find Bandera gazing down at me when I stopped at a pharmacy in a no-name town. To many Ukrainians he remained

a symbol of the struggle for independence during the twentieth
century, despite his hateful politics. In Lviv a statue of him had
been erected soon after he'd been named a Hero of Ukraine. At the
same time his effigy was burned in Odessa.

Of course the town didn't really lack a name. I simply hadn't
taken it in, my mind befuddled by the particularly nasty cold that
the steaming Dnipro bath hadn't nipped in the bud. En route to
Chernivtsi – or טשערנאָװיץ or Cernăuți – I'd managed to find
neither lemons nor apple-cider vinegar, the latter being a sure-
fire defence against an oncoming cough. Nor did I happen upon
a ready supply of *kogel-mogel*, a traditional Jewish raw egg and
vanilla cure-all. Thankfully the pharmacist behind the counter –
and under Bandera's flashing portrait (it was surrounded by
glittering fairy lights) – was sympathetic and helpful, although
she didn't understand a word I said. I managed to communicate
my symptoms by pointing at my blocked ears and clutching my
aching head.

I had no idea what drug she prescribed but, as far as I could tell
by miming my hands on a steering wheel, I would be safe to drive.
In the Skoda I took a slug of the raspberry flavoured liquid, then
another for good measure. Along the main street came a horse-
drawn cart, its workers returning from clearing snow with shovels
slung over their shoulders. A Ukrainian border-patrol unit trooped
past an ancient woman whose bowed pegs were wrapped in woollen
leggings and felt boots. Neither the march of time nor the tramp
of armies – Austrian lancers, Romanian Roșiori, Einsatzgruppen
death squads and Soviet commissars – had broken her step. In the
no-name town the twenty-first century seemed to have been tacked
on to the past like an afterthought. Or so it seemed as I drove on,
passing a wrecked Ikarus bus on the outskirts.

Ahead the road twisted higher still into the hills, through aspen
forests and past frozen waterfalls. With every mile or two another
isolated hamlet fell away behind me. At every other turn a new vista
opened onto glistening peaks. Stacks of winter firewood insulated
the walls of the last, remote farmhouses. A single, lone dog trotted
along the broken tarmac. Otherwise the place felt empty of life.

Zakarpattia, the west-facing nose of Ukraine, borders four countries: Hungary, Poland, Slovakia and Romania. In its hills, frontiers moved more often than people. A man named András Orosz had lived in the village of Novoye Selo, called Tiszaújhely in Hungarian. Over the course of his long life he had held five different nationalities: Austro-Hungarian, Romanian, Czechoslovak, Soviet and, finally, Ukrainian. Yet Orosz had never once left his village; the borders had been moved around him.

'Do you know the old joke about the baby who was born on the border?' asked a forester in German, the first living soul I'd seen in an hour and who I asked for directions. 'To find his true nationality his father picked him up and threw him in the air. If the baby landed on the Hungarian side of the border, he was Hungarian. If he landed on the Ukrainian side, he was Ukrainian. But if he landed on his head, he'd be Russian.'

On the snowy verge he drew a route map for me, over the pass to Bilky and Brid, uphill to Zahattya and Zavydovo. He too had heard about the golden church, although he had never seen it.

'But I know for certain it's here,' he insisted, stabbing at a point in the snow, laughing along with me. 'I have heard the story.'

I drove on, climbing even higher into the mountains, deeper into muffle-headed blurriness. The pharmacist's tonic may not have advertised its hallucinogenic qualities but the Skoda did develop a remarkable facility to sail over the potholes. I opened the window to gulp deep breaths of thin air, in the hope of clearing my head, but it only exacerbated the cough. I tried to focus on describing the scene around me – a peak enveloped in cloud, a curved ridge thigh-deep in snow, a dark abyss – but almost drove into the ditch while writing notes. I paused to align my road map with distant peaks and a frozen river, then carried on, the Skoda's tyres spinning on ice patches.

Gold had been mined around Beregovo since the twelfth century. In the Soviet years more than twenty miles of tunnels were dug into its ore-rich volcanic dome. On one of my orientation stops I spotted a mine-head of Avellana Gold, the Cyprus-based company that has sunk thousands of drill holes, hoping to revitalise the empty wilderness as a Carpathian Klondike.

An hour later the setting sun gilded an edge of mountain, casting a band of yellow across crag and scar. I realised that the nearest village lay miles behind me and I began to doubt that I could find my way back to it, despite my good sense of direction. Half a dozen switchback turns on labyrinthine forest tracks finally convinced me that I was lost. Ice crystals glistened in the snowfields, filling the air with a kind of magic, wrapping a halo around an old wooden building.

In any other light I'd have driven right past the church, tucked as it was amongst the spruce trees. But suddenly it was in front of me, and I wasn't the only visitor. I parked the car and walked into the bright halo, towards the sound of hammering. My footsteps crunched on the hard-packed snow as I pushed open the heavy wooden door. At the head of the nave were an elderly couple, and a coffin. She – in layered black skirts and embroidered *peremitkah* headdress – was crumpled upon it. He circled it and her, driving home the last nails, sealing its lid. In a pinewood pew stood another man – younger, perhaps a son, also dressed in black – who held a wilted bunch of flowers upside down.

The moment was sad and dark yet all around it spread fields of gold: rumpled golden altar cloths, iridescent cross, a lustrous shining sanctuary. Beneath Christ Pantocrator, the all-powerful judge of humanity, the church shimmered with light. It lit the naive iconostasis, glistened off the falling hammerhead, caught the tears on the old man's cheek. In that brief moment, I imagined generations of miners stepping forward, kneeling with humility, shaking out their hair around the altar. Never had I seen the like, and never would I see it again for outside the sun dropped behind a far peak and deep shadows fell across the earth. The golden light was sucked out of the day and the building revealed its true colours: dismal ash grey and weathered brown.

As I watched, the two men lifted the coffin onto their shoulders and carried it past me into the dusk. The old couple did not meet my eyes, did not speak, but once the coffin had been slipped into their pale van the younger man turned to me.

'*Mein Bruder*,' he said. My brother.

'No priest?' I asked.

He shook his head. 'All gone. Every person gone.'

'I'm sorry.'

He answered with the barest hint of a shrug then turned and opened the driver's door. His parents were already inside the van. I had no idea how the brother had met his end – war? Mining accident? Drug overdose? – but when the engine coughed into life, I had the presence of mind to spring forward, and tap on the frosted glass.

'*Ist das die goldene Kirche?*' I asked, gesturing at the sombre church. '*Die geheime goldene Kirche?*'

'*Da da*,' replied the young man in Ukrainian. 'But all gold gone. All stolen.' He wound up the window and added, 'Good night.'

I followed their tail lights downhill to another no-name town. I found a room in a no-name hotel and lay on the bed. In my head I watched the sun go down once again over fields of gold. I pitched the cold tonic across the room, and missed the bin.

Tomorrow I'll leave the bloodlands, I told myself, assuming I survived the night. Tomorrow I'll be in Hungary, with eyes sharp and emotions in check. I'll record my journey with clarity and cool objectivity, I imagined.

As I tried to convince myself of that impossibility, there came to mind a last story from the heartbroken borderland, about a boy and his mother. Years ago the two of them had tended a smallholding in the contested fragment of territory, near to where met the frontiers of Western Europe and Greater Russia.

'One morning at the end of the Second World War the son left home to work in the field across the river,' a storyteller had told me ten years earlier in a Tiraspol cafe. 'In the evening when he rowed back he found barbed wire and Soviet soldiers on the beach. The guards told him that the river was now a border. They wouldn't let him come ashore, wouldn't let him go home, and he had to find a place to live on the far bank. Every day he toiled in the field, calling across the water to his mother, until the soldiers ordered him to stop. The old woman then started to sing songs to him, sharing the news from home: who had married, who had had a baby, who had died.'

'In time the boy grew into a man, stopped farming the land and married. He trained to be a train driver, with a single, secret objective in mind,' the storyteller had recalled, taking my hand across the cafe table. 'Twenty-eight years after the border had torn his world apart, he drove a train across the river-bridge, stopped at his old village station and finally, at last, embraced his mother again.'

'Is that true?' I'd asked her, already reaching for my notebook, starting to jot down key phrases.

'It is a story,' the woman had replied, covering her mouth and laughing, laughing at the bittersweet tragedy. 'It's just a story.'

Hungary

25

Not Quite Spring

I knew the road of old, running south out of the Carpathians onto the Great Hungarian Plain. The mountains fell away behind me as the sun warmed the valleys ahead. Oaks and hornbeams clung to the slopes. Smoky hazelnut trees pirouetted in the breeze. Carpets of green inwrought with snow and flecked with lilac-cupped crocuses spread across the meadows. A river of viridescent verges, the Tisza, meandered through the fields, its oxbows glittering like twists of silver. I drank in the early spring as if it were an elixir, giving me life and revitalising my spirit. Already my return to Hungary felt like a homecoming, although in ways I hadn't begun to imagine.

'*Na, Kind,*' said Alajos, grasping me in his carpenter's arms. '*Du bist zu Hause.*'

Kid, you are home.

Thirty years ago he had welcomed me to Tokaj with the same embrace, wearing leis of dried paprika. He and his wife Panni had flung strings of garlic around my neck like garlands of flowers. Great sacks of cabbages, boxes of oranges and bags of sweet peppers, their skins as translucent as the skins of Klimt's women, had been stacked around the house. At the time of my first visit their son Sandor had just opened a grocery shop next door. I knew of Panni's death but the shop?

'Gone,' replied Alajos, gesturing towards town. 'Now we have Aldi.'

He stroked his white bristles with the stubs of his fingers, the tips severed long ago by a power saw, and limped ahead, ushering me through the coiling vines to the front door. He had aged of course, growing more stooped and grey, the skin under his eyes crosshatched with wrinkles, but inside the house was still as colourful as a painter's palette: red plaid curtains, blue twined carpets, a tablecloth edged in lace and embroidered with yellow blossoms. After Panni's passing, their three daughters – Lara, Lili and Szonja – had moved in to care for Alajos. Now they fussed him into a chair, scolded him for going out without his cane and brought us a dusty bottle of Crimean champagne, bought three decades before and set aside for the day of my return.

'I've worked up quite a thirst waiting for you to come back,' he said, wrestling with the cork, lacking the strength to dislodge it. Without a word, Lara eased the bottle out of his hands and opened it. As she poured our glasses, he said, with playful pessimism, 'The alcohol will help me to forget that life is worse than yesterday...'

'... but better than tomorrow?' I teased.

He lifted his glass. A ribbon of the national colours – green, white and red – was still stitched into his lapel but I noticed that the psoriasis had spread over his hands. He was over ninety now and I treasured him as friend, exemplar and a key source of stories in my first book.

'Remember what I told you: Hungary placed its faith in the losers of every war since the sixteenth century. This twenty-first century will be no exception.' Alajos said in toast: 'To a once hopeful Hungary. Long may we mourn her death.'

Unlike him, the ancient champagne hadn't aged well.

'Our history is complicated,' Alajos had once said to me, no more prone to exaggeration than any of his countrymen. The Magyars, a Mongol tribe, had first stormed across the steppes and into the embrace of the Carpathians around AD 895. Their fierce horsemen then raided deep into the west, ravaging Germany and Italy, playing their part in burying classical civilisation in the Dark Ages. Their enemies prayed, '*A sagittis Hungarorum libera nos domine*' – deliver us from the arrows of the Hungarians – and God answered by defeating them at the Battle of Lechfeld.

The vanquished tribe settled on the Central Plain, abandoned their nomadic habits and organised themselves into a state. In time that state fell under Habsburg rule, and later moulded itself into Austro-Hungary. At the start of the twentieth century Budapest was home to a dozen future Nobel Prize winners, the film-maker who would create *Casablanca* and the physicists who would help to spark the Manhattan Project and nuclear age.

But the Great War ended its heyday, reducing the kingdom to a quarter of its original size. In the hope of regaining its land, its embittered leaders forged an alliance with Nazi Germany, contributing 250,000 soldiers to its assault on Russia. When the tide turned against Hitler, Budapest tried to make peace with the Allies. In response, German troops occupied the country, installed a puppet government under the fascist Arrow Cross Party and set about executing or deporting more than half a million Jews. Another 280,000 Hungarians were raped, murdered or deported when the country fell to the Red Army. Next, a quarter of a million ethnic Germans were expelled and ten Soviet-style labour camps built within its borders, to save the trouble of transporting political prisoners to the USSR. Some 200,000 more Hungarians fled the country during and after the 1956 revolution. When the Wall fell and Hungary then joined the EU, Alajos (and I) had thought that the nightmare was over at last.

Late into the night I read aloud parts of my first book, recounting the stories that he had once told me, closing a circle. His eyesight had deteriorated over the years and in any case he didn't speak English so I translated his words back into German, leaning close to the lamp, watching expressions pass across his dear face.

'After the war I went back to school as a mature student,' I read out, quoting Alajos back to himself. 'One day – during Latin class – a man appeared at the classroom door and asked for me by name. I stood up. He showed me his identification card – he was ÁVH, state security – and he ordered, "Follow me." What could I do?

I followed. We walked to the police station. He showed me to an empty room. "Wait here," he said and left me for two hours. Then a man I'd never seen before came into the room.'

'Stand up!' barked Alajos, taking up his story again, recalling the new policeman's order. He lifted himself to his feet and said, 'The man asked me if I'd ever been to the West and I told him I'd been a prisoner in Belgium in the war and for that he slapped me hard across the face.'

Alajos snapped back his head as if he'd been hit again, as if the pain still stung across the years.

'Then he told me that I could go and from that moment I was a collaborator, as most of us were. I was frightened and fear made me cooperate. I had a wife and children. I didn't want to die. I wanted them to live. They gave half of my house to the policeman. I was permitted to occupy the remaining part, for which I was obliged to pay rent. My tormentor slept in my old bedroom.' Alajos paused and asked me, as he had done thirty years before, 'What would you have done?'

Thirty years on I still ponder that question, repeating it to myself again and again. Thirty years ago, in that same bedroom, I'd slept between cotton wedding sheets long stored in scented drawers, dreaming of lying in a bowl of potpourri, and waking into a time of hope after so much tragedy.

Now I woke to whispers, to the rustle of clothing and the muffled clink of crockery. Around Alajos in the next room whirled his three daughters and an indeterminate number of grandchildren, slipping in and out of the kitchen, balancing plates of smoked salami and buttered breakfast *kifli* bread rolls. I sat up in bed and watched the careful preparations by the half-light of the closed shutters, moved beyond words. My sudden laughter startled the family, sparking their own in turn. Alajos fixed his almond eyes on me and declared with mock severity: 'You can live a quiet life – drink my wine, go to bed and die early. Or you can get up and learn something.'

Suddenly everyone was talking, tempo and volume turned up as if by a switch. Bacon, eggs and potato pancakes sizzled in a pan.

A kettle whistled on the cooker. Four children pulled me from bed to table, giggling, trying out their German.

'*Hallo hallo.*'

'How are you?'

'*Mein Name ist Maria.*'

Coffee was poured and a dressing gown draped around my shoulders.

'Thank you,' I said as a fifth child placed a cinnamon pastry in my hand.

'*Nichts zu danken,*' said Alajos, welcoming me back into the heart of the family: modest, loving, without condition or expectation. He put his hand on mine and added, 'I'm glad you survived the night.'

As we resumed our conversation, I dropped a handful of coins on the table, mementoes from my last visit to Hungary. Alajos picked them up, saw the communist stars and threw them across the room.

'Worthless,' he said with a flash of sudden anger. 'Throw them away.'

He pulled a modern forint banknote from his wallet and warned, 'This also may be worthless. Our new government ordered special security paper from Germany and the border guards made sure that the freight cars were left on a railway siding overnight. I'm not saying that they had anything to do with its theft but they all drive Mercedes now.'

Alajos rubbed the note between his fingers.

'Good quality,' he said with a wink. 'The forgeries look better than the real ones.'

Thirty years ago – at the same table – Alajos had asked me about democracy and the rule of law, and now he recalled my definition. He said, 'If democracy is tradition then the sum of our experience is thirty-three months: in 1918 for two and a half years and in 1956 for ten days. We have no tradition of democracy here.'

'And today?' I asked him.

'You are wondering what has changed?' he replied and, when I nodded, his laugh was bitter. 'Everything and nothing.'

I told him of the changes that I had seen on my journey, of hopes betrayed, fears manipulated and people choosing to believe lies rather than face difficult questions. 'I also see that nobody in Hungary is in danger of losing weight,' I added.

Since the fall of the Wall, Hungarians had become the fourth most obese nation in the world.

'People eat well in our banana republic,' said Alajos. 'It helps them to overlook the ruin around us. Have some more coffee.'

'The ruin?' I said as my cup was refilled.

'Our judges have been tamed and journalists restrained, once again. Enemies are invented and loyal politicians given our property, once again. Now we are just their marketplace.'

'Including Sandor's shop?'

'Including Sandor. Aldi – with its Hungarian partner – bought the old co-op, undercut his prices, drove him out, drove my son out of his own home like the ÁVH had driven me out. *Und so weiter. Und so weiter.*'

And so it goes on and on, as ever.

'The only difference now is that ideology has been replaced by money,' he said. 'I'll show you after you've eaten another croissant.'

After breakfast I was bustled out of the kitchen and into my clothes. His daughters and their children then guided Alajos and me out to the car, holding our hands, asking more questions, helping him into the passenger seat. The oldest child asked how Britain and the US coped with the waves of crime committed by immigrants. When I told her that no such thing was happening, she pulled up a fictitious news story on her phone. As we drove away, I told Alajos that her question had reminded me of the pre-war anti-Semitic myths and hoaxes that had ended in genocide.

'*Und so weiter. Und so weiter,*' he said again.

Together we drove south from Tokaj, following another familiar road along the Tisza. Mosaics of light fell across our path, filtered through the poplars. Fens of reed and willow flanked the roadside. Once more I asked him about his son Sandor but he wouldn't be drawn.

'Gone, gone,' he simply replied.

When a great body of water opened before us, Alajos began to repeat himself. I let him go on not out of tolerance of an old man's forgetfulness, but because the story needed to be told again.

'The dam was built by Hungarian and German prisoners in the 1950s,' he said, lifting his cane to point at the wide sweep of concrete.

'I was working not far from here in Tiszalöki,' he explained, gesturing away to the west. 'One of the engineer's wives wanted built-in cupboards. They were popular in Budapest at the time and no functionary's wife could be without them. I agreed to make her a wardrobe of beech with walnut inlay and – when I was taking the measurements – she told me about the riot.'

Fifteen hundred POWs had been treated no better than slaves, building the hydroelectric dam. Beneath Soviet statues of valiant workers brandishing lightning bolts, they lived on water roots and horseflesh, surviving on 200 calories a day. The suffering was terrible, but there was a worse crime – the lie.

'This stretch of the river had been sealed off. No one could get near the site. It was isolated from the world. The men had been brought from Kiev at night in sealed cattle wagons. Their guards spoke Russian. Their letters to their wives were taken to the Soviet Union to be posted to Hungary. The prisoners thought they were in Russia, as they were supposed to think.'

'But they knew that the war was long over and they demanded to be returned home, home to Hungary, not knowing that they were home, here in Hungary, all the time. Permission was refused so they went on strike, four men were killed, another executed, but one man broke free.'

Alajos then said, 'One morning on my way to work – I'd nearly finished the wardrobe – I found an old friend. We thought he had died at Stalingrad, but he'd survived the war. He was the prisoner who had escaped from the dam. But he had become lost in the woods and, not knowing how close to home he was, he had given up hope. After walking for days he had hung himself from a tree not five miles from his village.' He paused for breath. 'I found his body, hanging, but I walked away. I told no one. I did nothing.'

Alajos looked at me, his eyes wide and round in confession. 'I knew. I said nothing. I lied.'

I felt the shame rise in him, realised that this dear, moral man – shaped by ethical integrity – would be forever haunted by his silence, humiliated by his acquiescence.

The Tiszalök dam, built by forced labour, had been owned by the state until last year when Nemzeti Vagyonkezelő Zrt. – the 'National Wealth Management Company' – quietly transferred its ownership to a private concern.

Once again no one objected, no one complained.

As we stood together in the cool sunshine by the Tisza, a sudden shiver ran through me, as if spring had not yet reached the country.

'My generation had not one day of peace,' Alajos confessed, his silhouette rimmed by the cold morning light. 'And when in 1989 peace finally came, when the chance to make a better life fell into our laps, when we could finally speak, everyone – even my own children – lost their voice.' He steadied himself on his cane, touched his tricolour lapel ribbon and asked, '*Was hättest du getan?*'

What would you have done?

26

Altogether Now

Steam, dense and opaque, rose with the voices. Bodies veiled in vapour glided through the heated air. Half-heard words evolved into intangible sounds, dropping into my ears like the beads of condensation off the vaulted ceiling. Half-seen bathers moved as if in a dream, stirring themselves from the tiled benches, looming out of the scalding, sulphurous clouds.

When I could stand it no longer, I plunged out of the steam room and into the cold bath, then back into the thermal pools. Around me skin blushed rosy red or glowed nebulous black. Sweat rolled down their arms, between breasts, dropped onto the octopus mosaic floor. The half-glimpsed bodies became talking heads, submersed to the neck, soothed into conversation. Tension shivered away as the medicinal waters tickled my upper lip. I let go, lay back and floated with so many others between the beams of light that fell from the hammam's copper dome.

Budapest had remained a city of curves, of underground springs, colonnades and crescents: the arc of the Kiraly baths, the bow of Chain Bridge, the Danube itself that rolled around the mock-medieval parliament building. Yet for all its soft curves it was not a feminine city, instead something hard and unforgiving still shaped it.

Terrorhaza, or the House of Terror, is a museum of horrors. On Andrássy Avenue – across the river from the hammam and up the road from the Hungarian State Opera – stands the former headquarters of both the fascist Arrow Cross and the communist secret police. These iniquitous opponents condemned thousands to death in this haunted villa. Now the place has become one of Budapest's most popular destinations, with an ominous stencilled steel blade projecting from its roof, and the shadow of the word 'TERROR' creeping across its elegant facade.

In the grey entrance hall visitors queue by the thousands in front of two massive tombstones – one black, one red. In front of them a Hungarian everyman, Mozés Mihály, pleads in an ever-looping video: 'So many people hanged. Why? Why? For what reason?' He is weeping over a grave. 'Young people whose thinking was different were sent to the hangman, the executioner. This was their *socialism*.'

On the monitor flash three words:

Fascism.
Communism.
Socialism.

In disbelief, I stepped into the deceitful museum, into a torrent of Death Metal techno pounding like gunfire. Banks of screens unleashed a staccato volley of advancing armies and armour, jumbling Hitler and Stalin, bombarding visitors with newsreel images of carnage and despair.

Budapest is devastated. Bulldozers clear away the dead. Outsiders are to blame. No mention is made that Hungary chose to ally itself with the Nazis as early as 1932, barely any suggestion that the Arrow Cross had been home-grown murderers.

In the next room, in a demonic Chaplinesque pantomime, a fascist manikin changes into a communist uniform, depicting an entire society *forced* to be turncoats. In the dead of night thousands of victims are rounded up to the sound of a haunting spy thriller score. In a political sleight of hand, Hungarians are absolved of responsibility for both holocaust and gulag.

The Terrorhaza mesmerises like a hi-tech movie, designed as it was by Attila Kovács, a talented set designer-cum-court-artist. Its heart-thumping soundtrack was composed by alt-right pop star Ákos. In its final scene visitors ride an elevator down to the prison cells and underground gallows, immersed in the vivid narration of a janitor who'd cleaned up after executions.

Fascism.

Communism.

Liberalism, reads the next screen.

At the House of Terror, Hungary is portrayed as a perennial victim, corrupted by foreigners and their ideas. Its new leaders alone can save the people from fascism and socialism, from Moscow, Berlin and Brussels. The horrors of the past have been manipulated to justify the oppression of the present. When he opened his museum, Prime Minister Orbán declared that Hungary had 'slammed the door on the sick twentieth century'. He didn't mention how he was poisoning the twenty-first century.

On Heroes' Square fearless, mounted, bronze Magyar chieftains – Ond, Tond and Huba with steed armoured in stag-horn antlers – lifted their swords and cudgels to defy eternal enemies, both real and imagined. Thirty years ago on the square the 26-year-old Orbán – a little-known, charismatic, football-loving village boy – had electrified an enormous crowd with a call for Russian troops to leave Hungarian soil. 'If we can trust our souls and strength, we can put an end to the communist dictatorship.' Back then he'd embraced human rights, a free press and the rule of law. He'd helped to lead Hungary towards freedom. He was elected to the National Assembly and in 1998 at the age of thirty-five became Hungary's second-youngest prime minister. Then he was seduced.

His transformation was neither violent nor dramatic. Orbán simply calculated that to retain power he had to win over the lower middle class, most of whom lived in the countryside, few of whom had finished high school. He reinvented himself by inventing enemies. He demonised intellectuals as well as the homeless, migrants and Jews. He took control of low-brow media to feed them his mythology. He bought their loyalty with government handouts. He played on the poor's sense of victimhood, cultivating their grievances.

Orbán – 'a thin-skinned opportunist who likes to command' according to former US Secretary of State Madeleine Albright – transformed liberal Hungary into a single-party state with a veneer of democracy. His home village, Felcsút (population 1,688), became the richest neighbourhood in the country. Its mayor – a former gas fitter and Orbán's long-time friend – came to own television stations, media companies, a bank and a nuclear engineering firm. The mayor's old firm – which was valued at less than $40,000 in 2006 – won contracts to build a bridge over the Danube and a football stadium. It also oversaw the closure of *Népszabadság*, the country's last major opposition newspaper.

At the same time Russia chipped in, loaning Budapest tens of billions of dollars, in part to expand a nuclear power plant but in truth to rebuild its rings of empire, perpetuating its imperial foreign policy. In thanks, Orbán obligingly criticised every EU action against Moscow.

Outside parliament, a dozen khaki-clad soldiers raised a 28-metre-square Hungarian flag on a needle-sharp pole. Around Kossuth Square, daffodils sprouted on once-noble balconies. Concrete lions roared over obscure military victories, forgotten by all but hoary historians and new nationalists. Retirees queued at post office counters to collect their pensions, eyes fixed on the twice-counted notes. At the Petőfi Sandor branch, an elderly woman handed hers back to the clerk, paid her rent, then tucked the meagre balance into an envelope secured with a paper clip.

I wanted to rediscover the city, to walk again from ancient Castle Hill on the Buda bank to bustling modern Pest. At Keleti station, its papal yellow wings taking flight from the wrought-iron entrance hall, I watched policemen scan the crowd for migrants, then lead away a Syrian family. Beneath its wide, arched roof a young man paid them no heed, awaiting the arrival of the Sopron train, clutching a bunch of flowers. A blind couple tapped across the forecourt, deafened by screeching brakes and the tannoy. I rode again the Budapest metro, the first underground railway on the continent. Half a lifetime ago I'd squeezed into one of its varnished wooden carriages with cellists and percussionists, flautists and violinists, all dressed in black tie, most carrying their instruments. At the Opera House stop, the musicians had piped me into the crowd, under the chestnut trees and up the grand spiral stairs into the horseshoe-shaped Opera.

But it wasn't only the street plan that felt familiar. In the air there lingered a feeling not unlike that of the communist days. It was no more than a fleeting sensation, like a draught of cold air in a hammam. I sensed that many Hungarians again radiated a certain caution, wary of stepping out of line, of people who had power over their lives.

On Liberty Square a vicious Aryan eagle swooped down onto the archangel Gabriel, its talons opened to seize Hungary's royal orb. Orbán himself had ordered the erection of the Monument to the German Occupation, in secret. 'In Memory of the Victims' was inscribed across its arch, making no distinction between Hungary's wartime Christian leadership and the slaughtered Jews, nor between Nazis and modern Germans, again manipulating the horrors of the past to poison the present.

In contrast to Orbán's offensive and gaudy bronze monstrosity, a simple, spontaneous living memorial had taken shape across a cobbled lane. Hundreds of small stones were inscribed with the names of the country's true victims. Candles burned between the stones. Flowers had been placed among them, as well as eyeglasses, shoes and small suitcases. Photographs of lost loved ones hung from strands of barbed wire. 'My mother was murdered at Auschwitz – thank you "Archangel"' read a bitter handwritten note, its ink running like tears in the rain. Beside it a length of railway track had been wrapped in ribbons of the colours of the Hungarian flag. A cracked mirror reflected the statue of Gabriel, demanding that Hungary face its past.

As Orbán reshaped Hungary, dividing it against itself, thousands of individuals had responded by creating the contrary *Eleven emlékmű – az én történelmem* memorial, marking their personal ties both to history and to modern Europe, gathering on the cobbled lane to sing Beethoven's 'Ode to Joy', the anthem of the European Union.

Hungary was not a victim, they knew. Hungarians had not been abandoned by Europe. Hungary had made its own destiny. But fewer and fewer people listened and Orbán laughed them off, declaring on his tamed television networks* that he – and his monument – served 'a greater calling', guided by 'the pain of the loss of our sovereignty'.

At end of the day I stood between the rival histories, overlooking their battlefield. At its edge rose *Hazatérés Temploma*, the Hungarian Reformed Church's Homecoming Temple. Every evening in the building, preachers and politicians advocated for the country's radical right, idealising its fascist past. Hungary must take back control, they crowed. Hungary must no longer be a victim.

At its entranceway was a flower-decked bronze bust of Admiral Miklos Horthy, the fascist regent who introduced the first anti-Jewish laws to modern Europe.

'Concerning the Jewish question, for all my life I have been an anti-Semite,' Horthy declared in the 1920s. 'I have never made any contact with Jews. I have found it intolerable that here, in Hungary, every single factory, bank, asset, shop, theatre, newspaper, trader, etc. is in Jewish hands.'

Europe cannot escape its history. Beneath the surface simmer dark forces, long unseen. Skilful and ambitious charlatans draw on them, exploiting prejudice, distorting the past and stealing the future. They claim to represent the people, the *real* people. Their

---

* In 2015 Orbán's friends owned some twenty-three Hungarian TV channels, newspapers and other media titles. Today they control more than 500, and have turned public broadcasters into mouthpieces for the government. 'Thirty years ago we thought that Europe was our future,' Orbán said recently. 'Today we believe that we are Europe's future.'

promise to save the nation from a corrupt elite is a fiction, of course, unlike their willingness to override constitutional checks and balances with 'the people's will'. In Budapest and Moscow, Westminster and Washington, these populists simply want power.

27

Down and Out in Buda and Kispest

With cracked fingers he combed the lice out of his beard. On the ground beside him a couple spooned in a nest of sleeping bags. Next to them a young woman slept uncovered, her tattooed stomach bloated and blue in the cold, undimmed neon. Above her swayed a man clutching a violin case to his chest, his eyes fixed on nothing.

At Kálvin tér station commuters glanced away and held their breath. But the sight of the poor held me, as it had done at another dozen metro stops across the city; bodies broken and collapsed against tiled walls, contorted figures crumpled onto concrete floors, filthy hands cracked with chilblains and gripping begging cups.

I'd heard the facts at A Város Mindenkié – the privately funded 'City is for All' homeless shelter: 7,500 people living rough in the capital, at least two deaths every winter night, vagrancy now criminalised in a draconian amendment to the Hungarian Constitution.

'People don't sleep on the street out of choice,' a volunteer activist told me. She had a pale, patient face but her voice was edged with anger. 'They sleep on the street because there is nowhere else to go.'

Nearby at the cramped and grimy Danko Utca shelter, over 200 lost souls squeezed onto barracks-like metal bunks. Men played cards or whispered to each other, guarding secrets. One wheeling drunk yelled coarse slurs across the room. His tone wasn't measured, his thoughts were unreasoned. A woman – with barely an ounce of

flesh on her bag of bones – had the air of someone long accustomed
to the ruin of dreams.

Gábor Iványi, the Methodist preacher who ran the shelter,
claimed that the ruling conservatives – specifically Viktor Orbán –
wanted to rid Hungary of the poor, along with everybody who
cared for them.

'The government has realised they can't play the migrant card
endlessly because there are obviously no migrants in the country,'
he said. 'Migration issues can still be useful for national campaigns
but for local issues they need a new scapegoat.'

Iványi had fought for the dispossessed during the communist
years. With their end he'd expected an easing of his workload.
Instead it had doubled when the new government had ostracised
the homeless, making them scapegoats along with the Romani and
refugees.

Humanitarian groups struggled to take up the slack. Iványi's
Evangelical Brotherhood provided shelter for hundreds every night,
cooking as many as 800 meals every day, until it was stripped of its
official status along with some 300 other religious organisations.

'I mourn for Viktor Orbán,' lamented Iványi. Hungary's prime
minister was 'on the road to damnation'.

'Sandor? Is it you?'

I'd not have recognised him were it not for the Hungarian lapel
ribbon. He wore it in the identical manner to his father, with tell-
tale twist, giving him away. Otherwise I'd have walked right by
him, his face and stature so changed by time. He was slumped
on a bench outside the shelter's office, trying to focus his watery
eyes, teeth crooked or broken, all but lost in an enormous, cast-off
Bundeswehr anorak.

'Who the fuck are you?' he snapped in response.

Thirty years earlier Sandor had opened his small grocery shop
but had then been squeezed out of business, Alajos had told me.
He'd left Tokaj and, with no word from him in so long, Alajos
had come to believe that he'd died. But in secret, his sister Lili
had stayed in touch with him, hiding the truth from their father,

knowing that it would have broken his heart. When I left for Budapest, Lili had told me that once a week Sandor collected her letters at Danko Utca.

'I can no face my father,' Sandor said to me an hour later at the Sza-Sa burger bar. 'I leave Tokaj for ever.'

He hadn't remembered me but he was willing to talk, and to be fed.

'Alajos thinks you are dead,' I said.

'Is better. No matter.'

'He's ninety-three and heartbroken.'

Sandor shrugged and said, 'Like Hungary.'

In the communist years everyone had a job. Everyone had a roof over their head. 'Workers pretended to work and the authorities pretended to pay them' was a well-worn cliché, meant as a joke, yet it contained a grain of truth. But the joke vanished with the Wall. In the early 1990s workers' hostels were closed, along with redundant factories, throwing tens of thousands onto the street. Many tried their luck at small start-ups, opening video-rental shops, nail parlours or a corner grocery, losing everything when their enterprises failed. They left their villages and towns in shame, escaping bad debts, joining the exodus to the capital.

Sandor had fallen into such a spiral. In Budapest he'd set himself up as a roast-chestnut vendor. But when he couldn't pay the weekly bribe, the police trashed his wheeled stove. He'd found casual work for a time with the city, weeding the central reservation of divided roadways in summer, scraping flyers off lamp posts in winter. After he lost that job, he turned to collecting discarded bottles and tin cans, loading them into a shopping trolley and living off the deposit refunds.

'Muslim steal jobs,' he told me, teeth bared in his ruined face. 'Muslim steal hostel beds.'

As a result of the war in Syria, some 400,000 refugees had fled through Hungary to reach Germany. Not one of them had taken someone else's job. In fact, almost none remained in the country. Yet the government had built a ten-foot-high razor-wire fence along its southern border. It had spun yarns about a 'Muslim invasion'. As in other parts of Europe, including the UK, the plight of refugees had been used to polarise opinion and hijack political power. As ever, an enemy was needed, and any enemy would do.

'Is like a thousand years ago,' insisted Sandor as he finished the burger, grease oozing onto the pumice-like skin of his hands. 'Hungarians again are border guards of Christian Europe.'

That wasn't true, I pointed out. About a thousand years ago it was the Hungarians who were the incomers. As for taking jobs or places in the hostels, I'd heard only Hungarian spoken at Danko Utca and the other shelters. Homelessness was a domestic problem.

I asked how Sandor was getting by – in the absence of government handouts – and he told me, 'I make business again. I show you.'

On the metro I tried to understand the change in Sandor. A loss of certainties played its part, of course, as did disappointment. Many Hungarians had expected their country to become as rich as neighbouring Austria within a year or two of the fall of the Wall. When it didn't happen, they lost faith in the future.

Hungary – again not unlike the UK – didn't know how to deal with its past. It harboured outdated notions of greatness, of superiority. As nostalgia replaced optimism as a ruling emotion, its people swallowed astonishing untruths about scheming enemies. They fretted that their identity was being undermined by immigration. On the seat beside me Sandor spoke of 'predators' and the 'Trojan horse for terrorism'. I couldn't blame it all on drink.

'Now Hungary is no longer sheep, is become lion,' he told me, clenching his fist.

Of course modern Hungarians – both drunk and sober – were not alone in imagining a lost Utopia, ruined by Jews, refugees, bankers or Brussels bureaucrats. To succeed, a political movement needed to find an 'existentially different and alien' opponent, according to the Nazi theorist Carl Schmitt. Eliminate that enemy, wind back the clock and restore lost glory, or so promised the fairy tale. Viktor Orbán is not the only contemporary politician who may have studied Schmitt's theories.

'Hungary must be great again,' he insisted.

As I tried to quell my anger, the train emerged from its tunnel and I caught a glimpse of the old Sandor, smelling a shrivelled apple in the fading daylight. He'd bought it for half price at the Lehel market, outside which he'd filched bags of rotten fruit from a skip. I remembered him whistling with pride as he opened his little shop thirty years earlier, fussing over a display of fresh oranges and peppers, wanting it to be just right.

Budapest's M3 metro line ended at Kőbánya-Kispest. At Köki Terminál mall, Sandor liberated a shopping trolley to haul the fruit through the housing estates and into a large belt of scrubland. In 1956 Soviet tanks had rumbled along Üllői Avenue to crush the Hungarian uprising. But suburban Kispest – literally 'Little Pest' – no longer worried about real invaders. Today Üllői Avenue had been cast into shadow by the ruling party's lying billboards.

'Did you know? The London and Paris terror attacks were carried out by immigrants?' shrieked their xenophobic propaganda. 'Did you know? Brussels plans to settle a whole town's worth of illegal immigrants in Hungary.'

I helped to hump the bags of fruit into the scrubland, the last few metres of the path being too rutted for the trolley. After a few steps we came upon a clearing and a rough encampment. Abandoned tents and torn tarpaulins had been cobbled together into half a dozen makeshift hovels. Within their rough circle, a clutch of six or seven middle-aged men – dressed in layers of hand-me-down clothes, warming their hands around a fire – called out in greeting. I held back but Sandor gestured me forward. His hut was a more substantial affair, held together by plastic sheets and a howling guard dog. As he released the padlock, the caged animal went crazy. He pushed the dog back with the slapdash plywood door to reveal tables, stoppered glass jugs and a mess of frothing buckets. A coil of copper tubing rose from a rusted kettle set on a wood burner. The air was filled with the smell of damp and yeast.

'Here I make best vodka in Köki,' Sandor said with pride, unpacking the fruit that would infuse the alcohol with flavour.

'Apples good. Chilli pepper too. One week must leave but sometimes I no wait so long.'

Sandor, who used to sell fresh fruit in the cheerful new age, had turned his expertise to blotting out its memory. He told me he'd found his way to Kispest's corrugated haven after a night in jail. Another down-and-out, also arrested on vagrancy charges, had waxed lyrical about the place, spinning a yarn about a green and pleasant community beyond the city limits. Of course it was nothing of the sort, but Sandor – after a few days sleeping rough beside its open rubbish tip, gagging for a drink – had hit on a way to survive; boiling up potatoes, adding mash, siphoning off the wash and earning a kind of living by bootlegging booze. He'd managed not to blind his undiscerning clients (more by luck than by design) and through his efforts had brought a hazy happiness to the encampment, helping its residents to avoid both clear thinking and sobriety.

I'd have expected to feel myself a complete outsider, in danger of being beaten up or robbed, but Sandor's welcome seemed sincere, and this was no clichéd vagrants' camp. Two of the men spoke English, the others had a smattering of German. One of the drinkers had been a primary school teacher in Pécs, until the government had handed his school over to the Church. Another said that as a student he'd once hitched all the way to Portugal's Cabo da Roca, the westernmost point of continental Europe.

As I found a place in the circle, they asked me about my journey and the UK, but I turned the conversation back to them.

'Migrants steal jobs,' I was told.

'Turkey will join Europe. We must save ourselves.'

On their island, Sandor and the other men talked, sharing stories, prejudice and tins of cheap food. Jam jars clinked together and Sandor's dog mauled a squirrel to death. I learned that the hitchhiker had earned a crust by repairing old fridges, until a new law made it illegal to collect appliances discarded in public places. Now only odd construction work came his way. Another man tightened a blanket around his shoulders and told me he'd been a bookkeeper at a Miskolc steel mill until he was laid off, fell into debt and lost his house. He made his money by unloading sacks of soil at a Kispest garden centre.

As the dark came, the men huddled closer together, bonded by sadness, alcohol and defeat. Around the fire they began to amplify each other's fears and fantasies, convincing themselves that they were not adrift in the world.

'All foreigners who threaten Hungary must be named as enemies.'

I have a calm nature. I like to settle, not to spark disputes. Once again I tried to be invisible. I went with the flow for an hour, hearing out their arguments, even at the cost of wreaking irrevocable damage to my liver. But I kept looking at Sandor, unable to fathom how the son of a lifelong freethinker could have surrendered himself to racist rhetoric. Finally I could no longer contain myself, due perhaps to his chilli-flavoured hooch.

'What does it mean? To take back your country?' I snapped at them. 'To take back the right to hate? To forget history?'

Silence fell between us, apart from the sound of the hound ripping off the squirrel's head. The men stared at me, sideways, bemused by my outburst. One of them reached out to pat my arm, as if to humour my faith in the future. Another refilled my jar. The moment was strangely touching and tender and I went wild. I yelled at the drunks in words they didn't understand, saying that lies had to be exposed and evil held at bay. I tried to draw a line between civic patriotism and xenophobic nationalism. I shouted out that Orbán was 'a showboat playing to the home crowd and no help in addressing the continent's broader problems' (or words to that effect, in the heat of the moment I was misquoting Albright again). Had they asked themselves why young Hungarians were now moving abroad in numbers greater than after the 1956 uprising? I bellowed.

I should have saved my breath.

At the end of my outburst only Sandor and the school teacher hadn't turned their backs on me. The teacher was the first to speak again. He'd maintained a tenuous hold on current affairs and – although his facts were out of date – ventured something about Britain distancing itself from Europe and congratulated me. I pointed out that Brexit had been a grotesque farce, dividing and diminishing the country, and that public opinion had been inflamed by reckless zealots, press barons and Russian bloggers.

'Then you say thank you to them all,' said Sandor, once again sunken-eyed and numb as he finished another jar of vodka. He blinked his watery eyes in an attempt to focus and looked across the fire at me. 'Europe is dead.'

Poland

28

Independence Day

'I have never been so frightened in my life,' said Kryśka. 'They kicked us and spat on us and dragged us to the side of the bridge. Of course we didn't stop the march. Of course our protest was symbolic. But we proved that the neo-fascists had stolen Independence Day.'

Thirty years had passed since our first and last meeting. Back then Kryśka had been a young medical student with spiky red hair and a dream fulfilled, grateful that Poland had at last the chance to become 'a boring country where people work hard and grow old in peace'. Thirty years on she was heavier around the jowls, her waist was a little thicker, but she remained as defiant as ever

'Today something horrible is happening in Poland,' she told me when we met in Warsaw, her voice exact and crystal clear. We'd shaken hands and then embraced, thinking of the shared values that had set our journeys in motion. 'The government has awoken our demons. People are not ashamed to show their hatred of strangers, of immigrants, of Jews. This is the last moment to act, before it's too late.'

For much of the twentieth century, Poles could only dream of freedom. During the Second World War Hitler had tried to reduce the country to a nation of serf-like 'helots'. Those not exterminated at Auschwitz would survive as slaves of the Reich. At the same time Stalin sent 1.5 million Poles to his gulags. By 1945 one in five Poles had been eradicated along with 352 hospitals, 5,919 schools, 17 universities, 25 museums, 22 million library books and 50 per cent of the road, rail and sea transport infrastructure. When Poland was 'liberated' by the Red Army, it was in ruins, and in chains.

Kryśka herself had rallied against the Soviet occupation on protest marches, in defiance of martial law, by printing banned literature. She had been born in leafy Żoliborz, Warsaw's *joli bord* – beautiful embankment – and home to the capital's intelligentsia. In the riverside neighbourhood of old villas and persistent ideals, she'd grown up with a sense that she was part of a greater community, with responsibilities towards it. She was seventeen when Solidarność, the first free trade union in a Warsaw Pact country, was founded. Aged eighteen she joined its student wing, Niezależne Zrzeszenie Studentów, and helped to print *Animal Farm*. Across the country hundreds of brave souls like her took huge risks to collect paper, type mimeograph pages, bind and distribute forbidden books and newssheets in secret. Everywhere lurked the danger of discovery, arrest, imprisonment – or worse. They published Orwell, Bulgakov and samizdat political brochures. Truth-telling – as she had told me at our first meeting – could have cost them their lives.

In the end the 'paper ammunition' helped to send communism 'to the mushrooms'.

'Suddenly we could breathe freely, people could associate freely, fear vanished.'

But after graduation and the fall of the Wall, Kryśka, then aged twenty-six and working as an anaesthetist in a state hospital, couldn't afford to feed herself and her young daughter. She joined Novo Nordisk, one of the Western pharmaceutical multinationals pushing into the burgeoning Eastern European market, and became its leading product manager.

'I chose Novo Nordisk because of its focus on education: running conferences, training medical practitioners, sharing knowledge. I used its expertise to help to build a better country, while building a new life for myself.'

As Poland became the most dynamic economy of the former communist states, Novo Nordisk, like other big pharmas, shifted its focus to profit. Kryśka resigned and returned to state medicine, her sense of social responsibility also driving her to build three educational medical websites: 'Others Like Me', a moderated platform for patients with chronic diseases; 'A Week for Your Spine', a physiotherapy programme for office workers; and 'Cure the Pain', which weaned doctors and nurses from prescribing opiates, the only pain medicine that had been available during the communist years.

Yet despite its economic success, Poland did not become a 'boring' country. Many Poles felt left behind – envious of wealthier Germans, allured by the solace of old, imagined certainties – and so turned to ethnic nationalism to fill the void in their lives. They wanted history. They wanted glory. Above all they wanted someone to blame for their perceived misfortune.

PiS, the so-called Law and Justice party, came to power by exploiting their anxieties. The party, led by twin brothers, campaigned on a strident anti-immigration platform. It claimed that migrants from the Middle East took Polish jobs, even though almost no Muslim refugees had settled in the country. It asserted that they brought cholera and dysentery into Europe, spreading 'various parasites and protozoa'. Then it cemented its rule with bribes – an unaffordable 'Family 500+' baby bonus scheme and a lowered pension age – and set about remaking the country as an illiberal democracy: taking overt control of the media, promoting civil servants according to their political allegiance, abolishing the state council tasked with fighting racism. To defend its attacks on civil society, the Law and Justice party spun a story that the transition from communist dictatorship had been a sham, and that it alone could protect – and lead – Poland.

At the age of forty-seven, Kryśka returned to political activism, outraged by the government's deception, as well as its exploitation of a tragic air disaster. In 2010 a Polish air force Tupolev Tu-154 crashed in thick fog killing one of the twin brothers as well as his wife, the chiefs of the army, navy and air force, the head of the National Bank and ninety other senior officials and veterans. The surviving twin became the country's leader and set about turning his brother into a martyr. On the same day every *month* (not just the annual anniversary), Jarosław Kaczyński – the surviving brother – stood in front of Warsaw's Presidential Palace to deliver a speech in honour of the dead, and to whip up fears of 'foreign interference'.

Obywatele RP – Citizens of the Polish Republic, the group that Kryśka would join – began its peaceful protest by holding aloft white roses during Kaczyński's divisive monthly rallies. When he set about politicising the judiciary, she and others paraded into the crowd a banner that quoted his dead brother on the need to 'fiercely guard' the courts' independence.

The leadership's response was swift and brutal. Police ripped down the banner and parliament outlawed demonstrations at regular political events. Within a month hundreds were awaiting trial for flouting the new, unconstitutional law, or for failing to pay its fines.

'We were called Poles of the worst sort,' Kryśka explained. 'We women and men who demonstrated against the governing party were said to have treason in our genes.' She rolled up her sleeve to show me her upper arms, bruised black and purple after police had dragged her away from four successive protests in as many weeks. Kryśka was only of medium height yet she always stood out in a crowd.

'*Jestem gorszego sortu!*' she told me, assuring me that she was among the 'worst sort'. 'It's a badge of honour for us, you know.'

Thirty years ago Poland had played a leading role in the collapse of the Soviet bloc. Solidarność had set the stage for the broader revolt across Eastern Europe. Its post-communist leaders had embraced market democracy, NATO and the European Union. But did most Poles no longer care about defending the principles and practices of a free society? Was the country making its own backwards journey, returning to an inward and illiberal past defined by family, church and home?

'No way,' replied Kryśka, shaking her head.

I feared the real answer was 'Not yet.'

Last November, Kryśka and thirteen other women joined Warsaw's annual Independence Day march. Around them on central Plac

Defilad gathered thousands of young couples, old patriots, families on holiday ... and a core of ultranationalists wearing Iron Cross hoodies and Polish eagle street wear.

As soon as the march began the extremists slid in from the fringes, chanting, '*Biała Europa*!' White Europe! They insinuated themselves into the crowd, perverting its party-like atmosphere, igniting flares to cast the square into smoky crimson light. 'Clean Blood! Pure Poland!' Their green and black flags stained the sea of Polish colours. Aggression was in the air.

'The police were afraid. We were afraid,' Kryśka told me. 'We had appealed to the city to ban the march, knowing that it would be hijacked but they refused, claiming that there was no proof.'

She and her tiny group walked with furled banner near to the front of the 70,000 marchers.

'But not at the very front. If we'd been there they would have killed us.'

At the place where wide Jerusalem Avenue narrowed onto the Poniatowski Bridge, her group – who ranged in age from nineteen to seventy-three years old – turned to face the crowd. They unfurled their long banner and blocked the march. '*Faszyzm STOP!*' it read in bold, red and black, hand-painted letters. Stop fascism!

Around them the crowd juddered to a stop. Two nationalists immediately tried to tear away the banner so the women – wearing woolly hats and Polish armbands – sat down on the pavement. Skinheads cursed them as terrorists, whores, enemies of Poland. A woman held up a cross and shouted: 'Satan is here in the world.' A man in battle fatigues radioed for back-up and within two or three minutes half a dozen heavies in balaclavas – perhaps from the right-wing Ruch Narodowy or Legionaries of Christ – mustered around them. They towered above the women with fists clenched, hurling abuse at them for dishonouring the national day. Red smoke rose from the spitting flares and stung their eyes but the 'Dirty Fourteen' – as they would become known – held their ground, kept on chanting, punching the air in determination.

'*Precz z faszyzmem*!' Down with fascism!

In their anger two of the hooded men started to drag away the encircled protesters, pulling on parka hoods, grabbing arms and legs. One of them, Kasia, was dropped, hit her head and lost consciousness. Another, Elzbieta, was kicked repeatedly in her back. The others again broke free, linked arms and lay down together to sing 'Prayer at Sunrise', their voices quivering with fear. In response the men began to spit at them, shouting more right-wing slogans, their rage drowning out the women's chants.

'Death to enemies of the homeland! Glory to Great Poland!'

In the crowd most families and couples looked on, passive and unthinking; some laughed, one or two snapped photographs, others simply turned away.

'We were alone,' recalled Kryśka.

In a handful of years, encouraged by PiS tolerance of nationalist factions, the Warsaw march has become the world's largest gathering of far-right extremists, drawing fascists from across Europe, Britain and the United States. Kryśka's protest went unreported on government-controlled channels, despite having been filmed by national television. Compliant news editors concentrated instead on Poland's interior minister praising the march as 'a beautiful sight'.

'We are proud that so many Poles have decided to take part in a celebration connected to the Independence Day holiday,' he said on air.

'Meanwhile we've been charged with obstructing a lawful assembly. Can you imagine?' Kryśka told me, back on the street after thirty years, fighting once again for her beliefs. She knew that freedom couldn't be taken for granted, that one had to be vigilant and be ready to act. 'This is a European disease. Unfortunately in my country it is very severe.'

In Warsaw's New Town, on the edge of the infamous ghetto in (or from) which earlier fascists had killed almost half a million Jews, I wondered if an entire nation could be stupid?

After my morning with Kryśka, I needed time to put her story into perspective. A milk bar – a dirt-cheap, canteen-style holdover from an earlier age – seemed a good place to start, unchanged as it was from my last visit and still serving bargain-priced *bigos*, a smoked sausage stew that, the Poles say, 'walks into the mouth'.

At the till the proprietress – in spotted purple pinafore and slippers – took my order. I passed the receipt through the tiled kitchen hatch. Behind a modest half-curtain three women in sleeveless blouses circled a heavy range, stirring pots, singing along with a song on the radio. A sparrow darted through the open door and alighted on the dirty dishes at a second, scullery window. When one of the cooks called out my order, pushing the plate out of the hatch, I found a metal chair at a melamine table beneath a bare light bulb and opened Czesław Miłosz's *A Book in the Ruins*.

'How is it, Chloe, that your pretty skirt/ Is torn so badly by the winds that hurt/ Real people,' the poet and philosopher had written in 1941 near to my unchanging milk bar. 'How is it that your breasts/ Are pierced by shrapnel…?'

In wartime Warsaw the Nazi occupiers had kindled a funeral pyre in the ghetto, wrote Miłosz, yet,

Before the flames had died
the taverns were full again.

In the square beyond my cafe window, an amusement park carousel had turned to the strains of a carnival tune, drowning out the salvos from behind the ghetto wall.

At times wind from the burning
would drift dark kites along
and riders on the carousel
caught petals in mid-air.
That same hot wind
blew open the skirts of the girls
and the crowds were laughing
on that beautiful Warsaw Sunday.

After the war, Miłosz had pondered the question of national stupidity, and the difference between the European and Anglo-American experience. In Europe 'the Spirit of History' had devastated the continent, 'wearing about his neck a chain of severed heads' and instilling a profound understanding of impermanence. In contrast non-Europeans had had a radically different war. Americans and Brits had been spared the wholesale destruction of their homeland and so continued to take for granted the permanence of their way of life. Now over a milky *bar mleczny* coffee, I wondered if national stupidity had come to have more to do with time than geography? With the passing of years, and the men and women who'd lived through the conflict, Poles (like Hungarians) had also begun to forget the twentieth century's bloody lessons.

Kryśka had never been a bystander, never laughed on a carousel while catching singed petals in mid-air. She continued to take risks, guided by her individual conscience. She took to the streets when photographs of six opposition politicians – who'd had the 'audacity' to vote against the government – were strung from a makeshift gallows in a public square. She drew attention to the means by which the ruling party extended its power. She demonstrated against its stringent abortion laws, enacted so as to secure the support of the Church (which demanded, for example, that doctors use the word 'baby' rather than 'foetus' even in the earliest stages of pregnancy). She saw it as her moral duty to protest against the systematic undermining of the legal order.

Yet for all her patriotism, all her dreams, I wondered if she was an exception.

'I – like many others – took advantage of the new opportunities after 1989. I profited from freedom,' she had admitted to me that morning: calm, dignified and compassionate. New opportunities and strong economic growth had shielded her – and many Poles – from the economic crisis. 'But I see now that others were less fortunate than me. I regret that I didn't have my eyes more open, that I didn't do more for them.' She'd paused and I'd noticed a frailness in her eyes. 'Poles are not stupid but we are uneducated: two hundred years of captivity during the Partitions, two world wars, seventy years under the Soviets, and now thirty years of galloping and unfair capitalism. We are not educated in democracy at all.'

In the milk bar the proprietress's slippers shuffled across the black-and-white checked floor, plates clattered into the sink, coins clinked into the till. I left the place empty but for a retiree in a felt hat and the sparrow, which the proprietress swept back onto the street.

In the late afternoon I circled Warsaw's unloved Palace of Culture and Science, Stalin's unforgettable 1955 'gift of friendship' to Poland. Its towering bulk and two of its stone-faced agitators – including a sightless author gazing towards a better tomorrow – were etched in my memory. Inside the socialist realist building, casinos and stylish shops now lined the endless marble hallways. The Marxist theatre troupes and Polish Academy of Socialist Scientists had been consigned to history.

Something else was new. In the square in front of the people's palace – across the road from TK Maxx and Pizza Hut – an 'ordinary' 54-year-old father of two had set himself on fire. On a balmy October afternoon Piotr Szczęsny, a grey haired chemist from Niepołomice, had distributed leaflets indicting the ruling party for its attacks on the rule of law. He wore an autumn-brown sweater and black woollen scarf. He poured flammable liquid over his body and immolated himself.

'I call on you all – do not wait any longer!' his leaflet begged his fellow Poles. 'This government must be changed as fast as possible before it completely destroys our country, before it completely deprives us of freedom.'

Szczęsny wanted his suicide to 'shake the consciences of people' and for 'the entire PiS nomenclature' to acknowledge that 'they have my blood on their hands'. He also wanted them to desist from perpetrating their divisive, inflammatory 'religion of the Smolensk air crash tragedy'. In response, the government-controlled media shrugged him off as mentally unstable.

On the spot where he'd set himself alight – surrounded by dozens of bunched flowers and votive candles – I stared at the paving

stone memorial into which were stamped Szczęsny's last words, '*ja,
zwykły szary człowiek*'.

I, an ordinary grey person.

Above Warsaw the evening breeze drew tiers of cloud across the
sky like runs of staggered curtains: hazy sheers, diaphanous lace,
heavy velvet drapes. Once or twice the veils parted and clear silver
light flooded over the broad avenues and wet paving stones. But
for the most part the clouds massed together, banishing the sun
behind their mottled screen, letting it cast neither shadow nor
clarity, lighting the city but illuminating nothing.

Thirty years ago when I'd first written about Kryśka, I'd changed
both her name and her occupation to disguise her identity, so as
to protect her. I did not suspect that, thirty years on, I'd consider
doing it again, as Poland – 'boring' Poland – stepped into the
unknown, into an era when nothing was certain, filling me with a
sense of awful premonition.

29

Devil's Domain

Poland, the Christ of nations.

Poland, martyred for the sins of man.

Poland, tormented by the devil.

In 1940, 22,000 Polish soldiers, surgeons, lawyers, landowners, fathers and sons were executed by Soviet secret state police – shot in the back of the head, their corpses dumped twelve deep in vast mass graves. All had been herded to that evil place beyond the eastern border. All were killed to wipe out the country's elite.

Seventy years later an aircraft plunged into the fog above the devil's domain. On board were Poland's president and ninety-five other senior officials. On the anniversary of the Katyn massacre they were flying to Smolensk, the nearest airport to the haunted forest. Bad weather made the landing risky but an urgent political incentive drove the president.

Three days earlier Vladimir Putin had stood in that forest, with the Polish president's political rival, Donald Tusk. In a rare demonstration of reconciliation, Putin had admitted that the Soviet crime 'cannot be justified in any way'. Russian and Pole had shaken hands over the graves. Their gesture promised a new era of cooperation between the two countries. It dominated the national news. Now the Polish president simply *had* to reach Katyn. He *had* to be photographed at the graveside. On its final approach, after speaking to his twin brother on the radio telephone, his Tupolev

Tu-154 slammed into the ground 200 metres short of the runway, killing all on board.

> Holy Poland,
> Martyred Poland,
> Pray for us sinners,
> Now and at the hour of our death.

Within hours of the accident, conspiracy theories seized – or were foisted upon – the Polish imagination. There'd been a bomb on board. The pilots had been lured to disaster. The fog around the airport had been artificially produced. None of the claims could be substantiated, but it mattered not for the tragedy – like that of the 1940 massacre – fed the cult of martyrdom, which was then exploited for political ends.

In 2016 *Smolensk* set out to legitimise the false narrative. In the Polish-made movie a fictional journalist named Nina refuses to accept the official version of events. Instead she launches her own investigation, interacting with other actors as well as actual persons, 'proving' that sinister forces caused the crash. Scripted scenes and documentary footage are intercut for dramatic effect: a mysterious 'International No. 1' instructs the presidential Tupolev to descend too low, KGB heavies seize a reporter's camera at the crash site, salvage workers smash the wreck's windows to martial music and the victims' metal coffins are welded shut to hide evidence. Finally, the ghosts of Katyn – dignified and tall in polished Second World War uniforms – greet Poland's newest martyrs to the afterlife, saluting the assassinated president, shaking hands with his dead wife, weeping together at the grave pit.

'I feel I need to make this film, even if it is me against everyone else,' its director Antoni Krauze declared with lashings of hyperbole. 'I intend to show the truth.'

In truth Krauze was far from being alone. As many as half of all Poles had been taken in by one or other of the conspiracy theories, and thousands of them donated money to finance the film. One pensioner gave three lots of ten złoty (about $3), apologising that it was all she could afford. Crowdfunding, topped up in part by the right-wing Smoleńsk 2010 Foundation, kick-started pre-production.

The rest of the budget was less easy to find. The Polish Film Institute – not yet controlled by the ruling PiS – did not fall for the celluloid yarn. No international distributor wanted to invest in it. The actor Marian Opania – who had been asked to play the part of the president – declared in public that he would not appear in a film 'based on lies'. As a result the project teetered on the brink of collapse, until an anonymous donor coughed up $1.5 million.

On completion *Smolensk* was awarded the 'Honourable Patronage of the President of Poland' (despite the president's wife and daughter missing its premiere to take in a new Woody Allen movie). It also picked up a record seven Polish 'Serpent' anti-Oscars, including worst film, worst director, worst female role and most embarrassing scene of the year. For all the controversy, one fact above all was undeniably true about *Smolensk*. It was a real turkey.

There were three of them, and I'd expected only one. Six months earlier he had flown to London to interview me about my books for his weekly arts programme. When I'd rung him to arrange a Warsaw meeting, he didn't mention his friends. Nor that he was now head of the network.

'Our duty is to regain Poland,' he said, pouring a fine Château Gruaud Larose (2ème cru, 2007). He was sandy-haired and pale of eye. I'll call him Janek.

'Think of it as a crusade,' suggested Mateusz. Again, not his real name. His sharp and craggy face brought to mind a prizefighter. He had just been promoted as well, from reporter to deputy controller of a 'rival' channel.

'A battle between good and evil,' specified the third man. He was different. He didn't work in television. He wasn't even a Pole. He was American.

All three men were in their mid-thirties. All wore leather bomber jackets. All were erudite, energetic and utterly sure of themselves. All had been thrust overnight into power.

'Europe is a leviathan overrun by the mass migration of Muslims,' stated the American: preppy button-down Hilfiger shirt, educated

Midwest accent, hyperspeed delivery. 'Poland will not surrender itself to this cultural suicide.'

We were in a lavish media wine bar near to Warsaw's trendy Plac Zbawiciela, home of skinny jeans, coffee baristas and TV studios. Around us well-to-do executive producers huddled at cosy tables in soft pools of light. Up-and-coming directors asked white-aproned waiters to uncork bottles of Pauillac and Pomerol. A news anchorman balanced on a bar stool by the open grill waiting to be called for the mid-evening bulletin.

As plates of tapas were laid on our table, the American said he'd read my earlier books and would like to discuss them. But I knew that they didn't want to chat about plot devices or character development. I understood they wanted to change my mind.

Over spicy *patatas bravas*, the American asked what newspapers I read. When I told him he shook his head in mock pity.

'Lies,' he said, dipping a *croqueta* into the tomato salsa. 'The people have had enough of mainstream media's lies.'

'The people?' I said, incredulous. I thought for a moment that he was taking the mickey.

'Your whole alphabet soup – *New York Times*, *Washington Post*, *Guardian* and the BBC – are history, elbowed out by infinite YouTube channels, infinite Twitter feeds. The people will no longer be silenced.'

I disagreed with him of course, arguing that 'the people' needed objective reportage and journalistic integrity now more than ever. How else could voters see through the fake facts and bogus promises?

'Journalistic integrity is dead,' replied the hack-cum-controller Mateusz, putting down his glass to interrupt me. 'There is no such thing any more.'

'We on the right are totally open about this,' said the American in cool confidence. 'We don't hide our personal bias. We're transparent and honest with our audience.'

'Here in Poland we fight for Polish ownership,' added network boss Janek, refilling our glasses.

'Meaning no dissenting views?' I asked flatly, thinking of the government's disinformation campaigns and state television's salacious, thinly sourced attacks on opponents. A few months later Gdańsk's liberal mayor Paweł Adamowicz – so often defamed as a thief and a homophile – would be murdered, live on air.

'Our country and our family come first, not the interests of globalists,' Janek continued. 'We'll drive a stake through the heart of the Brussels vampire.' His eyes seemed too far apart.

'We're fighting on the battlefield of ideas,' said the American while nibbling on cider-cooked chorizo. 'Politics is propaganda and information is a weapon.'

I sat back but couldn't make myself comfortable. I had wanted to meet Janek, to throw myself into his virtual lion's den. To be frank I also hoped to change him, or at least to remind him of the importance of pluralism and a free press. But as hate speech seeped into public discourse, he seemed content to toe a party line, shaping an expedient narrative to sustain the elite (and to empower a new one), while purporting to reflect the will of 'the people'.

'I suppose this new book of yours, about Europe's last thirty years, won't be a comedy?' ventured Janek.

'It isn't easy to raise a chuckle, given what I've just heard.'

'I'd be happy to check over the manuscript for inaccuracies,' cockily offered the American with no trace of irony.

Thirty years ago Poland had been a place reborn, free to shape its future. Adam Michnik, one of the leaders of Solidarność, had called for liberty, fraternity and normality. He wanted a revolution for a constitution, not for a paradise. But since 2015, the Law and Justice party has undermined the bodies that protect that constitution, turning parliament's lower house into a rubber stamp, forcing almost half of Supreme Court judges to retire.

'Achieve power by democratic means then kill democracy. You know you're not the first to hit on that idea?' I reminded my smart and stylish crusaders, likening their support for PiS to the betrayal of Poland by the Nazi's willing helpers.

'That's something you don't understand,' snapped the American. His hand shot out, unexpectedly strong, seizing my wrist. 'Do you think the old communists were just magicked away after the fall of the Wall? Poland's lurch to democracy was a sordid, stitched-up business deal.' His whole body stiffened, his movements became sharp and spiteful. He was volatile and belligerent. He hissed, 'At last we are rid of those apparatchiks and Solidarity has-beens, and their corrupt, nepotistic judiciary.'

On our table appeared a trio of fried oysters encased in crunchy batter and served on a bed of wilted spinach. The network boss offered one to me as the American explained that 'meaning and purpose' had brought him to Poland. His Jewish grandfather had been a Polish poet who'd fallen foul of the post-war leadership, he said. He'd emigrated to the States but – in the McCarthy years – could find work only as a motor mechanic. His poems, which somehow managed to juxtapose Polish folk tradition with interstate highways and car parts, had attracted little attention, even after he was crushed to death under a falling Oldsmobile V8 engine. The loud-mouthed prepster had grown up idolising the grandfather he'd never known, blaming the untimely death on both big government and the Warsaw Pact. In his late twenties, after spells at Princeton, in a Washington lobbying firm and at a Trump campaign office, he'd come to Poland in search of his roots, possessed by a dream of tribal loyalty.

'Poland is made up of Polish people. That may seem obvious to you but I'd never lived in a homogeneous country,' he said, calming himself by machine-gunning facts at me: 7 per cent of the people in the US aren't citizens, Mexican illegals account for 13 per cent of all crimes, Latinos commit nearly 12 per cent of all murders. He left me no time to reply or verify his claims but rushed on, 'As soon as I arrived here I wanted to be a part of this exclusive club, to help to make its history.'

Of course his alt-right insider knowledge made him of value to the PiS, and the leadership ensured that he did feel both useful and at home. Ministers began to consult him on the media and Breitbart. He brought access to analytics and specialised polling data to help them to target voters. He took every opportunity to big himself up, his arrogance tempered by nervy self-consciousness. 'As Donald once said to me, if you'll forgive the namedrop…' In no more than a couple of blog posts he found himself invited to the right parties, bought a Gucci dinner jacket and spoke about the historical parallels between Polish and American politics.

Poland had long been divided between *kosmopolici* and *patrioci*, he told me. 'Cosmopolitans and patriots are like coast liberals and ordinary Americans.'

Kosmopolici were an elite who derived their power from outside Poland, from 'imperial' Moscow, Berlin or Brussels, explained network boss Janek. They 'suppressed' ordinary 'patriotic' Poles.

'Since the eighteenth century it's been an historical struggle, that's now been overturned here and in America.'

Of course he didn't see himself as *kosmopolici*, despite his elitist education and designer dinner jacket. He was a patriot and a nationalist. The party even helped him to find a pliant publisher willing to print his grandfather's poems.

'To further US–Polish understanding,' he said without a flicker of self-mockery. 'Maybe you'd consider writing an endorsement to go on the jacket?'

The three 'Right hipsters' – as they called themselves with only half a smile – seemed at ease in their new skin, relaxed after another day's battle with pesky bogeymen. No mention was made of the independent journalists and programme makers who'd lost their jobs to make way for them, fired on the pretext of 'violating the interests of the nation'. No responsibility would be taken for the disaster that they were bringing on the country.

Over battered calamares, our conversation turned from politics to books, football (deputy controller Mateusz supported Lechia Gdańsk) and – inevitably – *Smolensk*. I told them that the film's producer, Maciej Pawlicki – who I'd met earlier that day – had said that the crash was 'the most important event in modern Polish history, for better or for worse'.

Janek nodded in agreement. 'In fact there are two tragedies: the crash itself and its treatment by the Left,' he said.

'Absolutely correct,' confirmed Mateusz. 'It wasn't the accident that changed me but the opposition's disrespect of its victims.'

He went on to explain that, within weeks of the tragedy, an opposition marcher had carried a banner through central Warsaw declaring: 'One duck down, one more to go.' (The root of the name Kaczyński is *kaczka*, the Polish word for duck.)

I pointed out that I'd heard the same story but could find no proof of it, apart from a rash of offensive memes online.

'It convinced me,' replied Mateusz.

'But it could be fake news.'

'If it's not true, it should be,' said the American.

All three of them truly believed that the Smolensk crash had been orchestrated – or at least abetted – on Moscow's orders, either by planting a bomb on the aircraft or by air-traffic controllers misleading the pilot.

'There is no doubt that the Kremlin wanted to be rid of the president because he was anti-Russian,' said Janek, pouring out the last of the wine. 'They created a fog within a fog.'

Quick-fire arguments then unfolded on destroyed and corrupted evidence as well as sealed coffins and the aircraft's black boxes. Once again I had no time to confirm or contest their facts, and no one was able to explain to me why the government hadn't released the recording of the last mobile phone call between the twins. I felt mobbed, overwhelmed by so much detail and so many rumours that, come the end of evening, I returned to fundamentals.

'Do you fear Poland becoming a one-party state?' I asked them.

'The real question is, do we need an opposition?' replied the American, almost impressive in his complete sincerity. 'There are such diverse opinions in the PiS.'

'And what about the party's tolerance of the far right?' I said, thinking of Kryśka and the Independence Day march.

'Our strength keeps them out of power.'

'As in Berlin in 1933?'

As we spoke I began to imagine a time – a society – without any agreed or verifiable forms of the truth. I asked if they knew that Tomáš Masaryk, the first president of independent Czechoslovakia, had likened democracy to a discussion, with the warning that 'a real discussion is possible only if people trust each other and if they try fairly to find the truth'. I don't think they bothered to listen to me. Certainly, I wasn't going to change them, no matter what I said. I bought neither their vision of 'licensed' journalists nor an agenda set by 'the people' (meaning *their* people). I felt an unbearable sorrow.

We finished the octopus and sparred with exaggerated civility over the remaining *gambas*. I took a last mouthful of the Gruaud Larose. Janek called for the bill then turned to me to say, 'Next time you are in Poland, let me know if there's anything you want. Anything at all.'

I didn't pay for the meal. In fact, no one seemed to pay for it. The 'Right hipsters' chatted to the owner of the wine bar and clapped him on the back. Janek the network boss then headed to a vodka bar to meet his girlfriend. Deputy-controller Mateusz threw on his bomber jacket and went off to a football match. The American gave me his business card (with a parliament address) and offered again to look at my manuscript. When I declined, he advised me not to use their real names in the text, adding for dramatic effect: 'This meeting never happened.'

I walked back to my hotel alone, looking over my shoulder, in no doubt that the devil drinks vintage Bordeaux.

30

Dementia

I woke to peals of bells, ringing from St Mary's gothic tower, tinkling above the ochre-domed Royal Chapel, chiming in St Katherine's fifty-bell carillon. The Old Town Hall clock beat out the patriots' anthem as Adam and Eve tolled the hour on the basilica's fifteenth-century astronomical timepiece. I didn't need my alarm.

I was back on the Baltic, a thin sea drizzle washing across the mullion window, softening my view of slender steeples and red-brick city walls. My room under the eaves was small, the bed large. I planned to take a few days to wander Gdańsk's Royal Way, to linger over coffee at the old port, to avoid argument.

My morning started well enough, over an idle breakfast of scrambled eggs, fried kielbasa sausage and potato cakes. My hosts were an elderly couple, retired teachers who rented out a spare room to augment their pensions. He refilled my coffee cup as she came in from the small back garden to arrange another vase of fresh flowers on the table.

'Thank you,' I said. Already there were four bunches set out before me.

Her husband said: 'That's enough now, *kotku*,' but she seemed not to hear him and turned back into the drizzle.

'I grow them and she picks them,' he sighed. 'Then she forgets what she's done. It goes right out of her head.'

I watched with a strange fascination as the woman pinched off the last of the morning's fresh blooms, arranging them carefully in her hand. Her movements reminded me of an animal following its daily routine. When she had finished not a single flower was left in their pocket-sized garden.

'Oh, did I do these?' said the woman when she returned indoors and saw the vases. 'Why is my hair wet?' she asked her husband. When she noticed me she said, 'Who are you? Who do you belong to?'

Her husband explained that I was a guest and that I was travelling alone.

'Then I must get you some flowers,' she said and went outdoors.

'Sometimes she even forgets my name,' he told me as if to share his pain. 'She lays out bread and cheese for our son, saying he'll want a snack when he comes home after his shift.' He paused then added, 'Our son moved to Australia twenty-five years ago.' The man looked out of the window at his wife, now picking leaves. 'What do we have if we don't have memories?' he asked.

Gdańsk, once the largest and wealthiest city of Poland, revealed itself in faux medieval lanes, fake princely gates and flagstone squares ringed by gabled merchant's houses reminiscent of Amsterdam. Its Renaissance doorways were capped with marriage stones and lintels carved with knights and sea serpents. Its salty air echoed with seagull cries and the rattle of wheeled suitcases on cobbles. Its restored Upland Gate had been embellished with three heraldic crests: Russian angel, Prussian unicorn and the lions of Gdańsk. Across the centuries, armies and occupiers had ebbed and flowed through the city, as they had all around the Baltic. Pomerelian dukes, Hanseatic traders and Nazi *Gauleiter* had all left their mark, until the Red Army washed them all away. Its ruined centre was rebuilt after the war, including St Mary's, one of the largest brick churches in the world. I climbed its massive tower, past its bells 'Gratia Dei' and 'Ave Maria', to gaze down on a picture-perfect cityscape of ersatz Flemish courtyards and Italianate facades, and caught sight of the real Gdańsk.

Beyond the city wall, monumental Teutonic schools hunkered across from crumbling modernist blocks and a decayed concrete flak tower, now the Klubogaleria nightclub. Between them broken pavements eddied and rolled like the Baltic itself, and pigeons washed themselves in the bath-sized potholes. One step further and I was at the Martwa Wisła or 'dead Vistula', the branch of the river that had opened Poland to the world. Here the Prussians had built a shipyard for their navy and German industrialists launched dredgers, trawlers and battleships. Dozens of U-boats had taken to the sea from its slipways and, in the communist years, the yard had grown to become the fifth-largest ship producer in the world. Here too the end of the twentieth century had begun.

In 1980 Gdańsk shipyard workers – including electrician Lech Wałęsa – laid down tools in protest against the firing of a crane operator, as well as plunging living standards and rising food prices. At Gate No. 2 of the then Lenin Shipyards, Wałęsa – fiery and affable with distinctive walrus moustache – inspired the strikers to go further. His demand for free trade unions (and press freedom) swept along the coast, closing ports and factories, then down the Silesian mines, paralysing the economy. After three emotional weeks, the government gave in to the protesters. Within a year some ten million Poles had joined Solidarność. Within a decade – in spite of an interval of brutal martial law and the arrest of 10,000 union members – Poles had dismantled the old order. They forged a model for compromise between ruler and ruled, and Wałęsa became the country's first freely elected post-war president.

To many, Wałęsa's negotiation for the withdrawal of Soviet troops marked the real end of the Second World War. So it was appropriate that now, in the shadow of the shipyard's chimneys and cranes, an extraordinary new museum to that war should thrust upwards out of the earth.

I stepped into its skewed glass and terracotta-panelled cube, and dropped into the four-storey-deep concrete bunker that lay beneath it. Around me sombre underground exhibition halls fanned out at unsettling angles: the Russian Revolution, Hitler's 'racial community', Japanese imperialism, air raids, death camps and the Battle of Britain. A wall-size map signed by Stalin and

Ribbentrop sliced Poland in half. In a black room entitled 'People Like Us' hung the framed portraits of hundreds of Holocaust victims.

In this haunting space, physical depth echoed emotional depth. Far below the sunbeams that glanced off its sheer walls, I paused to consider Łódź ghetto banknotes, minute figurines carved from toothbrushes at Ravensbrück concentration camp and doughy shards of china melted by the atomic blast at Hiroshima. The Gdańsk museum did not celebrate military heroism. It didn't propagate a patriotic, official chronology. Instead it focused on civilians – European, Asian and Middle Eastern – who'd endured terror, humiliation, hunger, bombardment, slave labour and forced mass migration. It recalled forgotten or marginalised victims from around the globe: 3 million Soviet POWs murdered – most of them starved to death – in German captivity; 2.7 million Chinese civilians lost during Imperial Japan's 'kill all, loot all, burn all' *sanko sakusen* operation; hundreds of thousands of Serbs, Jews and Roma exterminated by Croatia's Ustaša. The astonishing subterranean building was a *Gesamtkunstwerk*, a complete work of art, unlike any I had seen before, but the man who had overseen its creation was not there. He'd been fired.

'We inherited the museum six months ago,' said Aleks Maslowski, the museum's new press officer, an intense, distrustful, squirrel-faced man with an edge of anger in his voice. 'Its displays were *international*,' he went on, all but spitting the word. 'It taught that war is a *bad* thing,' he huffed, looking at his watch, ticking with impatience, making me aware that he had more important things to do. 'Now the message will be changed. We need to teach the Polish people that they must be prepared to defend our home.' He paused to emphasise: 'This is a *Polish* museum, financed by *Polish* taxpayers, so it must reflect the *Polish* perspective.'

In the exhibition I had noticed the new regime's first dozen changes, tacked on like emoji smileys on Goya's *Disasters of War*. Polish heroes were feted. New exhibits on resistance to Nazi Germany and the Western Allies' 'betrayal' of the country had replaced displays on the war in Asia. Victories were emphasised over pain.

But the most shocking 'correction' was saved for the final room. Originally a series of documentary clips had been projected above a stretch of the Berlin Wall, linking the war to the present day, from the arms race and Kennedy's assassination to Donbas and Syria. Mao Zedong had been juxtaposed with the Beatles, Vietnam with the Warsaw Pact, Polish strikers with moon shots. US helicopter gunships had come face to face with Tiananmen Square tanks. Taliban fighters had swept across Afghanistan as African refugees drifted in the Mediterranean. A weeping Aleppo father clutched his bloodied, dying son as the folk ballad 'House of the Rising Sun' warned, 'Oh mother, tell your children, not to do what I have done...'

Now, instead of a salutary anti-war message, a slick and derivative *Call of Duty* animation flashed across the screens. Above the real barbed wire, a cartoonish Polish martyr fought to hold back invaders. He flew a Hurricane against the Luftwaffe, survived (or at least respawned in) a Siberian gulag and led the Warsaw Uprising from a hi-tech *Matrix*-like base.

'We break the German enigma code, saving the lives of millions and in exchange for all that we do, we are betrayed, abandoned by the West behind the Iron Curtain,' trumpeted a brassy narrator, championing both victimhood and martyrdom. 'But we don't give up, despite being left on our own.' Then in a stagey visual finale, Polish shipyard workers in yellow hard hats knock down the Wall and Poland prevails 'because we do not beg for freedom, we fight for it'.

In front of my eyes, history was being rewritten.

'This process will never be finished,' press officer Aleks insisted when I asked him about the tacky, animated *Unconquered* video. 'We will find new facts. The displays must be changed whenever is needed,' he added without a hint of contrition.

'The story of the museum is the story of modern Poland,' said ousted director Paweł Machcewicz when we met weeks later, far

away from Gdańsk. After his dismissal he'd taken refuge in Berlin
and we met there in his temporary, sparse, stark white office. On
the desk in front of him lay a copy of Galasso Scotini's *Politics of
Memory* as well as his own book *Museum*. 'Our history is again
exploited as a political weapon.'

Since 1945, the monolithic mythology of the Red Army's glory –
and heroic communist resistance to Nazism – had been extolled
across Eastern Europe. That political tale crumbled along with the
Berlin Wall, in the same year that Machcewicz graduated into 'a
miracle'.

'After university I realised that I could do anything, become
anything: journalist, academic, historian,' he told me. His face was
long and lean, his lips pronounced, his shirt checked and his blazer
blue. 'I chose to be an historian so as to play a part in writing true
Polish history.'

His career ran in parallel with the new national narrative:
working as a research analyst at the Institute of History of the Polish
Academy of Sciences, writing books on the Cold War, serving at
the new Institute of National Remembrance. As the director of its
Bureau of Public Education, he encouraged the acknowledgement
of wrongdoing, as in the opening of Służba Bezpieczeństwa secret
police files. Alongside others of his generation, he was determined
to shape 'the new, democratic, independent Poland'.

'It was a heady time, a high point of Polish self-consciousness,'
he said, offering coffee, setting aside the morning to talk to
me. 'We were electrified by the excitement of truth-telling and
reconciliation.'

But then the Law and Justice party came to power, and recast the
Institute of National Remembrance as a tool for an authoritarian
assault on culture.

'When I saw their intention, I immediately resigned from
my post at the Institute.'

Machcewicz believed that Poles had something important to
say, both to themselves and to Europe. In the newspaper *Gazeta
Wyborcza*, he wrote that 'the most tragic conflict in the history of
humanity' had shaped Polish identity, as it had shaped the identities

of many other nations. He said that Poles needed to learn more about it 'to understand the way we are today'.

Poland's then prime minister, Donald Tusk, read the article and asked Machcewicz to create a special war museum in Gdańsk.

'Such an opportunity comes only once in the lifetime of an historian, and not to every historian,' he said with a laugh.

From the start the museum set out to transcend national boundaries as well as to show how the war had impacted individuals. Its collection would include thousands of items donated by both the public and by institutions: buttons and belt buckles retrieved from Katyn graves, the keys to Jewish homes (in the 1941 Jedwabne pogrom, some Poles had tormented and murdered Jews with the complicity of the German Ordnungspolizei), a cattle wagon used by the Soviets to transport Poles to Siberian gulags and by the Nazis to send them to Auschwitz. Through its exhibits visitors would come to understand that war does not lie in a remote past. The undertaking absorbed eight years of Machcewicz's life and some $130 million of taxpayers' money, until Tusk's party fell from power. Immediately PiS sought to 'liquidate' it.

'It was – and is – the largest historical museum in Poland but the government claimed that it wasn't patriotic enough,' Machcewicz emphasised with both defiance and an air of the hunted. 'PiS wanted to use it for propaganda purposes, to promote the idea of Polish heroism, martyrdom and uniqueness.'

The new government demanded extensive changes, including the repackaging of facts. For example, although the Soviet Union and Germany had suffered the greatest loss of life in the war, in order to portray Poles as the greater victim, they wanted deaths to be listed as a percentage of population.

'If I'd agreed, Poland would have come top of such a list, having lost 20 per cent of its people. But the figure is contentious as it includes Polish Jews, some of whom were murdered by their fellow countrymen. I refused to change a single detail of the exhibition under their pressure.'

As a result, the regime cut the museum's funding. They accused Machcewicz of overspending on building works, of sabotage and of working as an agent of Brussels and Berlin. They even conjured up a controversial law 'to defend Poland's reputation from historical inaccuracies' and thereby punish anyone who mentioned Polish complicity in Nazi crimes (such as the Jedwabne pogrom). Finally, as the museum became an ideological and political flash point, the regime fired him.

'They behaved like occupation forces, seizing and taking control of territory,' he said, containing his emotions while recalling their barbaric methods. 'Five years ago no Pole could have imagined that something like this could happen.'

But that wasn't the end of it. In an effort to defame and demoralise Machcewicz, the Central Anti-Corruption Bureau – a kind of political police invented by the first Kaczyński government – began to call at his home and intimidate his family. Then a criminal investigation was initiated against him and he was menaced by a charge of corruption with the possibility of up to eight years in prison, despite there being no evidence against him.

To tell the true story, Machcewicz fought back with appeals and his new book, *Museum*.

'I don't feel defeated by the government. These attacks are their revenge for failing to defeat me,' he said. 'In fact, I feel it is a victory. Half a million visitors saw the exhibition before the regime took it over and started to change it.'

He went on, 'Young people today are the first generation who may not have any family recollection of the war. So the museum's first task was to convey some basic knowledge as schools are not fulfilling this task in a sufficient way. On a deeper level we wanted young and old alike to become emotionally involved, to understand what war is, what violence is, what suffering is. We wanted to affect their values. I believe that has been achieved, half a million times.'

We spoke through the morning about responsibility, moral courage and politicians who retell stories of the past to justify their power. We looked back at moments in the twentieth century when one party eliminated its opposition and took control of the police and courts. I said it was no wonder that the PiS regime especially disliked his exhibit on the rise of 1930s nationalism.

'It has always been possible to destroy democracy from within,' replied Paweł Machcewicz. 'The difference today – in Europe at least – is that there is no direct physical violence.'

'Not yet,' I said.

'*That* is why it's so important to defend the museum,' he emphasised. 'To show that the war isn't a closed chapter, that it isn't the past. The propensity to violence is inside us; it is part of the human condition. Our task – as responsible and cognisant individuals – is somehow to avoid the repetition of such a nightmare.'

That night it poured in Gdańsk. Crocodiles of umbrellas skirted puddles in the half-light. Older locals stayed indoors, behind curtains drawn against the damp dark, while younger Danzigers stepped out, shaking off the wet like dogs inside candle-lit cafes. I lingered among them, over ginger tea, waiting for the torrent to subside.

It takes time to build an authoritarian regime, I thought, but in Poland democracy has been undermined at breakneck speed. As in Russia and Hungary, from which the Kaczyński twins took their lead, the country has come to be ruled by one man who claims that he alone speaks for 'the people'. He has eliminated his foes and gutted the democratic institutions that constrain him. He works to polarise the country, turning Pole against Pole to prevent them from uniting against him and defending their democracy. He exploits the myth of Smolensk for – whatever the truth – the tragedy serves him.

Of course a majority of Poles voted Law and Justice into power. The electorate chose to belong to the nation – a more primitive form of collective identity – rather than Europe's postmodern vision of community. But how could they – a free people – then allow their nation to be dismantled? How did they stomach the party's comic-book world view?

At times Poland struck me as an unknowable place, secrecy ingrained in it by centuries of occupation. Yet at the same time the regime's intentions are plain to see. Journalists and judges who want to keep their jobs now understand not to violate 'the interests of the nation'. The Smolensk crash investigation continues to be debased (the greatest cover-up 'in the history of the world' according to the PiS defence minister). New schoolbooks no longer name Lech Wałęsa as an important twentieth-century democrat, claiming instead that the true heirs of Solidarność are the Kaczyńskis.

'I am unsure whether they are enemies of Poland, traitors, agents or complete fools,' Wałęsa said in a recent interview, calling the PiS leaders narrow-minded demagogues who sow discord and incite hatred. 'They do not care what damage they cause as long as it helps them to win elections.'

As the rain eased off, I shrugged on my coat and wove back along the rain-slicked cobbles and beneath the Green Gate (Wałęsa's private office is in a room above one of its arched passages). On the Motława embankment, where sailing ships had once unloaded their cargo, two or three damp buskers vied for the attention of the evening's last tourists. I lowered my head to hurry past the riverfront cafes until I heard, 'Give me a word and I'll sing you a song.'

'Any word?' I asked.

'Any word,' replied the man.

His approach caught my attention. He had brown eyes and the sort of thin, colourless face that's so easily forgotten, so I stopped to look at him. He was no older than twenty-five and – I guessed – out of work. He stood about six feet tall with a thin beard, thin body and straggly dark hair. He wore wire spectacles. He was nobody's concern, or so I imagined. At his feet was a cardboard sign 'Your Song – 10 zł'.

'Love? Home? Heartbreak?' he prompted as if to help me to decide, stepping forward and unzipping his guitar case. On it raindrops glistened under the gaslight.

'I remember,' I said.

'That's two words,' he replied. When I laughed he added, with a crinkly smile, 'That'd be an extra 10 złoty.'

'Deal,' I said, reaching for my wallet.

He took the notes, tucked them carefully into his breast pocket and stared at me. 'I remember,' he repeated in English and then

Polish. *Pamiętam*. He turned to look out at the water and then he
started to sing.

'*Tak niewiele żądam, Tak niewiele pragnę*,' he warbled, strumming
his guitar. '*Tak niewiele widziałem …*'

I understood none of the words but I sensed his emotion, which
surprised me given the damp night and modest fee. He wasn't
begging, wasn't relying on handouts, but rather offering me words
in an exchange.

'*Tak niewiele myślę, Tak niewiele znaczę …*'

As he sang I couldn't help but wonder if his father had worked
in the Lenin Shipyard, standing alongside Wałęsa to change the
future. I imagined that his old man had then lost his job, laid off
in the first waves of privatisation and instead of the gift of freedom,
had found himself collecting unemployment benefits. I wondered
if he had begun to long for a lost life of yore.

'*Wolność kocham i rozumiem, Wolności …*'

'Your song,' said the proud, thin-faced young man when he had
finished. 'That's all I have to offer.'

I returned to the elderly couple's little house. My host was waiting
up, having put his wife to bed. It's the happiest moment of her
day, he told me, and I imagined the poor, forgetful woman tucked
under the covers and drifting off into contented oblivion.

I'd recorded the busker's song on my phone and played it back
in the cramped kitchen, asking the elderly man to translate for
me. Rings of withered flower petals lay on the table top around his
wife's sad little vases. After a minute he said, 'But there's nothing
here about remembering. It's an old song.'

'I don't ask for too much,' the busker had sung, 'I don't want
too much,/ I may lose everything …'

His song – my song – was 'Kocham wolność' or 'I Love Freedom'
by Bogdan Łyszkiewicz, the Polish John Lennon.

'But freedom, I love and understand it,/ Freedom, I'm not able
to give it away…'

Overhead the bells of Gdańsk tolled as night closed in on Poland.

Germany

31

Beyond the Horizon

Here it began, and ended. Here at the flashpoint of the world rose the Berlin Wall, and here it fell away as an historical aberration. Here in 1989 I made a trail of footprints across the smoothed sand of no-man's-land, believing that Europe had changed for ever.

I'd first seen the heinous barrier half a lifetime earlier. At the heart of the continent had been watchtowers, barbed wire and Grenztruppen border guards instructed to shoot fellow citizens who wanted to live under a different system. The sight of that great divide, between a capitalist West and a communist East, had shaken me to the core. I'd stood for hours on the wooden observation platform overlooking Potsdamer Platz and the Brandenburg Gate. I'd stared in silence across the death strip, stunned that a clash of ideas could be set in cement at the centre of a city.

Then one cool November night came the most unexpected and joyous moment of the century. *Ossis* and *Wessis*, East and West, danced together on the Wall, holding hands, waving sparklers, united in jubilation for the new beginning. Swarms of buzzing Trabants – the cardboard car for comrades, belching blue smoke, breaking down, being pushed – circled gangs of soldiers dismantling the concrete slabs. At Checkpoint Charlie the Russian cellist Mstislav Rostropovich – who had been harassed, intimidated and stripped of his citizenship by the Soviets – played an impromptu Bach suite. Bouquets of flowers covered the windscreens of police

vans. British squaddies served cups of scalding tea to the rippling
crowd. As they drank and sang, the East Germans glanced back at
the barrier, hardly believing they were finally free. Soon the slabs of
white concrete would be stacked in neat piles. The barbed wire was
coiled into tumbleweed balls. Within a year the entire Wall – bar
a few token stretches – truly vanished, leaving in its place only a
discreet line of paving stones. The two halves of the country were
reunited and Germans called the change *die Wende*.

The turning point.*

'How could such a dark period of my life have become a musical?'
laughed Thomas Brussig, the post-*Wende* wunderkind novelist and
screenwriter. 'I'll never get over the miracle.'

I'd known Brussig for more than a dozen years, having first met
him soon after the publication of his comedy of terrors *Heroes Like
Us*. The first great unification novel, it told the story of an East
German Forrest Gump (and wannabe Stasi spy) whose birth was
induced by the rumblings of Soviet tanks on their way to crush the
Prague Spring (his mother had paused in her labour to point them
in the right direction) and whose penis was responsible for the fall
of the Berlin Wall.

'*Heroes Like Us* brought a kind of relief that jokes could be made
about totalitarianism,' Brussig told me. 'And that such a crazy story
could be brewed from those dark days.'

Spring had arrived with me in Berlin. Lime-green buds burst on
the linden trees along Bornholmer Strasse and dappled shadows
whispered across the faces of the grand, ranked apartment blocks.
Sparrows fluttered and chattered in the dark ivy. A pair of dancing
shoes lay abandoned on top of a postbox.

---

* German reunification was a moment of unique historical significance, wrote historian
Ian Kershaw in *Roller-Coaster: Europe, 1950–2017*: 'It marked the symbolic end of an era in
which the German nation state had first inflicted unimaginable suffering and destruction
on Europe, then, divided for forty years, in its western part at least, had contributed
greatly to building the foundations of a new Europe resting on peace, prosperity and
stability.'

On that balmy morning, Brussig met me on Bösebrücke, the first border crossing to be opened in November 1989. It was still early when he mounted the S-Bahn steps and shook my hand. We planned to spend the day together, walking along the line of the old Iron Curtain, across the city's waist, to reach Potsdamer Platz where his 'miracle' Cold War musical – *Hinterm Horizont* – had played to sell-out audiences for the best part of a decade.

'As a young man I was fascinated by the West,' he said as we set off along Norweger Strasse towards Mauerpark. 'In the West one could read any book, go to any university. But it was a place I knew I'd never be able to visit, as long as there was a Wall.'

Brussig had grown up to the east of Mauerpark, a large linear park which in its time served as a drill ground for the Prussian army, a railway station and the death strip between the French and Soviet sectors. Around the same time I'd lived on the western side of the Wall. In those days neither of us had imagined the city – let alone the country – reunited.

'I did dream of free speech, of free travel, but I was unwilling to make that jump into the dark, to try to leave and risk imprisonment. Also I didn't want to be corrupted by the system.'

Nevertheless Brussig found the courage to join many East German protest marches, often fearing – as he closed his front door behind him – that he might never see his apartment again.

He also listened to Bruce Springsteen.

'In 1988 I had a job as a porter at the Palast Hotel. As I earned tips in West German Marks I could afford to buy a Walkman, and five Springsteen cassettes. I listened to them over and over every day on the way to and from work. When Springsteen came to East Berlin it was a concert I'd waited a lifetime to hear.'

That July 'the Boss' had played to 100,000 fans at the Weissensee cycling track, across town from the Mauerpark. The authorities had invited one of the West's most popular musicians to the people's republic in the hope that the event would vent mounting pressure for reform. The state newspaper *Neues Deutschland* championed Springsteen as a working-class American who 'attacks social wrongs and injustices in his homeland' with 'hard and unadorned songs about the shady side of American reality'. The article failed to mention the anxieties that mark his songs, and his rebellion against authority.

His four-hour concert, the largest ever staged in East Germany, did not relieve tensions. '*Es ist schön, in Ost-Berlin zu sein*,' Springsteen had called out with a clear political message. 'I'm not here for any government. I've come to play rock 'n' roll for you in the hope that one day all the barriers will be torn down.'

Then he launched into Bob Dylan's 'Chimes of Freedom', helping to inflame the spirit of rebellion, said Brussig.

'It was a big event but it wasn't big enough,' he told me, his aquiline features – pointed nose and slightly hooded eyes – accentuated by sparse, receding hair. 'By then we'd started to imagine new possibilities.'

The Berlin Wall was never a neat and orderly construction but rather a zigzagging atrocity, shearing across streets and through neighbourhoods, dividing families, built to stop East Germans escaping to the western half of the city. It encircled the west, cutting it off from the rest of the country, yet paradoxically it was the *Ossies* who were trapped.

Brussig and I turned onto Bernauer Strasse. Along it, yawning caretakers opened doors, raised electric shutters, lit their first cigarette of the day. Overhead balconies sprouted window boxes and a woman cleaned her windows. Every apartment building seemed to house one or two small businesses: a physiotherapist, a Chinese acupuncturist, a vet. In one – a reptile specialist – a metre-long albino snake sunned itself in the window. Children darted by it on their way to school, lugging colourful, oversized backpacks. A young mother cycled over the tram tracks towards a kindergarten, her toddler balanced on the back of her gleaming black bike.

In the Cold War only border guards had walked along Bernauer Strasse. As one side of the street had belonged to West Berlin and the other to East Berlin, the buildings themselves had become border fortifications. Dozens of East Germans had escaped through them and, after the doors and windows were bricked up, through tunnels dug in the city's sandy soil.

Brussig had also escaped, through words.

'I had no early ambition to be a writer,' he recalled, stopping and standing with hands on hips and elbows angled outwards. 'My father was an engineer, my mother a special needs teacher. In school I trained as a builder, taking odd jobs as a dishwasher and museum guard. I even worked on a light-bulb assembly line. I had no clear direction for my life.'

Then during a compulsory, unhappy spell in the Volksarmee, he discovered a love of reading.

'I found that words could articulate my contradictory emotions. Suddenly I saw that I wasn't alone, and I became fascinated by the ability to express myself on the page. I started to write as a means of helping me to make decisions. I realised that I had a talent for it.' Brussig laughed at himself. 'In other words, I began writing because I didn't know what I wanted to become, and in the process I became a writer.'

On the morning of 9 November 1989, Brussig submitted his first novel to the leading East German publishing house. But he wasn't the only writer to take advantage of relaxing censorship laws. Aufbau Verlag's office overflowed with hundreds of manuscripts, stacked in teetering piles on tables and radiators, crammed into cupboards. Some like Brussig's were new but others, typed on old yellowed paper, had been pulled out of secret drawers or unearthed after years of hiding.

'I dropped mine onto a pile, believing that I'd never see it again.'

That evening, at a press conference after the emergency meeting of the Central Committee of the ruling Socialist Unity Party, the East Berlin party chief, Günter Schabowski, made his bumbling announcement of a new travel law. Foreign travel was permitted, he said, 'with immediate effect'.

Within minutes, thousands of East Berliners took Schabowski at his word and headed to the border. At first the guards at Bornholmer Strasse had stamped and invalidated their passports, expatriating the holders without their knowledge. But as the crowd grew, the strategy was abandoned. The barrier was raised and within an hour, tens of thousands crossed the Bösebrücke into West Berlin. Similar scenes unfolded at Sonnenallee, Oberbaumbrücke and other checkpoints. One month later as many as half a million people stood on the Gendarmenmarkt to hear Beethoven's Ninth, with three united choirs – the East Berlin Radio Chorus, the West German Bavarian Radio Chorus and the Children's Choir of the Dresden Philharmonie – singing 'Ode to Joy' as a spiritual hymn to hope.

Die Wende gifted a lifelong subject to Brussig. Apart from in *Heroes Like Us*, he imagined in most of his novels that the Wall hadn't fallen. In his mock-autobiography *Das gibts in keinem Russenfilm* (*That Ain't No Russian Movie*), he conjured up a confident East Germany that did not humble itself to West German expertise but rather pioneered revolutionary technologies (including hybrid electric vehicles and wind-powered generators built by convicts and conscripts).

'My made-up alternative East Germany was ruled by the party and as successful as China,' he told me.

Of course East Germany provided him with rich material because of its inherent ludicrousness: the absurd iniquity of a death strip cutting through Berlin's heart, of the U-Bahn trains running beneath it, of a child spying on the Stasi.

Near Schwartzkopffstrasse, we paused at a corner cafe. An office worker perched in the sun on a chrome chair, breakfasting on sweet *Kirschstreusel*. A window cleaner abseiled down the front of a glass building. Outside a Lidl supermarket, Russian residents grumbled about the meanness of German child benefits.

As well as imagined worlds, we talked about the real past, for in Berlin one can never escape it, nor the noble and necessary act of remembering. Over strong bitter coffee I told him of my conviction that Germany had become an open and dynamic society as a direct consequence of its people taking responsibility for their history. In a courageous, humane and moving manner, they'd unearthed and memorialised their past for the psychic health of the country.

'That's true for the Nazi years,' he replied, shading his eyes with his hand. 'But of the socialist period that I knew, all that remains now is the TV Tower at Alexanderplatz. The Palast der Republik was demolished. The Rathauspassagen has been Westernised. Lenin's monument has been removed even though he can't harm anyone any longer.' Brussig nodded back in the direction of Bernauer Strasse where a single, short stretch of Wall has been preserved. 'Above all I feel sorry that nowhere can a long length of the Berlin Wall be seen, in all its naked brutality.'

We jerked south, passing one-time 'ghost' U-Bahn stations, closed for almost thirty Cold War years and now freed of their phantoms, and cut across Invaliden Strasse to reach the Spree. Here the Wall had once flanked both sides of the river. Now Norman Foster's Reichstag dome rose above it. Tourists swirled around the Brandenburg Gate, posing for selfies at the site of my long-vanished observation platform. Ahead of us the vast glass-roof parasol at Potsdamer Platz caught the sun.

As we followed the paving stones, stepping from east to west and back again, I asked Brussig about the other rock star who had touched his life. 'You told me once that Udo Lindenberg is world famous, throughout Germany,' I said.

Outside the country, the thick-lipped, cigar-smoking Lindenberg is almost unknown. But at home he is venerated as the godfather of *Krautrock*. He's especially honoured for having looked east, unlike his contemporaries with their ambitions to break into the British or American music scene. For over a decade he aspired to perform in East Germany, writing pleading letters to the Politburo, and even composed a pop song for its leader Erich Honecker. In 'Sonderzug nach Pankow' ('Special Train to Pankow'), he speculated – in a melody based on the swing classic 'Chattanooga Choo Choo' – that the dour Communist Party Secretary was in fact a secret lover of rock music.

'Udo tried for years to do a big tour,' Brussig told me. 'In the end he was given a single gig, but only because he shared an agent with Harry Belafonte. When the East Germans had asked to book Harry for a festival, the agent insisted they take Udo as well.'

In October 1983 Lindenberg performed three songs at Berlin's Palast der Republik, his only appearance in old East Germany. Brussig had been in the crowd outside the venue.

'I wasn't a particular fan but I simply had to be there. It may be difficult for you to understand but to us Lindenberg was more popular than the Beatles or even Springsteen.'

Twenty-four years later, after the fall of the Wall and publication of *Heroes Like Us*, Lindenberg rang Brussig – they'd met once during the intervening years at an awards ceremony – and asked him to write a rock musical.

'I'd never written a musical. I didn't even like musicals. But when someone like Lindenberg calls such details don't matter.'

Lindenberg, no stranger to self-promotion, wanted the story to revolve around his hit singles and the myth that he'd fathered a child in East Berlin.

'You know the scene in *Apollo 13* where NASA scientists cobble together parts to save the space ship?' Brussig asked me. 'That's what it was like for me, building a story around his songs.'

Hinterm Horizont (*Beyond the Horizon*) took shape as a fictionalised love story between Lindenberg and an East Berliner. The Wall, the Stasi, a Moscow tryst and an unexpected pregnancy came together in Berlin's most successful musical of all time, which would be seen by more than two million people. Across the stage lovers swooned, dancers danced and border police unwound barbed wire beneath a nine-metre-wide Lindenberg fedora, designed along with much of the set by Renzo Piano, architect of parts of revitalised Potsdamer Platz and the Shard in London.

'I make my living by telling stories about that time so I feel a responsibility towards all of us who lived through it,' said Brussig. We'd found a bench on the edge of the Tiergarten, Berlin's vast, wooded inner-city park. 'I'm happiest when I overhear people say, "That's exactly how it was." They are my true audience. They are my real readers. But I also want to win over those who did not experience life in the East.'

It was lunchtime now and Berliners spilt out of offices and into parks and outdoor cafes. They turned their faces towards the sun, set aside their salad bowls and inhaled clouds of lilac perfume. An African man and an Asian woman sat on the grass holding hands. Taxis drove by with open windows, trailing the music of Farid al-Atrash and Alisa's *Exile* in their wake. Thirty years ago at this very spot, I'd stepped through a hole in the Wall and made that trail of footprints across the sand of no-man's-land.

'Nostalgia is a sweet and cosy look into the past,' Brussig answered when I asked about the dangers of romanticising the past. 'Everybody feels nostalgic from time to time. It's part of human nature. But as long as political decisions aren't based on nostalgia, as long as nostalgia is kept in the heart and out of the mind, everything will be okay. For nostalgia lies about the past, just as Utopia lies about the future.'

He paused, then went on: '*Hinterm Horizont* is a musical, as is *Billy Elliot*. Both draw on historical events, the fall of the Wall and collapse of the British coal industry. Both tell a truth about those events. But if you want historical accuracy, you'd be better off reading history books.'

In spite of his success, Brussig remained a humble man – no designer shades, no mobile phone calls cluttering our conversation – and he radiated a boyish excitement over the unexpected nature of his success.

'I can't say that I miss the old East Germany, although I suspect – if the Wall really hadn't fallen – I would have still been an author. I might even have declared – as does my character in *Das gibts in keinem Russenfilm* – that I wouldn't visit the West or read Kundera's *Unbearable Lightness of Being* until everyone could do so. I might have become infamous for such a statement. I might even have been seen as a dissident for it, although in truth I was always too fearful to be a real dissident.' Brussig added, 'It's a different world now.'

His work has brought him into contact with writers and film-makers across Europe, in Latin America and in the US. While a writer-in-residence at the Goethe-Institut in New York, John Irving invited him to Vermont for the Halloween weekend. Over dinner Irving's son Everett – who was fourteen years old at the time – announced that he planned to dress up as Abraham Lincoln. In response Irving quoted the complete text of the Gettysburg Address, from memory, adding his interpretation from time to time.

'For me it was a Great American moment, a Great American writer quoting a Great American speech for his son.'

Over the years the two authors stayed in touch, Irving writing to Brussig soon after the election of Donald Trump, 'Hatred is everywhere, Thomas, but in the US hatred has been ELECTED.'

At the end of our walk, Thomas and I stood outside the Theater am Potsdamer Platz where *Hinterm Horizont* had played for so many years. Given the nature of my journey, I needed to ask him about identity and nationalism. We talked for a time about the concept of *Unbehagen*, the weighty unease of the unfamiliar that is shaping much of modern Europe. Then I reminded him he'd once expressed a fear that a reunified Germany might 'in a great failure of imagination' carry on where it had left off in 1945. Unexpectedly he didn't talk of neo-Nazis or the far right but rather revealed that his fear had been swept aside by football.

'During the Second World War the Nazis abused patriotic feelings. They created heroes who later turned out to be murderers. Then in the Sixties intellectuals responded by banning certain words and emotions. Since those days, there was a little man inside every German head telling us not to trust our feelings.'

Brussig went on: 'For Germans this changed during the World Cup. We saw – in a kind of patriotic virginity – that we could show our pride, and still be liked. This in turn helped us to like ourselves again. We felt a healthy new patriotism that celebrated our technology, our generosity with development aid, our protection of the environment, our society that is totally non-unilateral. Strangers put their arms around each other and sang the national anthem. We realised that we were patriots of a new stripe.'

Brussig's soft, low voice and stern expression often masked his true feelings so his wide smile came as a surprise.

'I never imagined such changes in my life,' he said again, echoing the experience of a once-divided generation. 'It's another miracle.'

32

Odysseys

The sea was like the desert. Charity's fingers trailed in the water. An hour earlier the fifteen-year-old had pushed out from the clutch of women and the stink of diesel. She had elbowed herself through the crush of crumpled Nigerians and Ghanaians. She had collapsed against the gunwales. If the boat hit a swell she would be thrown into the water. If that happened she couldn't save herself. She wouldn't have the strength. She didn't know how to swim. No one knew how to swim.

Yesterday the engine had stopped. In the night the boat had begun to take on water. Two corpses had been dragged below deck. The Senegalese boys wrote their parents' mobile phone numbers on their clothes, so their families would know their fate if their bodies were ever washed ashore. Under the Mediterranean sun, one hundred souls baked in the rolling steel hull. The Libyans had given them only enough fuel to reach the open sea, telling them that the Europeans would rescue them. But no one came to them, apart from the ghosts.

Charity watched them glide towards her across the glassy water. All her life ghosts had hovered at the edge of her vision but never in such numbers, and never walking on water. Now before her eyes they came by the dozen, the white hem of their skirts licking the waves. She lifted her arm to wave to them. She tried to stand and to step towards them. She wanted them to take her in their arms, and to pull her away from the searing silver sea.

One year earlier Charity's mother had taken her hand and together they had run across the border. There had been no life for them at home, in a country at war with itself. Both Charity's father and brother had died during their army service. In Eritrea, Christians could be jailed unless they renounced their faith. Their church elder had been executed. In Ethiopia Charity would be able to go to a Christian school, said her mother. She could teach herself Amharic. Yet she still lived in fear. They still went to bed hungry.

On her walk to school Charity met another Eritrean who promised to help her to find work as a maid in Germany. She gave her a printed blouse of white hearts. She said, 'Europe is where you will not be afraid.' Six months later Charity stole her mother's raffia bag and rode a truck into the desert.

No one chooses to be a refugee. Tens of millions of Africans have fled their homes in recent years to escape war, famine and drought. Half of them were under eighteen years old, risking their lives so they, and their families, may live. Charity is one of them, and this is the story that she told me.

She was slender and tall, standing two inches above the other girls in the truck. In Darfur she waited in a mud-walled connection house as other migrants arrived from Sudan, Mali and Chad. Recruiters took some of the boys to the phone shops or cash machines near the bus station. Those with no money were made to call home. If the family did not pay, they would hear the sound of torture. Charity told me that she kept quiet. She did not leave the compound. She had to trust the woman who'd paid for her travel.

Thirty people stood in the back of each Toyota Hilux, clutching phones and bottles of water. At the gates of the desert the Toubou drivers let air out of the tyres for better traction. Charity stood for most of the next week, her feet burning on the bare metal, her head exposed and pounding under the Saharan sun. One pickup lost a wheel and rolled down a dune, crushing its passengers. Another time a dozing Liberian girl fell out, but the convoy did not stop.

Days blurred into nights spent around rocky outcrops. In places the dead lay alongside the track, covered and uncovered by the shifting sand.

At the Libyan border a sleek black line of asphalt stretched north towards the sea. But on the outskirts of Tripoli, their pickup was stopped and the refugees taken by one of the fractured militias. Charity was locked in a cell with fifty-three other women, some of whom had been held for almost a year. In the first week two of them gave birth, on the floor, in the filth, passing their babies around to be suckled. Charity slept during the day and prayed through the night that the men would not come. Women who went to the toilet after dark were raped by the guards. Her head still ached from the sun. She had no papers. She was kept in the dark for a month.

The Eritreans were to be traded to another trafficker. The men would be sold on as labourers, the women to serve as prostitutes. But on the day of the trade, an Ethiopian consul happened to come in search of jailed Ethiopians. Charity begged for his help and he, moved by her soft Amharic, asked the militia to free her. Through him she found work as a kind of house slave in Tripoli. Her new owners fed her and beat her. She was too ashamed to call her mother. Instead she telephoned the woman who'd promised to protect her. Two nights later Charity stood outside the house as instructed, terrified and alone on the unlit street. A man in a long woollen *jurid* cloak approached her and she went with him.

At the water's edge, the heavy rubber dinghies were lugged through the press of sinewy black bodies. The migrants were divided into ranks of ten and loaded like goats into the craft. The smugglers knelt on the sand to pray then pushed them off, pointing at the sky and ordering, 'Look at that star. Follow it.'

Charity was climbing onto the ninth or tenth dinghy when it snared on a rock. As it began to lose air the Libyans shouted accusations at each other, waving their guns in the air. She was shoved back, crammed into a larger group then packed into a metal hull that had been beached further along the shore. Libya's coastline is more than 1,000 miles long. No one knows how many boats are lost en route to Europe, sinking without trace.

None of the passengers were silent now. Those not weeping were calling to God. As soon as their metal boat hit the waves the first of them started to vomit. Ahead the sea seemed endless, without beginning or end. To block out its emptiness, Charity hunkered down with the other women, warmed by their bodies and deafened by the throbbing engine. She took shallow breaths to keep down the sick. Spillings of fuel mixed with seawater burnt her skin.

Five hours later, at dawn, the rising sun drove away the cold as well as the North Star. The tillerman guessed at a heading, out of sight of the dinghies. No phone had a signal. No one had a compass. Around noon the engine ran out of fuel. The metal hull rolled in the swells, baking under the white-hot sky. People sheltered under plastic sheeting and folds of cloth, numbed back into silence. Charity tried to remember the dim coolness of her mother's thatched hut. She imagined lying on their raffia mat. She was so weary.

Later the setting sun flicked red fire across the wave tops and darkness shrouded them again. Above Charity, points of light glowed like the lights of a city. She clawed herself awake and to her feet, towards salvation and voices half heard, then realised that the lights were mobile screens, held up against the starless sky. Someone near to her had managed to catch a signal.

'I beg you sir, please rescue us,' pleaded a man, rancid with sweat. Others joined in, calling and crying into his phone in English. 'There are children.'

Charity heard the response, crackling from another world. 'What is your position?'

'In the Mediterranean Sea,' the man answered. 'Hello? Hello?'

When the signal was lost a wail rose out of their throats as if to swallow the world.

Another day and Charity stirred into its heat. Again there was no wind, no fuel, and now no water. She slipped in and out of consciousness as another soul – a pregnant Moroccan – slid from life. Charity managed to crawl out of the suffocating clutch of women. She elbowed herself through the crush of crumpled Nigerians and gaunt Ghanaians. She collapsed on the gunwales and tried to reach the water, to cup it in her palm, to drink. But she didn't have the strength. Her hand trailed in the water, and she saw the ghosts. They glided towards her by the dozen, the white hem of their skirts licking the waves. She tried to hold out her hand to them. She wanted them to take her in their arms. She lifted herself, and rolled into the searing silver sea.

On that same day, 800 miles away across the Mediterranean, another young woman went into the water. Behind her was the Turkish coast. Ahead the rocky grey hills of Lesbos were silhouetted against the setting sun. Yusra was seventeen, two years older than Charity, and also trying for Europe. Her sister Sara was already in the sea, clutching a rope, trying to steady the small dark-grey dinghy. Each wave spun the bow around ninety degrees. Every swell jerked the girls' heads against its rubber tube. Saltwater stung their eyes, filled their mouths, dragged and sucked at their clothes. On board eighteen fellow refugees prayed aloud.

Together the sisters kicked and steered the boat into the waves, pointing it at the island, keeping it from being swamped. Two of the men took turns in the sea while at the stern the Afghan pulled the starting cord again and again. Another boat passed them, its motor running, its passengers pointing at the stranded dinghy, but it did not stop. It ploughed on through the waves.

After three and a half hours in the sea, Yusra shuddered with cold, her limbs ached, her muscles seized. If I drown now, it will all have been for nothing, she thought, fighting down the rising panic. No time to live, no time to win.

Yusra could swim before she could walk. As a baby her father, a swimming coach, had lowered her into the shallow water at the pool's edge and taught her to kick her legs. At the age of four he'd enrolled her in swimming classes. Whenever she lost courage he threw her into the pool, pushing her to train with her older sister's group. By the time she started primary school she was practising two hours a day. Her father wanted Yusra and Sara to be the best, and his ambition fired their own. Yusra made the Damascus youth team and started to train with the Syrian national team, winning medals at home and abroad.

'If your dream isn't the Olympics, you aren't a true athlete,' her father told her.

But then a peaceful uprising erupted into civil war and tore apart the country. Russia entered the conflict to 'stabilise' the government with both regular and contract soldiers, the latter alleged to have been supplied by Yevgeny Prigozhin, the oligarch behind the St Petersburg troll factory.* The Kremlin wanted both to exercise its military muscle and to intensify the flood of refugees heading to Europe. Five million people – the majority of them women and children – fled their homes in the largest exodus in recent history.

Throughout it all Yusra lived for swimming. Swimming was the best distraction as friends and teammates left the city, as fire fights cracked along its streets. Her father was mistaken for the enemy, hung up by the feet and beaten. Government tanks destroyed the family home. A mortar shell hit the athletes' hotel, killing a fellow sportsman. On the nightly news a banner scrolled across the screen totting up that day's dead: 120 on Monday, 367 on Tuesday, 1,026 lost over a single weekend. One evening, as she swam lengths, a rocket-propelled grenade crashed through the roof of the Tishreen pool, sank to the bottom ... and did not explode.

Yusra's mother begged her to give up her training, to stay indoors in the belief that it would be safer. But the truth was not so simple. The choice was to stay home and die, or risk death to live abroad.

'Swimming is my life,' insisted Yusra, her ambition undiminished. 'I'll have to go to Europe.'

The sisters' father funded them to fly to Beirut and Istanbul. As the aircraft circled the city the stewardess warned passengers not to steal the lifejackets. Turkish smugglers agreed to put the girls on a boat to Greece, at a cost of $15,000 each. On an August night a curtained minibus slipped them beyond Ayvalık to a pine-clad slope

---

* In 2018 the US special counsel Robert Mueller indicted Prigozhin for his role at the Internet Research Agency. Other sources including the *Guardian* and Buzzfeed linked Prigozhin to a private military contractor known as The Wagner Group (which he denied).

overlooking the Aegean. For two days they waited for a calm sea. Their first attempt had to be abandoned due to a coastguard patrol. Then their boat was slashed by competitors. On the third try the sisters waded through the green shallows and lifted themselves into the overloaded inflatable. The vessel was absurdly small, no more than twelve feet in length, and designed for four people. Water brimmed over its edge.

The six-mile ride across the Mytilini Strait to Lesbos was to take no more than one hour but after fifteen minutes the outboard motor spluttered and died. The inflatable wallowed in the swells. Waves crested over it and water pooled on its floor. To lighten the load, bags and shoes were dropped overboard, followed by one of the men and Sara. Yusra slipped in after them, swinging her legs over the side and sliding down into the water.

No swimmer would have had the strength to tow the boat in such choppy seas, but the sisters could steady it and keep it from taking on more water. The Afghan continued to pull the starter cord in desperation. The passengers prayed for help and forgiveness. Hours passed and the swells rose as the sun set and Yusra's limbs went rigid.

Then the engine coughed miraculously to life and the sinking boat wrenched itself forward towards Greece. All shook with cold and fear. All were deathly pale. Thirty minutes later it hit the dark, stony shore. The men attacked the inflatable with their knives, shredding it in their fury. Yusra, her bare feet cut and bleeding, wept for 'the soul was still in my body'.

That night they slept in a small country church. In the morning the sisters boarded a local bus to Mytilene, the island's capital, where like the 80,000 others who'd landed on Lesbos that month they queued for temporary residence permits and then ferry tickets. In Piraeus, Athens's large industrial port, touts sold them seats to the Macedonian border. Both there and in Serbia, government coaches ran the refugees further north, to the next border.

Hungary in contrast worked to frustrate their progress; erecting barbed-wire fences, closing the frontier and arresting migrants and their helpers. As in Russia, the Church played its part – Cardinal

Péter Erdő, the country's highest-ranking Catholic official, declaring that to provide shelter for refugees constituted human trafficking. In the following months Bulgaria, Slovenia and Macedonia also sealed their southern borders with razor wire. But Yusra and Sara were ahead of the clampdown, hiding overnight in a cornfield, paying another small fortune to be driven to Budapest. At Keleti station, where I once had arrived and would arrive again, they bought tickets to Vienna. Within sight of the Austrian frontier, Hungarian border officials then arrested them and held them in a stable.

Yet Yusra and Sara managed to escape and, four weeks after leaving Damascus, they arrived with thousands of others at Vienna's main train station. Around them, and to their disbelief, crowds of Austrians applauded and cheered, offering food and flowers, holding aloft home-made signs: *Wilkommen Flüchtlinge.* Welcome Refugees. After a hot meal and medical checks, the sisters were put on another bus.

Eight hours later, in the depths of the night, they pulled off the autobahn and into a courtyard. Another crowd and another handmade sign awaited them: 'Welcome to Berlin Spandau.'

One hundred miles off the Libyan coast the ghosts wore white protective suits and spoke Italian. They pulled Charity out of the sea and into the Zodiac. She lay on its floor sobbing, as she and the others were ferried to the frigate. On board all were photographed, their nationality and age recorded. Charity claimed that she was eighteen years old. On windswept Lampedusa she was given dry clothes and flip-flops. In the shelter's yard, Malians wrapped in mylar blankets queued at the free payphones. Guineans and Ghanaians played football as Senegalese women watched from the surrounding balconies. Indoors, Gambian girls cut the blue string from their wrists, tied there by Médecins Sans Frontières nurses to show they were unaccompanied minors. Of the thousands of Nigerian women rescued from the Mediterranean in the last few years, 80 per cent were trafficked for sex work.

Charity hardly left her bunk for the first days. She kept her thoughts to herself, telling the doctors only that she had been kidnapped. Her details were registered with Frontex, the EU border agency, and she was transferred in a group to Messina and then to the Italian mainland. At the camp she was told that she was free, that she need do only what she wanted. But she had no money, and groups of West African men loitered on the breezeblock wall at the entrance. As soon as she received her travel document, she vanished.

Where she went, what she did, how she fed herself, she would not tell me. She simply dropped out of sight, leaving no trace: no mobile phone trail, no asylum registration, no claim for financial support. She ceased to exist, her name and number deleted from the Italian registry after a year. No one looked for her, and it seems no one looked after her, until she turned up in Berlin.

A couple of months before I reached the city she passed through the Moabit LaGeSo Refugee Welcome Centre – around the corner from Thomas Brussig's home – and was given a bed at Tempelhof. The old airport which had kept the city alive during the Berlin Airlift now sustained its newest residents. Its hangars had been lined with ranks of white tents. On its noticeboards German lessons were advertised in Arabic, Farsi, Russian, Somali and Vietnamese. Syrian fathers pushed hand-me-down prams along the airport apron. Young Uzbeks lounged at mobile phone charge points. To date Germany has given shelter to almost two million refugees in a noble and magnanimous act of humanity and contrition.

Vertriebene has a special meaning for Germans, the word understood more as 'the evicted' rather than 'refugees'. It is replete with the memory of the millions of ethnic Germans expelled from Soviet territories after the war. A Berlin friend of mine works as a volunteer at Tempelhof, manning its dozen washing machines. Every day, all day, refugees bring their clothes to her. Few words are spoken, no names exchanged. The work is numbing, humbling and essential. My friend puts the dirty laundry in a numbered basket and issues a numbered receipt, which is needed to retrieve it.

But Charity lost her receipt. She forgot her number. She hovered near to the machines for a day and a half, hoping to see her clothes. When she didn't spot them, she summoned the courage to approach my friend. In broken German she explained her loss. She fought to hold back the tears. Together the two women looked through the numbers and in cupboards. After an hour they found the clothes, in a machine that had broken down mid-cycle and was awaiting repair in a far storeroom. In the murky water was all that Charity owned in the world. My friend asked for her name, not her number, and Charity broke down and wept.

Over the next few weeks I met her four or five times in my friend's apartment. My friend – like tens of thousands of Germans across the country – acted as a kind of foster parent, guiding Charity through the bureaucratic jungle, helping her to translate and file the papers necessary to claim asylum. She also taught her how to ride a bicycle. During that time, when not filling out forms, Charity told me her story – her odyssey – while sitting with us by the kitchen window. There was a delicacy about her: oval face, plain headscarf, teeth as white as her eyes that were always focused on the floor. She sat by a window, she said, to forget the lightless Tripoli cell.

'*Hier bin ich sicher*,' she assured me, a breeze lifting the curtains. I'm safe here. But somehow I sensed that she didn't believe it.

Charity wanted to make herself useful, she said, and my friend found her unpaid work at a nearby cemetery. Sprawling Weissensee was the largest Jewish burial ground in Europe, the final resting place of more than 100,000 Berliners, yet today it is all but deserted. Ivy has crept into its pre-war tombs and cracked its stones. Brambles have swallowed its grandiose Wilhelmine monuments. Under the Nazis, Weissensee was closed and the city's Jews sent to distant death camps. Urn fields of ashes from Auschwitz, Bełżec and Bergen-Belsen now fan out from the old mausoleums. Almost no one remains alive in Berlin to remember its dead.

Charity pushed her wheelbarrow around the graves. She walked the overgrown paths and cut back the wild ivy from sunken headstones. As she worked her family often came to her in visions, she told me, her father staring from a far copse of trees, her mother's shadow falling across a collapsed tomb. She also said that she saw other ghosts but she didn't understand their language.

'Sometimes I feel so helpless. Sometimes I wake up asking, "Why did I wake?"' she told my friend in the quietest voice.

I wasn't in Berlin when she disappeared again. Her asylum claim had been refused, as first requests often are. My friend had sat with her, explaining how to reapply but Charity just stared out of the window as if she might slip through it. It was winter by then and she'd pointed at the bare chestnut tree in the courtyard garden and said, 'Soon there will be birds in the tree, and a nest, and leaves to hide the nest.' Together they'd drunk tea until the pot was empty. When Charity had stood to leave she'd added to my friend, 'God keep you.'

She didn't turn up for work in Weissensee. She failed to appear at the refugee cafe at the weekend. At the hostel my friend learned that she had simply left with her raffia bag, telling another Eritrean that she had to meet someone in Italy.

My friend mourned Charity's passing, blaming herself for not doing enough. She revisited the rejected application again and again. But then she moved on, as she had to do, volunteering to mentor twins from Iraq while keeping Charity's memory in her heart. She even persuaded two German neighbours to help her at Tempelhof.

'My neighbours were as scared as the Iraqi girls,' said my friend. 'I told them, "Take my hand, and you'll find a person that touches you, who opens your heart. You may even fall in love with their story and then really be able to help them."'

Mitläufer, the German word for 'fellow traveller', can be used in a metaphorical sense, meaning to walk alongside another person. I tried to envision myself in Charity's shoes. I wanted to imagine her experience: the feel of the clothes on her back, the reek of sun-blistered flesh in the drifting metal hull, the sound of a gang rape in the next cell. I tried to conjure up her missing year, about which she would not talk. I could only guess at the magnitude of her suffering.

At Schönefeld airport – predecessor to Berlin Brandenburg – a broad underground passageway ran from the S-Bahn station to the terminal building. On my last evening in the city I hurried along it to catch a late-night flight. At the tunnel's far end there appeared ten, then a hundred, perhaps a thousand people, led by a dozen uniformed officials. The mass of humanity filled the wide subway, blocking my path, threatening to overwhelm me. I stopped in my tracks and let the crowd flow around me: Romanian mothers in purple headscarfs, gaunt Africans clutching large official envelopes, teenage Pakistanis carrying sleeping bags in Ikea bags, an elderly Ethiopian walking with a cane. Almost none of the *Vertriebene* – the expelled – wanted to be there. Almost all of them had had to make an impossible choice. I could never know all the details of course, of decisions made when there were no good options, of stealing from a parent, driving a Hilux or shouldering a Kalashnikov to save oneself and one's family. All I could do was to pick out one or two faces in the crowd, to envisage their lives and to tell their individual stories.

'When I think of my journey, I can hardly believe it all happened,' Yusra Mardini told me. 'When I read about it in the book, and when I see the film, I cry. I laugh. Of course it isn't a hundred per cent as I lived it, no book or film can ever be, but in my heart is a sense of great responsibility, that my story can help people, that it can give them hope.'

We can stay, Yusra and her sister had realised on their arrival in Berlin. No more running. No more fear. No more war.

On their first Berlin morning, beside the shower block, trestle tables had been piled with gifted soap, shampoo and towels. In the red-brick camp building whole rooms were filled with donated clothes. Yusra chose white T-shirts and a jumper as well as black shoes and a pink scarf.

Wasserfreunde Spandau 04, a swimming club based at the nearby Olympic Park, took in the sisters and let them resume their training. The war and exhausting journey had sapped their strength, and a shoulder injury forced Sara to stop, but Yusra continued, determined not to give up on her dream.

When the International Olympic Committee decided to form a refugee team for the Rio Games, Yusra was asked to join it. But she hesitated. She didn't want charity. She wanted to compete in the Games because of her ability, not by virtue of being a refugee. Yet at the same time she realised that she could speak for those who did not have a voice. She saw a way to support fellow refugees by her example.

'I really wanted to feel their pain like I felt my pain. I know what pain is in this situation: to lose your country, your friends, to start a new life.' No one chooses to be a refugee, she repeated. 'Our choice is to die at home or risk death trying to escape.'

Yusra flew to Rio, joined the Parade of Nations, swam the 100 metres freestyle and the 100 metres butterfly. She didn't win a medal but her main focus was on telling her story. At press conferences, in her later address to the United Nations General Assembly, as the youngest UNHCR goodwill ambassador, she relayed a message of hope, determination and courage, aspiring to change perceptions, declaring for all to hear that those who flee their countries are capable of achieving great things.

When we met in Berlin she was already training for the next Olympic Games.

'Migrants can bring joy to their new home, as well as ideas and good food,' she told me with a disarming smile: big black eyes ringed with kohl, shoulder-length hair, gap tooth. 'Every individual has something special to give but they need to have both time and the opportunity to give it.'

As we spoke I wondered if she felt herself to be Syrian? Or Middle Eastern? European? German? Muslim?

'I am a bit of everything,' she replied with feeling. 'I can understand different cultures because of my experiences. I always try to empathise with another person.' She paused and added, 'I put myself in their shoes.'

Xenophobes only stand in their own shoes, of course. In Budapest and Baltimore, from St Petersburg to St Albans, their leaders empower themselves by exploiting doubts and fears. They place political ambition above humanity, blinding themselves – and their supporters – to compassion and generosity. As I'd seen a battle of ideas was unfolding in Europe, once again sweeping up the innocent, including now Yusra's sister Sara. She had also been determined to help refugees. She'd returned to Lesbos to volunteer for a migrant aid group. But in a nativist clampdown on civil society, she was arrested and imprisoned on trumped-up charges of people-smuggling.

In 1989, the year of the fall of the Wall, eleven countries had border walls or fences. Thirty years on, there are more than seventy around the world.

'What have I learned on the journey?' said Yusra Mardini, repeating my question as we parted in Berlin. 'Perspective,' she answered. 'Perspective.'

33

Wir sind das Volk

Thirty years have left little mark on parts of East Germany. Only a sheen of modernity seemed to have been brushed across much of the countryside. Beyond the train's window, communist-era breezeblock pigsties lined a waterlogged swede field. A farmer cleaned out her chicken shed, its tarpaper roof weighed down with rocks. Kitchen gardens awaited spring planting, the newly turned soil black against the sprouting green. Mossy mounds of salvaged bricks were stacked at the edges of fields, to be reused on a day yet to come.

After unification, some two million people opted to leave the eastern *Länder* of empty factories and closed collective farms,* the best and the brightest choosing to build their lives in Berlin and the West. Many of those left behind felt both abandoned by established politicians and resentful of migrants who, they believed, were competitors for jobs. Most succumbed to *Ostalgie*, forgetting the trials and troubles of the old East. 'Many now remember it as

---

* In 1992 former East Germany accounted for only 3.4 per cent of Germany's gross domestic product. Some 2.5 million state jobs were lost with the ending of the centralised economy and collapse of the old industrial system. The world order that so many had once known ceased to exist. Today after huge inward investment, its contribution to national GDP has risen to about 15 per cent but none of the thirty largest companies listed on the German stock market are yet based in the east.

a gentle country where there was full employment,' reported the *Berliner Kurier* newspaper. Some chose to idealise another disgraced doctrine, and channel their insecurities into hate.

Today Saxony, a state once more powerful than Brandenburg and Prussia, imagines itself as a kind of German Texas: conservative, authoritarian and bold. In Chemnitz, its third largest city, one of the first grand villas boasted a four-sided inscription: *Ich hab's gewagt*. I dared to do it.

I changed trains there, catching a double-decker Regional-Express to Leinefelde. The town's small Eichsfeldtag festival was no Woodstock or Rock am Ring, corralled onto a single sports field across from the KiK discount store. Only 1,000 sympathisers came on the day of my visit, the men sporting tattoos and T-shirts: Support your Race, Stop the Asylum Flood, *Feuer und Flamme für eure Demokratie*. The women wore baseball caps and shades, pushed prams, sipped beers. Their children darted between them and the bouncy castles, queuing at sausage stalls and having kaleidoscopic butterflies painted onto their smooth, white faces.

The family-friendly festival was hosted by the NPD, the ultranationalist Nationaldemokratische Partei Deutschlands that once preferred biker rallies and hard rock concerts. In front of the stage there seemed to be as many policemen and journalists as participants, especially when '*ein hohes Tier*' – a party bigwig – began to work the audience, raving about fire and blood, trying to instil in them a sense of fear and power. 'Either the German people expel the Muslims or the Muslims will enslave us,' he cried. 'We must fight for our country, peacefully of course.'

Other far-right factions have gone further to rebrand themselves. Generation Identity – a part-hippie, part-hipster, anti-Islam group – hosted its Europa Nostra summer fete in Dresden, as well as a traditional Christmas market in Halle (complete with flaxen-haired angels, ginger-scented mulled wine and choristers singing of their dream of a white Christmas). With even less subtlety, its activists stormed a migrant integration class at Klagenfurt University, sprayed fake blood on actors in a Vienna theatre (the performance was Nobel Prize-winning author Elfriede Jelinek's reworking of

Aeschylus's refugee tragedy *The Suppliants*) and hung banners on both the Brandenburg Gate ('Secure borders – Secure future') and Westminster Bridge ('Defend London – Stop Islamisation').

In its most elaborate media stunt to date, Generation Identity chartered an ocean-going ship to disrupt humanitarian rescue missions in the Mediterranean.

'Every week, every day, every hour, ships packed with illegal immigrants are flooding into European waters,' asserted its Defend Europe website, conjuring up a sense of existential crisis. 'This massive immigration is changing the face of our continent. We are losing our safety and our way of life and there is a danger we Europeans will become a minority in our own European homelands. Our future is under attack.'

Their ship – crowdfunded by high-profile US white supremacists and a former Grand Wizard of the Ku Klux Klan* among others – set to sea intent on sinking refugee boats and turning over would-be migrants to the Libyan coastguard. But on its maiden voyage, the ship – festooned with a banner 'No Way – You Will Not Make Europe Home' – broke down and was denied entry to both Malta and Tunisia, local fishermen blockading the harbours with small boats and waving signs: 'No racists'. When it did finally reach a European port, most of the Sri Lankan crewmen were found to be travelling on false documents and so were deported.

Yet despite such occasional farcical failures, fringe political groups – along with online communities such as Reconquista Germanica and its Discord channel – have become influential, radicalising 'the normies', promoting non-violence while enabling

---

* In the twentieth century, Europe's two great allies – the UK and US – 'had saved [Europe] twice from suicide', wrote Ian McEwan, Milan Kundera, Adam Michnik, Orhan Pamuk, Salman Rushdie and twenty-five other leading writers, historians and Nobel laureates in their 2019 open letter on the rise of populism. But now Europe has been 'abandoned from across the Channel and from across the Atlantic' with some Brits and Americans even helping to finance the 'explosions of xenophobia and anti-Semitism'. 'Three-quarters of a century after the defeat of fascism and thirty years after the fall of the Berlin Wall, a new battle for civilisation is under way,' stated the manifesto's signatories.

racist attacks and waging *Infokrieg* to advance the far-right
Alternative für Deutschland (AfD). Their avowed goal is to rout
liberalism and rid the continent of non-Europeans.

I didn't linger in Leinefelde. I didn't share a beer with the *hohes
Tier* at the Deutsches Haus or natter with bigots in biking leathers
about their claim that all refugees are soldiers of Islam. Instead
I backtracked to Chemnitz, to stand beneath the head.

Karl Marx's head – the so-called 'Nischel' or skull – is the second-
largest bust in the world. In 1971 the massive forty-ton bronze
was cast at the Monument Skulptura foundry in Leningrad
and transported in ninety-five pieces to the city, to mark its
(short-lived) renaming as Karl-Marx-Stadt. On its plinth on
Brückenstrasse, the towering thirteen-metre work glares down
at the individual, so stern, so *überdimensional* that it stuns most
passers-by into silence.

But not everyone. In the early hours of a late summer morning
in 2018, a fight broke out in the shadow of the Nischel. A 35-year-
old German carpenter was stabbed, dying later of his injuries. Two
Kurdish immigrants – one Syrian and one Iraqi who escaped from
the scene – were charged with manslaughter.

Within an hour mourners were on the street, their candles flickering
on the paving stones. At first there were only a couple of hundred
of them, but by the middle of the afternoon there were thousands,
standing together, chanting 'Germany for Germans' and '*Wir sind das
Volk*'. Their anger swelled with the news that the Iraqi had previous
convictions, that he should have been deported months earlier.

Beneath a sky cut with wispy clouds, protesters carried placard
portraits of the dead man as well as of 'other [Caucasian] casualties
of Germany's indiscriminate hospitality'. Banners read '*Ausländer
raus!*' and '*Multikulti tötet!*' Multiculturalism kills. Radicals from
the far-right Junge Alternative, National Socialist Underground
and Kaotik Chemnitz slid in from the fringes, as had hooligans on
the Warsaw march. One of them held aloft a crass caricature of a
thick-lipped African. NS Boys – some with itchy fists – began to
stalk their prey.

Police water cannons rolled in from Leipzig and Dresden in an attempt to maintain order, and to protect a smaller counter-protest across the square. Masked demonstrators from both sides then began to throw flares and fireworks at each other over the police lines. When a television journalist claimed that the marchers had made the Hitler salute, he was taunted as 'the lying press'. *Lügenpresse.*

'We don't want Chemnitz to become an Islamic city in twenty years,' protesters shouted into microphones. 'How about integrating us first?'*

Wir sind das Volk, the mob had chanted in Leinefelde and Chemnitz. *Wir sind das Volk* they cried while surrounding a refugee bus in Clausnitz. *Wir sind das Volk* yelled the thugs as they chased two dozen dark-skinned teenagers through the streets of Bautzen. Thirty years ago *Wir sind das Volk* – We are the people – was a cry for democracy, for freedom, for inclusion. Now the far right has co-opted the slogan, repeating it over and over, exploiting it to exclude those who think differently, who are different.

Saxony has a history of neo-Nazi protests. In the last election one in four Chemnitz voters cast their ballot for the anti-immigrant AfD. Dresden is the home of the nationalist movement, Pegida, the so-called Patriotic Europeans Against the Islamisation of the West. Leinefelde – population 19,617 – is one of hundreds of small eastern towns where far-right groups hold annual festivals, preaching a hate-filled, pro-white gospel. Berlin, only a few hundred miles distant, is another world.

But Berlin is not Germany just as London is not England, as New York and LA are not the United States. Berlin – for the moment at least – is different, a refuge for a reconstituted liberal order.

I returned to it by train, the journey taking a couple of hours, and changed onto the U-Bahn. On a bench, on the platform, a

* At the time no more than 3,000 Syrian refugees lived in Chemnitz, and barely 1,000 Afghans. Yet for over a year, weekly far-right protests have continued in the city, local people venting their anger at being 'left behind'.

young mother waited in silence with her two young sons. She
wore a headscarf and voluminous black abaya. The boys sported
new Germany football shirts and back-turned caps. All had heavy
shadows under their eyes. I guessed that they were newcomers.

As a U-Bahn train glided into the station, they seemed to lean
back as if in awe. A twenty-something man – the boys' father –
stood apart from them, close to the platform edge. When the
train doors opened he nodded and his boys leapt to their feet to
dart into a carriage, laughing with sudden excitement. To ride
the underground was so much more fun than being driven out of
Damascus or Aleppo by Russian bombs, than travelling across the
continent in the back of trucks. Their mother – who I imagine had
wept throughout the journey in fear for her children – followed
them onto the train, taking a seat and gathering her sons around
her skirts like a mother hen.

But the younger boy, who was not much older than a toddler,
was too excited to sit down. As the doors closed and the train
jerked forward, he rocked back and forth on his feet, shouting to
his father who sat across from the small, tight family. The child was
thrilled by the noise of the wheels, by the strobing lights, by the
novelty of the smiling faces of the Berlin commuters. His parents
and older brother tried to quieten him, hushing him in Arabic. But
he would not be restrained and stuck out his short, pink tongue
at them.

Then his father – in his embarrassment, in jest, in a gesture
unseen by me in Germany in all the years I've known the country –
curled his fingers into the shape of a pistol and took a shot at his
son. In a flash the boy responded, firing back at his father with
both hands, taking cover behind another seat, imagining the crack
and ricochet of gunfire around the now hushed carriage.

No one on the train was smiling now.

Switzerland

34

Waiting for Gorby

'Who did you meet?' exclaimed Dmitri Denisovich, the chicken tsar, his crooked gob open and teeth jagged as a broken Moskovskaya bottle.

'Mikhail Sergeyevich,' repeated Vasya, his driver.

Six months had passed since we'd parted in Moscow, six months since I'd sampled Putin's Pecker, stood on top of the world, and endured the most stonking hangover of my life. Now I sat with Dmitri on a Philippe Starck sofa staring open-mouthed at Vasya. He stood in front of us, silhouetted against a broad balcony window, backed by a chocolate-box sweep of mountains, telling us about his astonishing encounter.

'I was waiting to pick up puppy from beauty shop. I walking to next door park. I sit on bench beside a man. It seem like nothing special.'

'Mikhail Sergeyevich *Gorbachev*,' said Dmitri, putting down his drink, lifting the coiffed dog off his lap and handing it to the Moldovan maid. 'The man on bench was Gorbachev.'

'He not look like on television. He look so ... old.'

'Did you talk to him?' I asked. I'd trekked all the way to Crimea to stand in the footsteps of the former Soviet leader, only to have him rock up in person around the corner from Dmitri's Swiss penthouse.

'When I recognise him, I think how he change world, and how now he not so busy,' Vasya answered me. 'So I ask him just one word. I say, "*Skuchayete?*"'

'Are you bored?' repeated Dmitri, translating for me, in disbelief. 'You asked Russia's greatest leader if he's bored?'

Vasya nodded. 'And he answer: "Very much." It was honest and simple answer. It was Russian answer. More time passing we just look on lake. I start thinking about my childhood, about time of perestroika. So I ask him one more thing. I ask: "Why?"'

'"*Tak bylo nuzhno*," he say back to me. "That's the way it had to be."'

Dmitri reached for his glass without looking and knocked it onto the floor. He kept his eyes fixed on Vasya as the maid darted to the sideboard to pour him a new drink.

'We not say more but I feel like we talking,' Vasya continued. 'I feel warmth coming from this old man. I feel magnet in him. Then time coming for collect dog from beauty shop so I say goodbye. He looking at me and ask me if I want his phone number and for some reason I say, "Why?"'

'*Da, navernoe ne zachem*,' Gorbachev had replied – Yes, I guess there's no point.

'So I leave him on bench,' Vasya concluded.

Dmitri stared at his driver, speechless. A helicopter passed by the window. A speedboat sliced across the glass-smooth water. The dog lapped the spilt vodka.

'Mikhail Sergeyevich Gorbachev offered you telephone number and you did not take it?' said Dmitri, pulling the silk dressing gown around him. '*Gospodi, pochemu menya okruzhayut odni ty?*' Lord, why am I surrounded by idiots?

Gorbachev had been a hero for both minigarchs and oligarchs. Without him the world might still be locked in a Cold War. Without him Russia's new elite would still be slumming it in cold-water Soviet blocks. But as I'd learnt on my travels, almost every other Russian blamed Gorbachev for all the country's woes. To them, the great reformer was the devil incarnate.

'What time did this happen?' Dmitri asked Vasya.

'This morning near twelve noon,' he replied.

'So tomorrow we go at same time to same park and we meet him.'

Montreux has been a Russian village for over a century. On its vine-clad slopes Gogol put pen to paper to draft *Dead Souls* and Tolstoy dashed off short stories while 'risking his health by chasing chambermaids down the Montreux Palace's endless hallways' (according to Vladimir Nabokov, who later lived in the same lavish hotel). Both Tchaikovsky and Stravinsky composed music in its belle époque salons and, more recently, the oil tycoon Mikhail Khodorkovsky – once Russia's wealthiest man – took shelter after his release from a Moscow prison (and from fabricated charges). Then as now the air smelt of Alpine rivers, ripening grapes and starched tablecloths. Palm trees and tropical flowers lined the waterside promenade. A view of the lake added a million to a property's price.

It was no surprise that both Gorbachev and Dmitri favoured this 'rosy place for riparian exile' but I'd never expected the chicken tsar to fuss so much about what to wear to meet the last General Secretary of the Communist Party of the Soviet Union. The next morning Vasya laid out his Gieves & Hawkes sharkskin suit, his navy blue houndstooth blazer, wine-coloured corduroys and both cashmere polo and racing green merino sweaters. Yet none of them seemed to satisfy him, nor for that matter did his Crockett & Jones Oxfords after the dog nibbled one of its fine calfskin toes.

'*Chyort vozmi*!' he cursed again and again, pacing from bedroom to balcony and back again as the maid ironed yet another shirt. The devil take me! Then a eureka moment stopped him in his tracks. '*Evrika*! Mikhail Sergeyevic's Labrador has died so we will bring puppy dog to make him happy.'

In the months since our parting, much had changed for Dmitri. Life had become risky at home, he told me in the car. He'd dropped the movie idea and decided to go into exile. He wasn't in danger of being gunned down in the street, those Wild East days having passed into legend, but certain bodies had wished to acquire his assets and he wasn't in a position to refuse them. In Russia the swashbuckling sole operator had been elbowed aside by savvy business syndicates.

Smooth corporate strategy had replaced crass amateurism. The change pleased the Kremlin as it polished the country's image abroad (and spilt much less blood on stately carpets). Oil, weapons, drugs and women were now sold in executive boardrooms by Harvard Business School graduates. The new home-grown syndicates also found – with Putin as guarantor of their assets – that they could muscle into European energy conglomerates and football clubs, American steel mills and basketball teams. The Bank of Russia even joined the buying spree, stashing away gold and billions of dollars of US government bonds for future use.

For all his arrogance, Dmitri had recognised that, in the slick and striving corporate environment, he was out of his league. He'd play no part in the revival of Russia's global ambitions. So he took the less-than-ideal-but-not-altogether-insulting payment, got out of town and called me.

'I am now free man. Ha ha,' he said with a mocking laugh, as mercurial as ever. 'So maybe you will write true book after all.' As he lifted the dog off his lap to kiss it, flashing those terrible teeth, his and Vasya's eyes met in the rear-view mirror.

Gorbachev was not at the park bench so we settled down to wait for him. Lake Geneva sparkled in the late morning light. In the distance the Chablais Alps gleamed in ethereal silver. The faintest scent of apple blossom drifted on the warm breeze. Dmitri told me that he had much to be thankful for, even though he could no longer afford a proper yacht.

'I do not need money now,' he said as Vasya parked the Range Rover. 'Money has become like toilet paper.'

I looked him in the eye. He knew it wasn't true. He was still playing a game.

'But I do have story for you,' he added.

Together we watched the puppy chase pigeons along the promenade. It was a handsome creature with intelligent eyes, a muscular body and a dark red coat.

'He's a corgi, yes?' I asked as it gambolled in the balmy air.

'The best. His genes are from your old queen's dog Monty,' he told me, explaining how he'd bought the puppy from a 'top high-class' Kennel Club breeder, hired France's leading trainer and entered it in Geneva's prestigious Exposition Canine. 'Trainer spent ten days with him, learning Swiss technique and what judges like: good posterior, strong back quarters. All very expensive but no matter, all was for good ending. My puppy dog won best in show.'

Purebred dogs had become the latest status symbol for the powerful. Putin owned both an Akita Inu and a Central Asian Shepherd dog. His prime minister kept two English setters, a Golden Retriever and also – in a respectful nod – another Central Asian Shepherd dog. His defence minister had a Mongolian Tuva and his press secretary a Pomeranian spitz. Now Dmitri – like both Roman Abramovich and the First Deputy Chairman of the Russian Government – had a Pembrokeshire corgi. Every time it tumbled over its oversized paws, Dmitri barked at Vasya, ordering him to look after his 'prize-winner'.

'I didn't know you were interested in dogs,' I said.

'Not so much,' he admitted with a shrug.

'Then why?'

'Why?' he repeated as if the answer were obvious. 'So people in Moscow say that Dmitri Denisovich raises top dog. So they not say Dmitri Denisovich is dust.'

As well as money, Dmitri had lost more than a little of his edge. He still strolled about with haughty self-confidence, thrusting out his chest, flaunting his newest Rolex, but he no longer had the air of a fighter. The wild wolf tattoo that had leapt across his torso, bringing onto the surface that which lay beneath it, seemed to be at rest after a long hunt. The change in him also affected our relationship of course. Yet he remained a survivor, and in more ways than I then imagined.

When he sent Vasya off for vodka and champagne (the latter for me as I'd said it was too early to drink), he chatted about Gorbachev's infamous successor.

'To common Russians – to *bydlo* – Putin is superman,' he told me with new and surprising candidness. 'But any clever dick apparatchik could do same job.'

'That's not what you said before.'

He ventured that Putin was a symptom, not a cause. Another charmless and little-known bureaucrat could have become an action-man president, posing without a shirt, practising judo and scheming to reassert the nation's power. In Russia politics is simple, he said: vote for the leader and then move on.

'No oligarch likes him or his KGB. You know about Berezovsky?'

I nodded. Boris Berezovsky was the oligarch who had made Putin, then turned against him.

'After he died, Putin told other businessmen, "Support me or say goodbye like Boris".'*

'And he took a cut for himself?' I asked.

'Fifty per cent,' Dmitri told me, a figure that I found hard to believe. Surely no individual – even in such an audacious kleptocracy – could pocket so much of a nation's wealth.

'Now when we see his face on TV, bragging about latest Russian victory or new nuclear torpedo, we think, "Oh God, not this thief again. Time to leave country and learn new language."' Dmitri sighed and added, 'For sure, I could not tell you this in Moscow.'

Again I wondered aloud about patriotism, and how Putin's actions often seemed at odds with the national good.

'He is proud to be Russian,' replied Dmitri. 'But with his billions who needs to love his people?'

As morning turned to afternoon, and Montreux residents strolled to silver service tables at La Véranda, Dmitri swigged vodka from the bottle. Vasya fed the dog morsels of steak tartare that he'd fetched from the Brasserie des Alpes.

'Cut it up so he does not choke,' ordered Dmitri.

---

* Another critic, the liberal politician Boris Nemtsov – who'd called the president a 'specialist in lying' – was assassinated in 2015 on a bridge near the Kremlin. Fresh flowers still appear every morning on the spot where he was gunned down. Every night the police sweep them away.

It was pleasant in the sun, rolling Moët bubbles across my tongue, waiting for Gorby. But I couldn't relax with Moscow, the Solovetsky Islands and the homeless shelters of Budapest not so very far away.

'I will survive crack-up,' said Dmitri, all but reading my mind.

'What crack-up?' I asked. I couldn't imagine what he might say next.

'Crack-up of Europe,' he replied. 'End of Europe. End of Euro. End time coming and I will survive.'

Doomsday fears were as old as religion, as old as man. On the day of the Last Judgement, Jesus will descend from Heaven to battle Masih ad-Dajjal and Vishnu will ride a white horse to end the Kali Yuga. But before that day, Europe really was at another liminal moment, on the threshold of a perilous new age.

'I'm not joking,' insisted Dmitri, in his cups yet with eyes full of brightness. 'My money is now in land, and sheeps.'

'Sheep?' I repeated. 'In Russia?' I'd heard rumours of unnamed oligarchs buying vast tracts of Siberian forest. One was said to have acquired a retired Soviet missile silo and converted it into a hardened bolthole. Likewise a few hundred wealthy Americans – including hedge-fund managers and dot.com executives – had bankrolled extreme makeovers on Atlas missile silos in Kansas and Wyoming. But I couldn't imagine any of them linked to sheep farms.

'I won't live in hole. I go away, for sure.'

'Where?' I asked.

'New Zealand,' answered Dmitri, lowering his voice in a conspiratorial whisper. 'I have Learjet on standby.'

'You'll need a pilot,' I said.

'Vasya is pilot,' he replied, again with a twinkle as I hadn't spotted the obvious. 'Balls *and* brains,' he said again, tapping his temple.

Dmitri explained that, in common with more than a thousand foreigners over the past decade, he'd purchased New Zealand residency. The process was easy enough, especially if one was willing to drop a couple of million into a 100-acre South Island property. He'd done just that, equipping it with solar panels, generators and thousands of rounds of ammunition. In exclusive chatrooms he'd then discussed second passports, gas masks, electrified fences and air filtration systems. He insisted that as many as half of Silicon Valley's billionaires had taken out similar 'doomsday insurance'.

'But you once told me that man without a homeland is like a nightingale without song,' I reminded him. *Chelovek bez rodiny, kak solovei bez pesni.*

'I tell you, I will survive,' he repeated with a shrug. 'But why you not writing this in your notebook?'

On the lush lakeshore, over vintage champagne and nibbles of a Maï Thaï green curry takeaway, we talked about economic meltdown, plutonium half-life and the top ten DVD films needed to see out a nuclear winter. Vasya returned from town with another bottle and sat between us on the bench, the corgi dozing at his feet. Around five o'clock an old man walked out of the sun and seemed about to stop but then carried on towards Chillon Castle. As dusk gathered around us, and birds took to their evening roosts, it seemed less and less likely that Gorbachev would make an appearance.

'He not coming,' said Vasya, unexpectedly reaching out to touch Dmitri's hand.

'Then we will return tomorrow,' declared Dmitri, clutching the bottle, somehow finding his feet. 'And tomorrow after tomorrow after tomorrow until we meet great man.' He swayed towards the lake, caught himself then announced, 'But first we toast.'

As I poured out the last of the champagne, he embarked on a convoluted tribute to Gorbachev. He took so long about it that my arm grew tired. A wave lifted itself from the placid water to rock the sailing boats moored along the shore. Their rigging chimed like St Basil's bells and an evening breeze stirred the purple bougainvillea. The corgi peed on my shoe. I looked at my watch. I didn't understand a single slurred word.

After he finished and we'd drunk to whatever, Vasya picked up the corgi.

'I forgot to ask, what's the dog's name?' I said.

'Winston,' replied Dmitri.

'Winston?' I repeated in incredulity.

'Like your dead prime minister,' he explained, rather
unnecessarily.

Long ago I'd written about another Winston and the coincidence
delighted me. When I explained he declared, 'My friend, this calls
for another toast!'

And so it was that beneath the night's first stars, Dmitri
Denisovich lifted his bottle for the last time and called out to
anyone who would listen to him, 'To all God's creations, may they
never die.'

On reflection I shouldn't have accepted the invitation to spend the
night in the spare bedroom. It wasn't the promise of steam showers
and crisp Egyptian cotton that seduced me, but rather my fascination
with power. In the lap of luxury I lay in bed unable to sleep, and
not because the filet mignon had been overcooked. I gazed out of
the open French windows at the dark water ringed by a necklace of
light, wondering about that inherently corrupting force.

Globalisation had empowered a new elite, leaving the rest
behind. *Eight* billionaires now own the same wealth as the world's
3.6 billion poorest people. Russia's richest 10 per cent possess 87 per
cent of the country. In the United States twenty-five hedge-fund
managers make more money than all the kindergarten teachers
combined. By 2030 a top 1 per cent are predicted to have amassed
two-thirds of global assets.

The unequal distribution of wealth has shaped our age. In many
parts of the world, the have-nots' bitterness – and racial resentment –
has been channelled into a kind of class war. In voting for Donald
Trump, Fidesz, Brexit and Alternative für Deutschland, millions
of ordinary men and women believed – and believe – that they are
taking on the establishment, that they can return to an imagined
golden (white man's) age. Once again, the truth is otherwise. The
newly rich have simply tapped into public frustrations, masking
their own ambition as a battle between the little guy and a corrupt
elite. It is a power game, pure and simple, between new money and
old. To both of them 'the people' will always be *bydlo*. The rabble.
Pawns. Scum.

Whether or not Dmitri deserved his success, he was savvy enough not to squander his luck. He had the resources to ensure that – if civil disorder overwhelmed Europe, if Gieves & Hawkes was acquired by Primark – he'd be all right, Jack. He'd get out of town to look after Numero Uno (and their dog). He'd neither take responsibility for society's future nor search for solutions to inequality. Instead he'd fortify himself against his fears.

When I finally fell asleep I dreamed that dozens of rats were nesting in my bed, curled around each other in a tight ball at my feet. I kicked them away, shearing off their moulting coats, streaking grey and black hair across the sheets.

In the morning I didn't join Dmitri at the park bench. I had a last flight to catch and two final meetings to make. Later I heard that he never met Gorbachev. He never received the old man's blessing. Nor did he assuage his deep anger at those whom he suspected of looking down at him. Soon afterwards he and Vasya moved to the southern hemisphere to breed sheep, watch movies and await doomsday. As far as I know neither man ever returned to Europe.

Britain

35

Jolly Ol' England

When I arrived in England his letter was waiting for me. I caught a train north from Euston and changed at Preston. Six out of the ten poorest areas in northern Europe are in the UK and his Lancashire market town is in one of them.

Its muddled high street was drowning under a fury of rain. Late-evening shoppers huddled in a bus shelter outside the sham Gothic town hall. Pale boys in soaked hoodies slinked by the grim black rectangle of a closed factory. A hard-eyed woman gazed at a glossy mobile phone window display. I splashed past boarded-up stores, payday lenders and Poundland. Once this mill town had helped to clothe the world, now it boasted the most charity shops in the county.

I found the Blue Nile in a redbrick cul-de-sac behind Gala Bingo.

'In Calais me and two brothers cut the wires on the hatch when the driver went for a piss,' said Sami, as lean and lithe as ever, his dark brown eyes gleaming again in his slender face. 'We climbed out of the cold and into the warm chocolate. It felt good at first. We was holding onto the rim of the hatch with one hand and the other on the next man's shoulder. But we couldn't touch the bottom. If we lost our grip we'd go under. We panicked when the tanker started to move.'

A young couple stepped out of the rain and Sami paused in his telling to take their order, limping between counter and fryer, wrapping their chicken and doner specials in waxy white paper. I leaned back into the plastic chair to watch, touched once again by his wounded-animal walk.

'Like I said, we started to panic,' Sami went on after the door had closed behind them. At the corner table a crop-haired drunk dozed over his half-eaten kebab. 'But like always I didn't give up. When things got hard, when my knees started to buckle, I kept going, kept moving my legs so as to not get totally sucked under.' To reach England he'd almost drowned in a tanker of molten chocolate while waiting to board the ferry. 'Man, it was only twenty minutes till the tanker stopped but I was so near the end. We stayed cool for as long as we could, stayed cool then pushed ourselves out, one by one, pulling against the chocolate. It was sticking like glue. It kept sucking us back down. But we got out, thank God, and we was on the ferry and the ferry was going. We'd made it.'

At Dover, Sami had stowed himself in the luggage hold of a London-bound coach. He'd walked from Victoria to his uncle's address in New Cross and slept for three days straight. At the asylum screening unit in Croydon he'd applied to be recognised as a refugee. He wanted to continue his studies, he'd said. He still hoped to become a bookkeeper. The caseworker told him no, he could not work. He had to get by on £37.75 a week. The application process would take at least six months. Sami spent the first payment on a last-minute ticket for *Thriller Live* in the West End. He rode the 273 bus from Lewisham to Foxbury Manor, the Chislehurst mansion where Michael Jackson had planned to live until his sudden death. Then he went north.

'So here I am. Here I am.'

The takeaway's door opened again, and again. It was pub closing time and the pre-midnight rush. His manager Nigel – a sour Mayfield School dropout – sauntered in from the Britannia and turned up the deep-fat fryers. Sami stood at the vertical grill, scorching the rotating kebab cone, shearing off thin slivers of meat. He knifed open toasted flatbreads and filled them with greasy lamb shavings and sliced tomato. Most nights the queue of customers stretched out onto New Cheap Street.

In the doorway three lads in their late teens clutched tins of Carlsberg Extra, chasing every other mouthful with swigs of vodka, a potent mix judging from their eagerness to chat. They were apprentices, they told me, but not for long.

'Closing down, see,' the taller lad said. 'Only way out of this town is to be a singer. Yea, that's the ticket.'

'I write the songs, he sings them,' volunteered his mate. 'Yea, he can sing.'

The taller lad hit a high note, in tune but with sobering words, a lament for a trackless future, as Nigel bawled from behind the counter, 'Leave it out, mate. This ain't *Britain's Got Talent.*'

The left-behind Lancashire town abounded in nicotine-stained pubs, neon-lit chippies and a couple of all-night clubs, one of which was the three lads' destination.

'It'll be wicked tonight – great band, great craic – but you need to be tanked to enjoy it,' the singer called over his shoulder as they tipped out into the drizzle with tinnies and bags of chips in hand.

Every morning Sami started at seven, cleaning the floor and frying range, refreshing the oil, peeling potatoes and logging deliveries of frozen fish, burgers and spicy wedges. He handled lunches alone but come the evening Nigel took charge, dragging himself in from the pub with the heavy step of the condemned. He always reeked of cigarette smoke.

Yet Sami was no zero-hours automaton like those trapped in the town's warehouses and call centres. He knew his luck and moved like a dancer while he worked, from cutting board to microwave, between chip pan and till. He mixed batter with cold water, added a teaspoon of baking powder and listened to the fizz of the fish as it hit the sizzling palm fat. Sometimes he helped to clear the few melamine tables with Floriana, the Romanian waitress who worked weekends. On Saturday nights after closing, when the neon lights had been switched off, he liked to sit and listen to her complain about her aching feet and Bulgarian boyfriend. At the same time his eyes were always on the door, fearful of an immigration raid, detention and removal from the UK. More than once Nigel had threatened him with the sack.

The Blue Nile differed little from a thousand other Lancashire takeaways, except in one peculiar aspect. Its owner, who lived upstairs, was a recluse. It was more than a decade since he'd last been spotted at the Britannia. He stayed indoors, relying on Nigel – his nephew – to run errands and do his weekly shop.

It also fell to Nigel to cash up at the end of the day. He hated lugging the takings upstairs, and the obligation to stay and listen to the 'right scally' grumble about falling profits and soggy chips. 'But there's nowt to do about it,' Nigel moaned, irritated yet accepting of his lot. 'You don't bite the fooker that feeds you.'

One Saturday, Nigel called in sick. On the phone he told Sami to cover for him, even if it meant leaving Floriana alone to clean up at closing time. To get ahead Sami pre-cooked extra cod and haddock. He deep-fried a mountain of chips and nuked two dozen servings of frozen chicken wings. He managed to keep up with orders until the last plastered punter staggered away into the night.

Sami had never met the uncle. He had never seen him leave the flat. As a result a kind of lore had grown up around the old man, about his moods and bloody-mindedness, all of which Nigel did his best to embellish. He owned half a dozen chippies and kebab shops in the north-west, said Nigel. He bought only British fish and New Zealand lamb. He was a bastard landlord who hassled incomers even though his eateries and tenements wouldn't survive without them. He was also a 'totally mental' hobbyist.

At the till Sami sorted the grimy notes, bagging them with the loose change, then – with a nod to Floriana – limped around to the side door. He stood there for a moment, pressing the thick envelope against his chest, looking up and down the empty street. He could be gone in an instant, he realised. He could swing by his room, grab his few possessions and catch a night bus to Blackburn. By morning he'd be in Leeds or Bradford. He'd never be found. He jabbed the intercom button and was buzzed up to the flat.

Alongside the stairs rose a line of framed movie posters: *The Dam Busters, Sink the Bismarck, Battle of Britain*. On the landing Sami stepped over a mechanical bulldog and around a battered pre-war globe ringed with pink-coloured colonies. A three-carriage Hornby model railway steamed around the edge of the sitting room, along a hip-height track and through miniature English villages. Tiny apple orchards, rustic pubs and rose-wrapped cottages spread across shelves. Cheery figurines played cricket on a table-top village green. A toy ferris wheel turned in a make-believe fairground. A model station master signalled to the locomotive, motioning it around and around the closed circuit. Rain beat against the real window.

'Who the fook are you?'

Sami hadn't noticed the man – Nigel's uncle – in the clutter. He sat sunk in a deep discoloured armchair; white, wispy-haired and wearing a particularly patriotic jumper that blended in with the flat's tatty chaos.

Sami introduced himself, explaining that Nigel was unwell. He gestured with the envelope and asked, 'Where do I put the money, boss?' He couldn't spot a single uncluttered surface.

Nigel's uncle levered himself to his feet and snatched the envelope. 'So you're the one,' he said, an account ledger falling onto the carpeted floor. On the walls portraits of Churchill and Thatcher – clipped from the *Daily Mail* – were decked in Union Jack bunting. Queen Elizabeth statuettes waved from another time. At least five empty beer bottles lay around his slippers or under the chair.

The man was seventy-something; oily-eyed, large-gutted, heavy-limbed and obviously a bachelor. As he collapsed back into the armchair he brushed by a pair of Airfix Spitfires suspended in an unending victory roll above a model church steeple. Sami couldn't take his eyes off the display.

'You like it, lad?'

'Lot of work, boss.'

'Oh aye yea, hundreds of hours. Hundreds. You speak English?'

'Of course.'

'Many of your sort don't. That's why I ask,' he said then instructed: 'Sit.'

'I need to close up the shop.'

'Take the load off your feet, lad,' he went on and, as Sami hesitated, he insisted, 'Who pays the brass round here?' When

Sami balanced on the edge of the chair, he passed him a bottle.
'Where you from?'

'Africa,' replied Sami. He was wary of saying more. He wanted
to leave yet at the same time there was something intriguing – even
intoxicating – about the overheated flat and its locked-in-aspic
world. 'Boss, I have to get back to work,' he repeated.

'You know if they nab you it's a fookin fine for me,' threatened
the uncle.

Sami yielded and sat back. He accepted the beer and
pretended to listen, as Nigel had instructed. It did feel good not
to stand. Between thirsty gulps, the old man droned on about
the economy, the weather and the 'ever-expanding population
of mosques'. Sami picked at the moist label with his thumbnail
while staring at the circling train and nostalgic scenes. He took
in a miniature theme park with jousting knights and a turreted
castle.

'Mark my words, one day immigrants will build a shanty town
down New Cheap Street and English kids will go to a madrasa
rather than Sunday School.'

Then he paused, realising that Sami was paying no attention.
'You *do* like it,' said the old man, following his eyes. 'Nigel thinks
it's total shite.'

Now he began talking instead about the layout. He was back on
his feet, unsteady but animated, explaining that this was Hoole and
that was Croston, idealised notions of the villages where he'd grown
up. Here was the Crown where he'd had his first drink. There was
the bicycle shed behind which he'd had his first kiss.

'And that there, that's Camelot. You heard of it, lad?' When Sami
shook his head, he went on. 'Oh, you missed something special.
See the figures on the hill above it?' With ham hands he gestured
at a plastic couple locked in an intimate clinch in a cornfield
overlooking the theme park. 'That's me having it off.'

The old man laughed with such sharp and sudden sorrow that
Sami turned his head back towards him.

'It's got history, this town,' he went on, digging another bottle
from the stash beneath the Hornby's control panel. 'Roman road

across the Yarrow, bouncing bombs made in Euxton, Cromwell tanks built down Pilling Lane.'

He spoke then of a King Cotton town, of Lancashire men civilising India and Africa, of wartime heroism, of Malcolm Campbell's *Bluebird* parked behind the Anderton Arms while its lorry was repaired on the journey to Coniston Water.

'That's it there,' he said, jabbing a sausage-thick finger at a miniature speedboat beside the model Euxton pub.

He didn't dwell on the closure of its Royal Ordnance Factory – at one time the biggest munitions-filling factory in the world – or the complete disappearance of the coal and textiles industries.

'It's home and you have to love it.'

The unexpected intimacy astonished them both, rising as it can between strangers. They held each other's gaze until Sami reached again for the bottle in an effort to hide his eyes.

'You're a long way from your home, lad.'

Sami hadn't intended to talk but his tongue felt loosened, perhaps by the longing in the old man's voice, perhaps due to the fumes of the dodgy Calor gas heater. Suddenly he was talking about *his* history, about ancient Hausa Kingdoms and the trans-Saharan city states seized by British colonial forces, their rulers co-opted or killed, their neighbourhoods set on fire. He remembered the tropical green mornings of childhood and Sokoto's twinkling city lights beneath a pitch-black sky. He spoke of the dust-dry Bukkuyum gold mine, the brutal Moscow convent and the molten chocolate tanker. He said that he had been frightened before and after every border, that he was frightened even now downstairs behind the counter. The words spilled out of him, falling like tears, silencing the uncle.

When he finished, the only sound was of the Hornby train rattling over the points. The old man blinked his oily eyes as if wrestling with something he had never imagined, another world, another history.

On the floor beside the armchair was a paper pad. After a moment Sami reached down to pick it up and wrote his name across the top of the page in big block letters.

'Number one: I am a high-school graduate with a year's training as a bookkeeper,' he said. 'Number two: I speak English, Hausa, some Ashanti and Russian. Number three: I am healthy, apart from the toe. Number four: I can dance.'

On the pad he composed a kind of résumé, recording his birth date, parents' names and nationality. As he quelled his fears, he thought of the troubles that had cut him deep. He heard Michael Jackson sing, again and again, 'Beat It'. He wouldn't be defeated. Nor would he just survive. He wanted to work, to live. The model train went around and around. The Spitfires soared in frozen victory rolls. On the village green, a miniature cricketer stood forever poised to catch out the batsman. When he had finished, he handed the pad to the old man.

'What's this?' he asked.

'This is who I am,' answered Sami.

It was after two when Sami finished telling me his tale. He and I sat together at a table dusted by the half-light of the street. The formica was still sticky to the touch, the air so saturated with chip fat that it could be wrung out like a flannel. Nigel and Floriana had left for the night, binning the waste, swabbing the floor and switching off the buzzing neon strips.

'Like, I believe in fate,' Sami assured me. 'I believe I was fated to meet him like I was fated to meet you.'

'He gave you a proper job?' I repeated.

'Man, I'm managing his accounts now, keeping his books.'

We laughed together then lapsed into silence. I wondered what it was that he and Nigel's uncle had recognised in each other? A mutual vulnerability? An acceptance of loss? I guessed only that it had been something to do with frailty, and the nobility of that frailty. Outside the rain fell in sheets.

Sami and I have stayed in touch over the last year. He's filled in the missing bits of the story, enabling me to tell it to you. Of course I've constructed it from notes, evidence and known facts, as do all writers. Gaps have always had to be filled in for, as we know, every history involves narration of one kind or another.

Sami's story could have ended another way. He could have stolen the money and been tracked down in Bradford. In Toxteth he might have been spat on every time he left the squat. He could have worked as a dishwasher in Sheffield until his arrest. In the Gatwick Immigration Removal Centre he might have fallen into such a black depression that he couldn't get out of bed for a week. All these realities are the truth, for the tens of thousands who make it to Britain's shores.

'I looked at the man in the mirror, like my father told me,' Sami had said again at the Blue Nile, the tone of his voice lifting and falling in its flight, dignified yet humble, proud and honest. 'That's what I done.'

In the morning I rented a car and drove west to Charnock Green. Across the M6 was Lancashire's 'real' Camelot. For almost three decades, hundreds of thousands of punters had ridden its Knightmare roller coaster, bumped and ground on the Jousting Knights dodgems and risen above themselves on the Kingdom in the Clouds ferris wheel. But then Camelot – and its owner the Story Group – had gone into receivership. The 'land of great knights and amazing days' had ceased to be a fairy tale, except in the old man's scale-model world.

I found a hole in the security fence and stepped through it into Merlin's crumbling castle. In the courtyard, plaster knights had been decapitated, the Magic Spell souvenir shop pillaged for its timber. Nature had reclaimed the Dungeons of Doom ghost train. No strolling minstrels sang in the Avalon Arena. No heroes splashed in Pendragon's Plunge water slide.

I settled on a broken seat in the Maid Marian cafe and thought about England. I wondered if Sir Lancelot really had been raised in Martin Mere, the waters of which had long ago covered the grounds of this mock-medieval theme park. Or if Godiva, Countess of Mercia, had actually ridden through the streets of Coventry clothed only in her long hair. Was the heroic tale of a doughty nation standing alone against tyranny now only a tool to unite the isles' diverse peoples? Had the country really punched above its weight and 'taken back control'? Or was it blinded by a kind of dreamy narcissism, believing in its own unparalleled greatness?

In Russia, Poland, Transnistria and Hungary, I'd seen people force-fed myths. But I couldn't understand how the same had come to pass in Britain, or at least England? How could the English – a people raised in a stable, peaceful and prosperous society with centuries of democracy and freedom – have swallowed the vapid promises of restored glory? How could they – we – have allowed ourselves to be played like puppets?

In its post-imperial confusion, England – once renowned for its pragmatism, common sense and political stability – had become a hollowed-out country, ill at ease with itself. Over the last three decades, its near neighbours had learned to thrive in a multicultural world. Scotland had understood the benefits of being Scottish, British and European. Ireland had rebuked absolutist fantasies. The Netherlands had come to terms with its own guilty history of colonialism, accepting itself as part of an imperfect family. France and Germany had deepened the embrace of a common idea to end centuries of animosity. Yet jolly ol' England had harked back to an older and cruder form of nationalism, wrapping itself in an empire comforter to protect it from chilly reality, unable to face its fading significance.

In the rickety remains of Camelot, the crack of gunshots startled me out of my reverie. Cries of angry voices cut through rapid machine-gun fire. But it wasn't the sound of a revolution, at least not yet. Beyond the headless plaster knights and faded Crosses of St George were a couple of small adventure parks. At Battlefield Live Pennine, local kids celebrated birthdays with simulated 'authentic combat experience'. Next door, TerrorFest UK promised that 'screams come true'. In their muddy trenches and burnt-out buildings, stag and hen parties undertook 'hard-core, pre-wedding missions before hitting the town and drinking like off-duty squaddies'. At both venues Morita sniper rifles were said to be the weapon of choice for brides-to-be.

'We persist in regarding ourselves as a Great Power, capable of everything and only temporarily handicapped by economic difficulties,' Sir Henry Tizard, chief scientific adviser to the Ministry of Defence, had said at the end of the Second World War, the moral victory that today's self-styled 'patriots' have twisted into so many immoral lies. 'We are not a Great Power and never will be again. We are a great nation, but if we continue to behave like a Great Power we shall soon cease to be a great nation.'

Nearby a robin moved through a thicket of ash. A woodpecker's laughing call echoed from a far copse. Overhead the sky filled with skylarks. The British will sort themselves out, I know, but it will take a generation. England will survive, but not in a form that any of us have known. I walked back to the car, broken glass crunching beneath my feet.

36

Fog in the Channel

Lunch was twenty minutes. That was all she could spare and she made sure that I knew it. Fennel risotto with pine nuts and *cavolo nero*. Bitter-leaf salad on the side. No wine. All pre-ordered and laid on the table as soon as we sat down.

'Talk', she instructed and I did, quickly. I told her about my journey to the end of Europe, and my return to the city that I have so long loved. I told her about my dread of blood-and-soil nationalism, and of a London fractured by racists and Little Englanders. I even said that I feared that the time was ripe for civil unrest.

Across the white tablecloth she listened with an intensity that belied intimacy. When I finished she put down her fork. She took a sip of Waiākea volcanic water. She leaned forward and said, 'It won't happen.'

Jenny was a banker: cropped auburn hair, shrewd green eyes, Dara Lamb suit. As a child in Virginia, she had learned German from her VW exec father and ambition from her antitrust lawyer mother. As head girl at Chatham Hall, she'd made the finals of both the National Speech & Debate Tournament and the US junior squash championships. Citibank had recruited her straight out of Wharton and dropped her into the firestorm after the collapse of Lehman Brothers. She cut her teeth on the international side – leveraged trades, currency hedge funds, credit default

swaps – before leaving the States for spells in Frankfurt and Tokyo.
A rival megabank poached her by offering the UK and, as she was
good with clients, made her a senior investment manager. She
liked to stand out as 'our girl in London'. She didn't miss the daily
commute from Connecticut to Manhattan. She sublet a flat in
the Barbican and indulged her passion for classic Mercedes-Benz,
racing her 220 Fintail at Silverstone. She played to her strengths,
stayed disciplined and avoided excesses, apart from the car of
course. A holiday home in the Hamptons would come in time.
Perhaps even a step through the revolving door to the Treasury or
SEC. Until then she worked so late that some nights she measured
her sleep in minutes. Her contrarian strategy netted in excess of 20
per cent per year on investments. Three analysts worked under her.
She reported directly to a VP. She was on a roll.

'It won't happen?' I repeated.

'Two reasons: first, Brussels's mind-blowing regulations had to
be circumvented and, second, our customers trust the fairness of
English law.'

'So Britain will become the Singapore of Europe?'

'Will become?' she laughed, her East Coast accent overlaid
with English vowels. 'Look at the history: East India Company,
Triangular Trade, Imperial Tobacco, Lloyd's, Eurobonds, non-
doms. Enterprise is in England's DNA. The country is already
there.'

I'd been introduced to Jenny by the same friend who'd led
me to Dmitri. Her private clients – most of whom had at least
$25 million of investible assets – came from Moscow, Kiev, Caracas
and Chipping Norton. They entrusted her with their wealth and
she multiplied it, advising them on innovative trades, tax regimes
and the state of the US debt bubble. Through her, Russian agri-
industrialists financed Turkish chicken farms, Mexican family
firms broke into Japanese shipping and Cotswold old money
shorted market sell-offs. In return those grateful clients introduced
her to 'special friends' and government officials from Osaka to
Astana whom she charmed with her fluent German or a dozen
endearing Japanese axioms. Over vintage Bollinger they whispered

of emerging opportunities and looming time bombs, details of which she passed on to New York. She became 'a trust pillar on a two-way street', according to our mutual friend; 'the gilded hub of a virtuous circle'. The flexibility of the British authorities – Inland Revenue, Bank of England, Financial Conduct Authority – also resonated with her clients. 'You know where you stand with them,' she assured me.

'So the UK has found its role at last?' I mocked, recalling US Secretary of State Dean Acheson's 1962 quote that Britain had lost an empire and not yet found a role. 'As a tax haven laundering dirty money.'

'You tell me which economic model will succeed in the twenty-first century? A low-wage, free-trade model of shredded rules or an over-regulated behemoth…'

'Which protects citizens' rights and the functioning of the rule of law.'

'Oh, please,' said Jenny, rolling her eyes and pushing aside her risotto. 'No nation has ever achieved – or maintained – greatness by giving its people an extra serving of gruel.'

'Maybe that's all some families can afford now, after being burnt by the last crash.'

I couldn't forget that her work – or at least that of her peers – had concocted the toxic brew that had poisoned the global economy.

'Listen, change is life, and change is growth. Gently rising markets and low volatility are yesterday. Ten per cent of the world's money is now offshore. Flexibility is the new reality, with the broken and rebuilt global connections. Even chaos brings opportunities.'

I looked doubtful, but she went on. 'How, after 1945, did Germany rise to become the most powerful nation on the continent? Through trade. Through rebooting the Holy Roman Empire and capturing a market for its goods. How will Britain now keep its head above water? Not by selling Big Ben tea towels.'

Jenny caught the waiter's eye, who whisked away our plates. As he poured coffee, she went on: 'The EU has always been too beautiful to be true. It's not a natural development from centuries of European civil war. Plus the Euro was a huge strategic mistake.

A sharper capitalism is essential for survival. When the next recession comes, there will be a price to pay. But my people won't be footing the bill.'

'Your people?'

'It's a new beginning.'

I didn't believe it – or rather I didn't want to believe it. After the horror of the Second World War, Germany and France had cast off their enmity and Europeans embraced the idea of a shared future. They undertook to set – and to uphold – values and rights across a continent, promoting peace and freedom, protecting human rights, abolishing borders. In such an open society, war would not happen. Prosperity would strengthen democracy, solidarity and well-being.

'The liberal agenda has failed in the West,' said Jenny. 'Middle-class Peter will no longer be robbed to pay working-class Paul.' She likened liberal democracy to a criminal cartel that forced citizens to surrender much of their wealth to pay for welfare, hospitals and state schools. She advocated for the necessity of self-interest and unilateralism 'in the coming half-century of nationalism'.

'We are living through a revolution, but almost no one sees its true colours,' she said in conclusion, adding in cynical jest, 'And those who do? Let them drive Audis! Let them buy iPhones! Consumerism is the great pacifier.' With a smile she rose to her feet and said, 'That's my time. Don't print my real name.'

I looked at my watch. Twenty minutes, almost to the second. We shook hands and I watched her walk away between the tables of market-makers and FX traders, Lloyd's underwriters and a pair of Conservative ultras. In Lutyens, the Conran restaurant in the former Reuters building, stock price ticker tape was immortalised in the marble mosaic floor. The City would survive, of that I had no doubt. But at what cost to those outside the Square Mile? In the last financial crisis, millions of jobs had been destroyed by the economic contraction. Massive government intervention transferred wealth from taxpayers to the banks. In Greece and Spain, two out of every five young people became unemployed. Italy suffered the longest recession in seventy years. France's sovereign debt soared to near

100 per cent. Collapsing tax revenues then forced severe cutbacks in public services, and austerity fuelled discontent across Europe. Yet throughout it all, oil men lunched at West End sushi bars, oligarchs dropped their sons off at Eton and Harrow, and bankers kept hold of their bonuses. Britain's top executives now rake in on average £4.4 million per year while median national pay hovers around £26,000. I sat back down, and ordered a big glass of wine.

London – dirty, thriving, patched-together London – had long been the centre of my world. Years ago I was drawn to it by its history and openness. I walked its streets by day, collar turned against the winter rain, listening and looking, enthralled by its unfolding story. I loved the city at night: the empty avenues, the clutching couples, the smell of autumn leaves, a single office light glowing on Whitehall. In summer I lay on the grass in Holland Park – never in a pay-for deckchair – or sat under a catalpa tree watching Wimbledon, the television's extension lead snaking out from my flat. I felt myself at home in the British Library and Canada House. I made movies at Shepperton and Pinewood. I cycled to work at the World Service and Goethe-Institut. I met my wife in SW10. David Bowie invited me to Dingwalls. Now when I return, I retrace the old paths and remember the conversations that I'd had along them, reviving them and the countless other voices that I hear suspended in the ether, above Piccadilly and Soho, on Chelsea Bridge and Highgate Hill, in a dozen languages and at a thousand points from Green Lanes to the Pimlico Tandoori.

After lunch I caught the number 9 bus to Kensington Gardens to stroll beneath the plane trees on Lancaster Walk. On that sunny afternoon I circled the Round Pond and paused for breath under the sweet chestnuts on South Flower Walk. Around me idled Spanish students and Australian au pairs, Kuwaiti non-doms and tight-knit bands of Chinese tourists. Russians – so many Russians – pushed prams, walked dogs and looked over their shoulders before waiting Mercedes-Maybachs whisked them back to Harrods. Nearby, along the Long Water, Southwark Park school kids ate packed sandwiches after their visit to the V&A. SOAS and Alliance

Française language teachers sat together on the steps of the Albert Memorial. American expats played softball across West Carriage Drive while a Polish mothers' group practised t'ai chi alongside the Rotten Row bridleway. Their London – our London – felt closer to New York than Newcastle, more like Paris than Preston. For beneath the continent, tectonic plates had shifted, twisting both it and Europe away from England.

Thirty years ago Europe became whole again. I wrote then that the Wall, the late great division of the world, had passed away as an historical aberration. In Berlin, Prague and Moscow I'd danced with so many others on the grave of dictatorships, in an act of defiance, in a celebration of the resilience of the human spirit. I convinced myself that our generation was an exception in history, that we'd learned to live by different rules, that we were bound together by freedom. I believed that the horrors of the twentieth century – the traumas of which had driven me to become a writer – could never return.

I've remade this journey – backwards – to try to understand how it went wrong. I've tried to catch a snapshot of ordinary people living in an extraordinary time, in fear in St Petersburg and Donbas, with courage in Tallinn and Warsaw. I've seen how Vladimir Putin capitalised on a series of terror attacks – real, dubious or fake – to muscle himself into total power, bringing to my mind the Nazis' seizure of control of Germany. I've watched him grab parts of a neighbouring country with an audacity unseen in Europe since the days of Stalin and Hitler. I've understood why he ordered his Sukhoi Su-34 fighters to bomb Syria.

In Germany the flood of refugees – even though now much reduced – has roused extremists. Populists have taken Poland and Hungary by demonising illusory enemies who threatened the 'purity of the nation'. Finally at home, I've witnessed another insular elite – in their quest for power, in their bigotry, with or without *pipiska putina* – exploit public grievances, mutilate truth and try to hijack democracy.

Under the lime trees, with my notebook open, the emotion took me by surprise, so much so that my eyes stung. For many years

I have travelled and lived with certain principles, prizing certain values, with a firm and unwavering belief in the promise of the future. Now I realise it's us who must fulfil that promise. We kid ourselves if we believe that one day the tectonic plates will simply shift again, that in time the demagogues and xenophobes will retire to Foros, Key West or Clacton-on-Sea, that we need to do nothing. History does not move in repeating cycles; rather it shows us patterns and trends. Change is life, on that at least Jenny and I could agree. Either we shape the future or we sleepwalk into it.

Europe and Britain need a new story, a true story. Perhaps it's here that it will begin, rather than end. I want to believe that Londoners won't be told what to do or how to live, that they'll never accept a stifled media or a single version of reality. Perhaps this open, patched-together capital can show us how to respect rather than scorn our neighbours, can help us to abandon divisive nativist notions as well as grand fancies of empire or a harmonious superstate. Perhaps London – in its diversity and untidiness, in its dissonance – can illuminate for the whole continent (including this island on the edge) how to stop being slaves to illusions.

Where then is the real end of Europe? I once thought it to be a physical place, perhaps the line of the River Oder or the Urals. I realise now that it is not a freak of geography and far more a question of culture and morality, a matter of principles. It's the point where antique forms of identity clash with modernity, where tolerance, decency and a certain way of thinking end, where openness meets a wall.

Acknowledgements

Some names have been changed, others not. In Russia many of those who I need to thank are protected with a pseudonym. In Germany I am grateful to Prune Antoine, Holger Böken, Corinna Bröcher, Molly Brown, Martin Dammann, Nigel Dunkley MBE, Victoria Gosling, Matthias and My-Linh Kunst, Helena Palsson, Johannes Vogel and Yusra Mardini who took time away from her Olympics training and let me read the proofs of her biography *Butterfly*. In the Baltics I thank Jason Finch of Turku's Åbo Akademi University, Kätlin Kaldmaa, Kristjan, Piret and Markus Moora and Keith Shannon, British Ambassador to Latvia. Elsewhere in Europe, the help of Paul-Henri Arni, Clifford Corzatt, Canada's Ambassador to the EU Daniel J. Costello, Pascal Cuttat of the International Committee of the Red Cross and Jakub Kalensky of the East StratCom Task Force was invaluable.

In the UK, I am grateful to Lady Plaxy and Sir Michael Arthur, Rick Ball, Carole Cadwalladr, Clementine Cecil, David Chater, Susan Crean, Nick Danziger, Michael and Marlie Ferenczi, Ed Jones, Toby Latta, Rachel and Neil Moss, Mary Price, Joanna Prior, Douglas C. Rice, Varvara Shavrova, David Thomson and Marcus Warren. I am indebted to my agent Peter Straus, my editor Michael Fishwick and above all my resplendent wife Katrin (cue fanfare of trumpets) without whom neither *Stalin's Nose* nor this book would have been written.

Finally, special thanks to Ekaterina Petrovna for sharing the secret of *pipiska putina*. Some days I wake up with my brain still sizzling. *Nu pravda ze?*

A Note on the Author

Rory MacLean is one of Britain's most expressive and adventurous travel writers. His books – which have been translated into a dozen languages – include UK top-ten bestsellers *Stalin's Nose* and *Under the Dragon* as well as *Berlin: Imagine a City*, which was named a Book of the Year by the *Washington Post*.

A Note on the Type

The text of this book is set Adobe Garamond. It is one of several versions of Garamond based on the designs of Claude Garamond. It is thought that Garamond based his font on Bembo, cut in 1495 by Francesco Griffo in collaboration with the Italian printer Aldus Manutius. Garamond types were first used in books printed in Paris around 1532. Many of the present-day versions of this type are based on the Typi Academiae of Jean Jannon cut in Sedan in 1615.

Claude Garamond was born in Paris in 1480. He learned how to cut type from his father and by the age of fifteen he was able to fashion steel punches the size of a pica with great precision. At the age of sixty he was commissioned by King Francis I to design a Greek alphabet, and for this he was given the honourable title of royal type founder. He died in 1561.